THE NEW
CANADIAN
PENTECOSTALS

Editions SR / Éditions SR

Editions SR / Éditions SR is a general series of books in the study of religion, encompassing the fields of study of the constituent societies of the Canadian Corporation for Studies in Religion / Corporation canadienne des sciences religieuses. These societies are: Canadian Society of Biblical Studies / Société canadienne des études bibliques; Canadian Society of Church Historic Studies / Association canadienne des études des patristiques; Canadian Society for Study of Religion / Société canadienne pour l'étude de la religion.

Submit manuscript proposals to:

Lisa Quinn
Acquisitions Editor
Wilfrid Laurier University Press
75 University Avenue West
Waterloo, ON N2L 3C5
Phone: 519-884-0710 ext. 2843
Fax: 519-725-1399
Email: lquinn@wlu.ca

THE NEW CANADIAN PENTECOSTALS

Adam Stewart

WILFRID LAURIER
UNIVERSITY PRESS

This book has been published with the help of a grant from the Canadian Federation for the Humanities and Social Sciences, through the Awards to Scholarly Publications Program, using funds provided by the Social Sciences and Humanities Research Council of Canada. Wilfrid Laurier University Press acknowledges the financial support of the Government of Canada through the Canada Book Fund for its publishing activities. This work was supported by the Research Support Fund.

Library and Archives Canada Cataloguing in Publication

Stewart, Adam Scott, author
    The new Canadian Pentecostals / Adam Stewart.

(Editions SR)
Includes bibliographical references and index.
Issued in print and electronic formats.
ISBN 978-1-77112-140-8 (pbk.).—ISBN 978-1-77112-142-2 (epub).—
ISBN 978-1-77112-141-5 (pdf)

    1. Pentecostalism—Canada. 2. Pentecostal churches—Canada. 3. Pentecostalism—Ontario—Waterloo (Regional municipality). 4. Pentecostal churches—Ontario—Waterloo (Regional municipality). I. Title. II. Series: Editions SR

BR1644.5.C3S74 2015   289.9'40971   C2015-901592-8
                                               C2015-901593-6

Cover design by Blakeley Words+Pictures. Front-cover image by Christopher Ewing/Ackleyroadphotos/Dreamstime. Text design by Lime Design Inc.

© 2015 Wilfrid Laurier University Press
Waterloo, Ontario, Canada
www.wlupress.wlu.ca

This book is printed on FSC® certified paper and is certified Ecologo. It contains post-consumer fibre, is processed chlorine free, and is manufactured using biogas energy.

Printed in Canada

Every reasonable effort has been made to acquire permission for copyright material used in this text, and to acknowledge all such indebtedness accurately. Any errors and omissions called to the publisher's attention will be corrected in future printings.

No part of this publication may be reproduced, stored in a retrieval system, or transmitted, in any form or by any means, without the prior written consent of the publisher or a licence from the Canadian Copyright Licensing Agency (Access Copyright). For an Access Copyright licence, visit http://www.accesscopyright.ca or call toll free to 1-800-893-5777.

DEDICATED TO DAVID SELJAK

teacher, mentor, advocate, colleague, friend

CONTENTS

List of Tables ix

Acknowledgements xi

CHAPTER 1 ⽌ 1
INTRODUCTION

    The Canadian Decline of the World's Fastest-Growing Religion *1*
    The Transformation of Pentecostalism in Canada *6*
    Methodology *11*
    Outline of the Chapters *19*

CHAPTER 2 ⽌ 21
THE PENTECOSTAL TRADITION

    Defining Pentecostalism *21*
    Pentecostal Beginnings *23*
    Traditional Canadian Pentecostal Identity, Belief, and Practice *30*
    Conclusion *41*

CHAPTER 3 ⽌ 43
THE CHURCHES AND THEIR PASTORS

    Freedom in Christ *43*
    Elmira Pentecostal Assembly *50*
    Elevation *59*
    Conclusion *74*

CHAPTER 4 · 77
Generically Evangelical Religious Identity

Generic Evangelicalism 79
Traditional Denominational Identifiers 86
Latent Denominational Identifiers 89
Non-denominational Identifiers 99
Conclusion 107

CHAPTER 5 · 109
Spirit Baptism and Speaking in Tongues

Ignorance and Confusion regarding Spirit Baptism 110
Spirit Baptism and the Question of Subsequence 114
Speaking in Tongues as Evidence of Spirit Baptism 118
The Purpose of Spirit Baptism 125
Conclusion 135

CHAPTER 6 · 137
Healing, Miracles, and Other Supernatural Phenomena

Divine Healing 139
Miracles 148
Angels, Demons, and Exorcism 154
Conclusion 163

CHAPTER 7 · 165
Conclusion

Notes 171

References 179

Index 189

LIST OF TABLES

Table 1	13	Basic demographic information for the interview cohort
Table 2	17	Basic demographic information for the survey respondents
Table 3	28	Highlights from the congregational surveys on religious identity
Table 4	111	Highlights from the congregational surveys on Spirit baptism and glossolalia
Table 5	138	Highlights from the congregational surveys on healing, miracles, and other supernatural phenomena

ACKNOWLEDGEMENTS

WITHOUT THE CONTINUED AND UNWAVERING SUPPORT I received from the dedicatee of this book, David Seljak, I would not be where I am today, nor have achieved half as much. Thank you for believing in me even when I sometimes did not believe in myself. I am a changed and better person for having known you.

Michael Wilkinson invited me into the world of Pentecostal scholarship when I was still very much wet behind the ears. He continues to offer his expert advice and help whenever it is asked of him, and has influenced my own thinking and writing on Canadian Pentecostalism more than any other person. He deserves my thanks, and the thanks of a great many others, for repositioning Canadian Pentecostalism from the periphery to the mainstream of the academic study of religion in Canada.

I would be remiss if I did not recognize the role that the friendships of Amarnath Amarasingam and William Rory Dickson have played in the development of this book, not to mention in the development of myself as both a scholar and a human being. For several years they weekly (and more often daily) listened to the methodological and theoretical challenges that I encountered in the researching and writing of this book, and generously offered their advice and encouragement. Moreover, they were always quick to celebrate my successes even when we competed for the same scarce resources. They were and are models of academic collegiality.

The unconditional love that I receive from my wife, Rebecca, and my son, Alasdair, provides the foundation on which all of my accomplishments are built. They are the motivation for everything that I do and I love them very much.

Finally, I gratefully acknowledge the financial support that directly funded this book from the Social Sciences and Humanities Research Council of Canada in the form of a Joseph-Armand Bombardier CGS Doctoral Scholarship, the University of Waterloo through its very generous scholarship and professional development funding, and the Federation for the Humanities and Social Sciences by way of its Awards to Scholarly Publications Program Publication Grant. The fact that so many different people have considered this book worthy of funding in ever-increasing times of austerity is a great encouragement to me.

1

INTRODUCTION

The Canadian Decline of the World's Fastest-Growing Religion

PENTECOSTALISM—often described as the fastest-growing religious movement in the world (Jacobsen 2011, 354; Westerlund 2009, vii)—includes as many as 600 million adherents, or approximately one out of every ten people on the planet (Johnson and Ross 2010). Although such estimates are often prone to exaggeration, the undeniable growth of Pentecostalism over the last hundred years has caused many scholars of religion to regard it as, in the words of historian Philip Jenkins, "perhaps the most successful social movement of the past century" (2002, 8). The results of a survey conducted by the Pew Forum on Religion and Public Life, for instance, reported that as many as 5 percent of Indians, 11 percent of South Koreans, 26 percent of Nigerians, 30 percent of Chileans, 34 percent of South Africans, 44 percent of Filipinos, 49 percent of Brazilians, 56 percent of Kenyans, and 60 percent of Guatemalans practise some form of Pentecostal Christianity (Lugo et al., 2006, 76-94).[1]

The remarkable growth of Pentecostalism in many parts of the world during the twentieth century meant that the results regarding religious affiliation released by Statistics Canada in 2003 caught Canadian sociologists of religion completely by surprise. The census showed that Canadian Pentecostalism registered a staggering loss of 15.3 percent, or 66,960 affiliates, between 1991 and 2001, the first decline in Canadian Pentecostal history. What was so puzzling about this change was that Pentecostal affiliation had reached an all-time high in Canada just a decade earlier.[2]

The 1991 census showed that 436,435 individuals (approximately 1.5 percent of the Canadian population at the time) identified as Pentecostal (Wilkinson 2006, 16–17; 2009, 4). In fact, the number of Pentecostals in Canada had grown remarkably since 1911, the first year that Pentecostals appeared in a census. In that year the census recorded 515 Canadians who identified as Pentecostal in what would have been only a handful of churches located largely in the provinces of Ontario and Manitoba, where the two earliest centres of Canadian Pentecostalism—Toronto and Winnipeg—were located. By 1921, the number of Canadians identifying as Pentecostal grew to 7,012, marking a 1,361 percent increase in just a decade. Canadian Pentecostalism continued to grow for the next seven decades with little sign of slowing down. At the dawn of the new millennium, the success of Pentecostalism in Canada was so apparent that Canadian sociologist Peter Beyer confidently claimed that "Pentecostalism is growing in almost all regions of Canada" (2000, 85).

In the decade between 1991 and 2001, however, something changed. Upon closer examination, it became clear that after several decades of consistent growth in conservative Protestant affiliation, a number of these denominations experienced marked declines. The relative decreases in affiliation between 1991 and 2001 within the Salvation Army, Pentecostalism, and the Christian Reformed Church, for instance, each exceeded decreases within the United Church of Canada, the Anglican Church of Canada, and the Evangelical Lutheran Church in Canada, three of the fastest-declining Christian denominations in Canada just a decade earlier. It appeared that in just ten years, Pentecostalism had transitioned from one of Canada's fastest-growing Christian denominations to one of the fastest declining. What was perhaps most perplexing was that no one was able to explain why this had happened.

One obvious way to account for the apparent decline of Canadian Pentecostalism is to interpret these census results as representing a real decrease in the actual number of Canadian Pentecostal adherents. Could Pentecostals be experiencing an upward climb on the socio-economic ladder, and, as a result, be leaving behind "a sect of the poor" for one of the "churches of the middle class" (Niebuhr 1929)? Could higher levels of respect, education, and income mean that Pentecostals are now leaving a religious tradition intended for the socially, culturally, and economically deprived for more respectable religious options (Anderson 1979)? Or could Pentecostalism, along with several other Christian denominations, be the victim of a prevailing loss of religiosity within Canadian society that has caused many of its adherents to simply drop out of its ranks altogether (Bruce 2002)? Despite the plethora of theoretical options available that might explain the decline in Canadian Pentecostal affiliation as representing a real decrease in the actual number of Pentecostal adherents, there exist at least four main problems with any such explanation.

First, denominational statistics collected by the Pentecostal Assemblies of Canada (PAOC), which accounts for as many as 60 percent of all Canadian Pentecostals, did not reveal the kind of decreases in attendance, numbers served, or number of congregations that would normally accompany such a dramatic decrease in adherence as that recorded by Statistics Canada. In fact, between 1991 and 2001 the PAOC recorded an *increase* of 10,000 members. While certainly not as large as the increases of previous decades, this casts serious doubt on any attempt to explain the decrease in affiliation recorded by the census as representing an actual decrease in Canadian Pentecostal adherence (Wilkinson 2006, 17-18; 2009, 4-5).

Second, census data on religious affiliation does not correspond to the actual number of adherents within any particular denomination. These numbers simply represent the percentage of people who report a certain religious affiliation or identity. Question twenty-two on the 2001 census instrument—the only question on religion—included the following information to guide census takers: "What is the person's religion? Indicate a specific denomination or religion even if this person is not currently a practising member of that group." What this means is that the numbers collected by Statistics Canada only point to religious self-identification, and, at best, is only ever an approximation of the actual number of practising adherents in any given denomination. As Paul Froese explains, "Individual religiosity is usually measured by belief, behavior, and identity. But these aspects of religiosity are by no means in perfect correlation" (Froese 2008, 106). In other words, someone can self-identify with the

United Church of Canada but never actually attend church or believe or practise any element of the United Church tradition. Conversely, someone might self-identify as a "Christian" or "evangelical," but regularly attend, and be a committed member of, a Pentecostal church. The numbers of actual practising adherents within any particular religious tradition, then, can be either much lower or much higher than their religious affiliation or self-identity may otherwise suggest.

Third, Statistics Canada recorded an increase of 121 percent (approximately 427,000 individuals) among those who reported a generic Christian identification such as "Christian," "Apostolic," "born-again Christian," or "evangelical" between 1991 and 2001. These titles and others are used synonymously by Pentecostals across Canada and around the world in order to describe themselves (Wilkinson 2006, 17; 2009, 6). Thus, a number of the respondents whom census enumerators lumped into this amorphous category would actually be practising Pentecostals. Furthermore, since at least the early 1990s, a number of sociologists of religion in both Canada and the United States have observed the rise of "generic evangelicalism." One important component of generic evangelicalism is the increasing tendency to avoid identifying oneself according to traditional denominational categories (i.e., Anglican, Baptist, Lutheran, Methodist, Pentecostal, Presbyterian, etc.), but rather as simply "Christian," "evangelical," "born-again," or "Christ-follower," as well as a whole host of other generic monikers (Ellingson 2007; Miller 1997; Reimer 2003; Sargeant 2000).

Not unlike those individuals that sociologists of religion call "spiritual but not religious" (Fuller 2001), increasingly, many North American Protestants are claiming that their experience of Christianity is not a religion, but rather a "faith," "journey," "lifestyle," "relationship," or "spirituality." In *The End of Religion: Encountering the Subversive Spirituality of Jesus* (a book read and discussed with me by many of the participants in this study), Canadian pastor Bruxy Cavey (2007) argues that Christianity is not a religion, but rather a unique form of spirituality. He writes: "The Jesus described in the Bible never uses the word *religion* to refer to what he came to establish, nor does he invite people to join a particular institution or organization. When he speaks of the 'church,' he is talking about the people who gather in his name, not the structure that they meet in or the organization that they belong to" (2007, 43; emphasis original).

Cavey's sentiments are echoed by several other popular Protestant authors who have similarly attempted to reframe their traditions in much more individualistic terms (Bell 2005, 2007, 2011; McLaren 2001, 2004, 2006, 2010; Miller 2003; Pagitt 2003; Rollins 2006, 2008, 2009, 2011; Tomlinson 2003). Bearing these observations in mind, it is easy to see how even a small portion of this large increase among those who reported a generically Christian or evangelical religious identity could more than account for the decline among those individuals who no longer chose the term "Pentecostal" to describe their religious affiliation on the census, but who may very well continue to attend Pentecostal congregations.

Finally, the census also recorded an increase of 43.9 percent (approximately 1,460,000 individuals) among those who chose not to report any religious preference between 1991 and 2001. Question twenty-two allowed census takers to record one of two possible responses to the religion question. The first simply included a space to write the individual's religious preference with the instructions: "Specify one denomination or religion only." The second option contained a circle that could be marked with an "X" in order to record "No religion." Contrary to some simplistic interpretations, the so-called religious nones category is not composed of only atheists and agnostics. Sociologist David Eagle, for instance, explains that while most religious nones in Canada "rarely attend church," the results from the General Social Survey administered by Statistics Canada reveal that 7 percent of religious nones report attending church at least yearly and 3 percent attend church weekly or monthly (2011, 188, 194). This means that 10 percent (or 146,000) of all the additional Canadians who were recorded as "religious nones" in the 2001 census actually attended church, and some could have certainly been Pentecostals. Furthermore, Siobhan Chandler has successfully demonstrated that many Canadians who call themselves spiritual but not religious could certainly be described as "progressive, liberal seekers," but that they also simultaneously maintain "some connection to organized religion" (2011, 33). This observation casts serious doubt on the outmoded idea that religious nones and the spiritual but not religious are not present within institutional forms of religion. They certainly may have a deep suspicion of religious institutions and a loose relationship with religious tradition, but this does not mean that they have completely jettisoned these institutions or traditions.[3]

The Transformation of Pentecostalism in Canada

THESE OBSERVATIONS led me to initiate a study of both individual and congregational religiosity in three Canadian Pentecostal churches in the Regional Municipality of Waterloo (or simply, the Region of Waterloo) in an attempt to better understand the decline in Canadian Pentecostal affiliation. Other than being certain that this decline was not the result of a decrease in the actual number of Canadian Pentecostal adherents (due to the reasons just discussed), I began this study with no clear idea of how I was going to explain the dramatic change recorded by Statistics Canada. This uncertainty, however, quickly dissipated after the first few weeks of fieldwork.

Following one Sunday morning service at Freedom in Christ (one of the three congregations where I conducted the research for this study), my wife and I were invited along with a few others to have lunch in the home of a couple from the congregation. Once the dishes were cleared following the meal, we gathered in the living room to talk. I immediately saw the opportunity to informally ask a few questions related to my research. Before long, I asked a man in his early thirties who had been attending Freedom in Christ with his wife and two children for more than six years, "Is it important to you that Freedom in Christ is a Pentecostal church?" After I asked the question, he stared at me with a puzzled look on his face for several seconds, then said, "Freedom in Christ is a Pentecostal church? I didn't know that." Without a second thought, and as casually as if I had just asked him whether it was important to him that the chicken we ate for lunch was free-range, he refocused his attention and joined another conversation. Although my interviewee did not display even the slightest sense of concern regarding what he had learned about the denominational identity of his congregation, I, to say the least, was shocked.

I wondered how it was possible for someone not to know (or even appear to care) that the church that he and his family had been regularly attending for more than six years was Pentecostal. I immediately thought that perhaps this individual was particularly unobservant or especially disinterested in the matter of denominational identity, and, as a result, this fact had gone unnoticed by him. I attempted to hide the perplexed look on my face and proceeded to pose similar questions to about a half-dozen other people gathered in the same living room that Sunday afternoon. To my astonishment, I heard person after person give nearly identical answers: "Freedom in Christ is a Pentecostal church?" Many of these individuals—most of them highly committed and regularly involved members—apparently had been attending Freedom in Christ for years without being aware that it was a Pentecostal church. Furthermore, one man who was aware that he was attending a Pentecostal church did not appear to know what this meant. He responded to my question by saying "Yes, I knew that Freedom was a Pentecostal church, but aren't Pentecostals just something like Baptists?" Suffice it to say, I left lunch that afternoon with a hunch—later confirmed by a year of fieldwork—that provided a possible explanation for the puzzling 2001 census results.

The decrease in Canadian Pentecostal affiliation recorded by Statistics Canada does not provide adequate evidence to claim that Pentecostal adherents have abandoned their churches at a rate of more than 15 percent in the decade between 1991 and 2001. Instead, my hypothesis is that this decrease in affiliation can be explained by the fact that Canadian Pentecostals are experiencing a significant transformation of religious identity and experience from traditionally Pentecostal to generically evangelical categories.[4] In other words, I propose that a significant proportion of those individuals who attend Canadian Pentecostal churches are simply no longer identifying, believing, or behaving as they did just a few decades ago and that this transformation accounts for the dramatic, if misleading, census results.

This development represents a reversal of the phenomenon described by Grace Davie as "believing without belonging" (1994, 2000) and more accurately represents what Danièle Hervieu-Léger calls "belonging without believing" (2006). It is important to note that most Canadian Pentecostals have not become as religiously inactive as the Europeans that Hervieu-Léger describes with this term. Nonetheless, many Canadian Pentecostals appear to be "belonging without believing" in their own way, that is, attending Pentecostal churches without acquiring the degree of commitment to traditional Pentecostal identity, belief, and practice that is necessary in order to influence their religious self-identification on a census form.

Over the last two decades, Pentecostal pastors and denominational leaders from Newfoundland to British Columbia have noticed a significant change in the way that Pentecostals self-identify, what Pentecostals believe, and the ways in which Pentecostals practise their faith. If one were to walk into many present-day Pentecostal churches in Canada on a Sunday morning, one would no longer find evidence of the ecstatic and emotive practices traditionally associated with Pentecostalism, such as being baptized in the Holy Spirit, speaking in tongues, publicly proclaiming a word of prophecy, being slain or falling down under the power of the Holy Spirit, or dancing in the Spirit. Rather, one might wonder if they had accidentally wandered into a Baptist, Brethren, Christian and Missionary Alliance, or Mennonite church. In many Pentecostal churches, the songs sung, the topics of the sermons preached, the rites performed, the curricula used to educate, the books being read, and even the terminology, would be very similar, if not identical, to what they would find within a whole host of other conservative Protestant churches across Canada and the United States.

What is perhaps more interesting is the question of whether or not the average church seeker would even be able to find a Pentecostal church in many communities across Canada. This is not because they do not exist, but because many Pentecostal churches have removed the word "Pentecostal" from their names. A random examination of the names of the ten churches affiliated with the PAOC in Mississauga, Ontario (where the national office of the denomination is located), in 2009 revealed the following: "Christ for Life Ministries," "Faith Alive Christian Centre," "Gift of God Church," "Heartland, A Church Connected," "Iglesia Evangelica Hispana Emmanuel," "La Semance de Vie," "Logos Christian Family Church," "Portico," "Victory Community Church," and "West Edge Community Church." The term "Pentecostal" is not found in the name of a single one of these churches, a phenomenon by no means unique to the city of Mississauga. Changes made to church names may appear as a rather weak indication of a shift in religious identity. Names, however, convey meaning, mark identity, and can reflect much deeper transformations that are occurring below the surface of ordinarily observed religious life.

This rather simple illustration demonstrates the complex process that some scholars of American Pentecostalism have identified as "the evangelicalization of Pentecostalism," which describes the gradual alignment of American

Pentecostalism with the broader American evangelical tradition, often at the expense of Pentecostal denominational and theological distinctiveness (Blumhofer 1993; Patterson 2007; Poloma 1989, 2006; Poloma and Green 2010, 25; Robeck 2002, 922–25; Spittler 1994, 112). These changes are not unique to Pentecostalism but form part of a much broader phenomenon occurring within many other North American Protestant denominations (Ellingson 2007; Miller 1997; Reimer 2000, 2003; Sargeant 2000; Wagner 1997). Sam Reimer describes this trend as the emergence of a "transnational generic evangelicalism," while Stephen Ellingson refers to this process as an evangelical "colonization" (Ellingson 2007, 178–85; Reimer 2000, 242; 2003, 15, 39). Conservative Protestant churches in North America are undergoing a gradual but continual transformation from traditional and denominational identities, theologies, and practices to homogeneous, generic versions.

Nancy Ammerman has also documented a similar homogenization within liberal Protestantism that she calls "Golden Rule Christianity." This form of religious commitment is defined by an ethical interpretation of Christianity where, she found, "the most frequently mentioned characteristic of the Christian life was that people should seek to do good, to make the world a better place" (Ammerman 1997, 197). Sociologist Christian Smith has uncovered an analogous religious attitude among American teenagers that he identifies as "Moralistic Therapeutic Deism." He argues that the defining features of this religious outlook include the following convictions: "1. A God exists who created and orders the world and watches over human life on earth. 2. God wants people to be good, nice, and fair to each other, as taught in the Bible and by most world religions. 3. The central goal of life is to be happy and to feel good about oneself. 4. God does not need to be particularly involved in one's life except when God is needed to resolve a problem. 5. Good people go to heaven when they die" (2005, 162–63).

While some very limited attention has been paid to the evangelicalization or homogenization of American Pentecostalism, this phenomenon has been largely ignored in Canada. The overarching objective of this study, then, is to provide a detailed description of how, in many respects, the religious identity, belief, and practice of the members of three Canadian Pentecostal congregations conform more closely to generic evangelicalism than they do to traditional Pentecostalism. This description will, in turn, provide some admittedly preliminary evidence to help support my hypothesis that the changes in Canadian Pentecostal affiliation recorded by Statistics Canada are the result of a shift in Canadian Pentecostal identity and experience, a shift that has spawned a new kind of Canadian Pentecostal.

Before the discussion moves any further, I need to be very clear about what this book does and does not promise. From the outset, it must be understood that this book is a foray into what is an otherwise unexplored area of research, a lacuna within both the study of Canadian Pentecostalism and the sociology of religion in Canada. As a result, my objective from the beginning was to keep my research extremely focused in an attempt to generate as precise a theory as possible that might explain the decline in Canadian Pentecostal affiliation recorded by Statistics Canada—nothing more, nothing less.

This objective has two important consequences regarding what this book promises to do. First, my explanation of the decline of Canadian Pentecostal affiliation being the result of a transformation of Canadian Pentecostal identity, belief, and practice remains, for the time being, only suggestive of a transformation that may be happening on a much broader scale across the entire spectrum of Canadian Pentecostalism. Without additional research, this hypothesis must remain just that, a hypothesis. If I can convince the reader that the religious identity, belief, and practice on display within the three congregations that I studied is substantially different than it was within the tradition as a whole a generation ago, then I will judge this book to be a success.

Second, the close reader will discern that I do not develop a definitive, overarching explanation regarding what larger social impetus may have initiated this transformation of Canadian Pentecostal identity, belief, and practice. I make no attempt to attribute this change to upward social mobility, secularization, or any of the other numerous metatheories of religious change contained within the common arsenal of sociologists of religion. I agree with Mark Chaves, who writes, "Too often, we develop explanations and interpretations before we are clear about what the facts are" (2011, 4). Basic sociological facts and descriptions of Canadian Pentecostalism are so scarce that I believe the field is best served at the present time by conducting primary research that contributes to the stock of shared information that might enhance our currently impoverished understanding of this important religious tradition. The type of careful, ethnographic research that is at the heart of this study is most helpful for uncovering specific, complex cultural patterns that suggest theories that have relevance for understanding the attitudes and behaviour of communities which share a common culture, such as congregations and denominations. The further the researcher attempts to stretch the implications of ethnographic research beyond the original context in which it was first conducted, the less precise and less helpful it is. I leave this work to social theorists whose job it is to stitch together the diverse tapestry of primary data generated by scholars such as myself who are more interested in answering very specific questions and problems, such as why a group of people suddenly change the way that they respond to a census questionnaire.

Methodology

DUE TO THE LACK OF EXISTING RESEARCH on Canadian Pentecostalism, the primary data that I use in order to demonstrate my hypothesis is derived from ethnographic fieldwork conducted in three churches belonging to the PAOC. The PAOC is the largest Pentecostal denomination in Canada and includes approximately 232,000 adherents, 1,100 congregations, and 3,500 ministers (Wilkinson 2009, 4). All three of the churches are located in the Region of Waterloo in the province of Ontario. The three churches, which will be introduced in much greater detail in chapter 3, are Freedom in Christ, Elmira Pentecostal Assembly, and Elevation. Fieldwork was conducted during a twelve-month period of study beginning in September 2009 and ending in August of 2010.

My ethnographic research yielded two primary sources of information that form the basis of this study. First, and most important, are a series of in-depth interviews that I conducted with forty-two individuals—fourteen from each congregation. All of the interviews were audio-recorded and transcribed in their entirety. Interview participants were recruited by sending an electronic invitation to all members of each congregation for which the churches had active email addresses, as well as through making a brief in person invitation on one Sunday morning within each congregation. All participants except five of the pastors—Tracy Dunham and Del Wells from Freedom in Christ, Hansley Armoogan from Elmira Pentecostal Assembly, and Brandon Malo and Steve Tulloch from Elevation—were given pseudonyms in order to protect their identity. The five pastors granted me permission to use their real names because it would have been impossible to guarantee them anonymity while at the same time using the actual names of the congregations. Interviews were conducted in participants' homes, in interview space generously provided by each of the churches, and at the University of Waterloo.

The interviews consisted of seventy-two semi-structured questions, meaning that I followed a pre-established set of questions with each participant. Interviews ranged in length from 30 to 130 minutes, with an average interview length of 60 minutes. A number of individuals were interviewed more than once when clarification was needed, and some also provided me with additional information through email. I also interviewed denominational officials at the district (provincial) and national levels, and attended denominational meetings and events, where I gathered field notes.

Basic demographic information was gathered from the interview participants by using an interviewee information form that I requested that each participant complete prior to beginning the interview (see table 1). Not including the five participants who declined to provide their age, the average age of the interview cohort was forty years, the median age was thirty-three years, and the youngest and oldest participants were nineteen and seventy-two years of age, respectively. Twenty-four of the participants were men (57 percent) and eighteen were women (43 percent). The higher proportion of male participants was the result of the greater number of both pastors and lay leaders who were men. Of the seven pastors who were interviewed, for instance, five were men.[5]

Some readers familiar with hearing about Pentecostalism's phenomenal growth in many other parts of the world may be surprised that I do not spend more time discussing the relationship between the congregations that I studied and the much larger movement of which it is a part. The reason that the global Pentecostal movement does not feature more prominently in this book is because the three congregations that I studied exhibited neither large numbers of multi-ethnic adherents nor strong relationships with Pentecostals outside of Canada. Twenty-two participants, for instance, described their ethnicity as "Canadian," another eleven as "Caucasian," two as "White," two as "Dutch," one as "USA," one as "Trinidadian," and one as "Jamaican," while two gave no response. In other words, only 5 percent of both interview and

TABLE 1. Basic demographic information for the interview cohort

Name or pseudonym	Date of interview	Church	Age	Marital status	Reported religion	Occupation	Highest level of education
Trevor	11 Sep 2009	Freedom	36	Married	Non-denominational	Professor	Doctorate
Mavis	4 Oct 2009	Freedom	54	Married	Christian	Manager	Master's
Arthur	5 Oct 2009	Freedom	26	Married	Christian	Foreman	College diploma
Colin	19 Oct 2009	Elmira	29	Married	Christian	Financial advisor	Some college/uni.
Caroline	22 Oct 2009	Elmira	24	Single	Christian	Pastor	College diploma
Gordon	22 Oct 2009	Elmira	27	Married	Pentecostal	Student	Some college/uni.
Amy	22 Oct 2009	Freedom	47	Married	Christian	Admin.	Bachelor's
Harold	27 Oct 2009	Freedom	nda*	Married	Grace-centred	Director	College diploma
Derek	2 Nov 2009	Elevation	34	Married	Christian	Teacher	Doctorate
James	28 Nov 2009	Elevation	48	Married	Christian	Software architect	Bachelor's
Steve	2 Dec 2009	Elevation	52	Married	Christian	Pastor	Master's
Del	2 Dec 2009	Freedom	57	Married	Pentecostal	Pastor	College diploma
Martha	7 Dec 2009	Elevation	25	Single	Christian	Social worker	Master's
Brandon	14 Dec 2009	Elevation	32	Married	Christian	Pastor	College diploma
Hansley	16 Dec 2009	Elmira	38	Married	Christian	Pastor	Bachelor's
Alice	18 Dec 2009	Freedom	29	Single	Christian	Student	Some college/uni.
Gwen	19 Jan 2010	Freedom	nda*	Married	Christian	Customer service	High school

Continued …

Name or pseudonym	Date of interview	Church	Age	Marital status	Reported religion	Occupation	Highest level of education
Mike	19 Jan 2010	Elmira	33	Single	Christian	Auto mechanic	College diploma
Kelly	21 Jan 2010	Elevation	31	Married	Christian	Admin.	Some college/uni.
Tracy	22 Feb 2010	Freedom	29	Married	Christian	Pastor	Bachelor's
Thomas	22 Feb 2010	Freedom	33	Single	Pentecostal	Sales	Some college/uni.
Shane	23 Feb 2010	Elmira	27	Married	Christian	Pastor	Some college/uni.
Dennis	24 Feb 2010	Elevation	36	Married	Christian	Civil servant	Bachelor's
Annie	1 Mar 2010	Elevation	33	Married	Christian	Marketing	Bachelor's
Isabel	16 Mar 2010	Elmira	52	Married	Christian	Homemaker	High school
Emily	18 Mar 2010	Freedom	53	Married	Christian	Admin.	High school
Albert	31 Mar 2010	Elevation	20	Single	Christian	Student	Some college/uni.
Edward	31 Mar 2010	Elevation	38	Married	Christian	Admin.	Some college/uni.
Jeremy	5 Apr 2010	Elevation	20	Single	Christian	Student	Some college/uni.
Elizabeth	7 Apr 2010	Elevation	29	Married	Christian	Homemaker	Bachelor's
Sidney	7 Apr 2010	Elevation	35	Married	Christian	Sales	Some college/uni.
Henry	8 Apr 2010	Freedom	32	Married	Christian	Insurance	Bachelor's
Jennifer	21 Apr 2010	Elmira	19	Single	Christian	Student	Some college/uni.

Continued ...

Name or pseudonym	Date of interview	Church	Age	Marital status	Reported religion	Occupation	Highest level of education
Ben	23 Apr 2010	Elmira	70	Married	Pentecostal	Retired	College diploma
Clarabel	23 Apr 2010	Elmira	72	Married	Pentecostal	Retired	College diploma
Elsie	26 Apr 2010	Elmira	29	Married	Born-again	Homemaker	College diploma
Kevin	27 Apr 2010	Elmira	nda*	Married	Christian	Firefighter	High school
Lucy	27 Apr 2010	Elmira	61	Married	Christian	Admin.	High school
Ruth	28 Apr 2010	Elmira	nda*	Married	Pentecostal	Homemaker	High school
Percy	3 May 2010	Elevation	50	Married	Christian	Director	College diploma
Jane	7 May 2010	Freedom	44	Married	Christian	Accountant	Bachelor's
Toby	30 Aug 2010	Elevation	nda*	Single	Christian	Social service	Master's

*no data available

survey participants identified themselves as visible minorities, which appeared to accurately mirror the demographics of the three congregations. Due to the lack of any serious transnational dynamic at work within the congregations other than with other largely white evangelicals in the United States, I restricted myself to discussing the specifically Canadian context in which these churches were primarily embedded.

Six participants had a high school education, eleven had some college or university education, ten had college diplomas, nine had undergraduate degrees, four had master's degrees, and two had doctoral degrees. A little more than 35 percent of participants had at least an undergraduate degree, which is more than four times greater than the national average for Pentecostals (8.2 percent), and more than two times greater than the national average for all Canadians (15.4 percent) (Statistics Canada 2001).

There exist at least three possible explanations for participants' above-average educational attainment: (1) the presence of seven universities within a hundred-mile radius of the Region of Waterloo could mean that university education is accessed at a higher rate by people living in the region; (2) those individuals with higher levels of education might have been more inclined to participate in the study as is typical in social research of many kinds; (3) the pastors might have encouraged their more educated members to participate in interviews.

The second primary source of information for this study was provided by a fifty-six-question survey that I administered within each of the three congregations using the online service SurveyMonkey (see table 2). The survey included five categories of questions and was intended to collect information regarding participants' religious identities (questions 1–10), religious beliefs (questions 11–23), religious practices (questions 24–33), social values (questions 34–45), and demographic information (questions 46–56).

Because I had access to the entire population of these congregations, I did not use a random sampling, but rather conducted a census enumeration, or entire population survey (LeCompte and Schensul 2010, 97). In other words, I made the survey available to every adult member of the three congregations. The survey yielded 158 completed responses (50 from Freedom in Christ, 38 from Elmira Pentecostal Assembly, and 70 from Elevation) from the total adult population of 515 people (125 from Freedom in Christ, 90 from Elmira Pentecostal Assembly, and 300 from Elevation), for a response rate of just over 30 percent. The 158 completed responses include all those individuals who read through the entire survey, but this does not necessarily mean that each respondent answered every question. The total adult population, or sample frame, was derived from a combination of congregational statistics, head counts that I conducted, and the churches' contact lists.

The survey revealed some important demographic information concerning the members of the three congregations. For instance, 56.7 percent of respondents indicated that they had been attending their current church for five or fewer years, suggesting a relatively high turnover rate. Only 47.4 percent of respondents indicated that they had attended a Pentecostal church prior to coming to their present congregation, and 37 percent of respondents reported that they had attended a Pentecostal church most frequently as a child. This

TABLE 2. Basic demographic information for the survey respondents

	Freedom in Christ	Elmira Pentecostal Assembly	Elevation
Number of respondents who completed the survey	50	38	70
Percentage of adult population who completed the survey	40.0	42.0	23.0
Median age range of respondents	31-35	41-45	26-30
Percentage of respondents who were men / women	56 / 44	44 / 56	42 / 58
Percentage reporting a visible minority status	7.0	4.0	6.5
Percentage who were married	86.1	92.0	67.7
Median household income range in 2009 before taxes	$85,000-$89,999	$75,000-$79,999	$50,000-$54,999
Percentage with at least a bachelor's degree	39.5	20.0	53.2
Most commonly reported occupational category	Professional (34.9%)	Professional (25%)	Student (33.9%)
Percentage who owned their own home	78.0	88.0	56.5
Most common city of residence	Kitchener (74.4%)	Elmira (66.7%)	Waterloo (59.7%)

means that the majority of respondents came to their current churches from non-Pentecostal backgrounds.

The survey also showed that 56.7 percent of respondents reported that they attend four Sunday morning church services in a typical month and 52.3 percent of respondents claimed that they give at least 10 percent of their income to their church, the traditional Pentecostal expectation.[6] The median age of respondents was thirty-one to thirty-five years of age, while 47 percent of respondents were men and 53 percent of respondents were women. Other than two respondents who described their ethnicity as "Other," two as "Black," and four as "Asian," the rest reported their ethnicity as "White." Twenty percent described their marital status as "never married," 74.6 percent as "married, never divorced," 3.8 percent as "divorced," and 1.5 percent as "separated." All but 5.7 percent of married respondents indicated that their spouse attended the same congregation. Respondents' median annual household income was $65,000–$69,999, with 17 percent of respondents reporting an annual household income greater than $100,000. A total of 42 percent of respondents—7 percent greater than the interview participants—indicated that they had earned at least an undergraduate degree. Only 3.1 percent of respondents indicated that they were "laid off, looking for work," with the single largest group of participants (28.7 percent) describing their occupation as "professional." Seventy percent said they owned their own home, and the majority of respondents indicated that they lived in either Kitchener (34.1 percent), Waterloo (32.6 percent), or Elmira (15.5 percent).

The interviews and survey were supplemented by a few other important sources of information. These included twelve months of sustained participant observation within each of the three churches, interviews with denominational leaders, content analysis of the sermons and songs performed at each of the three churches, and an examination of the material culture present at each of the churches. Some of the materials that I analyzed included annual business meeting reports, curricula, orders of service, promotional materials, religious literature, and website content. The personal interviews, surveys, participant observation, and content analysis provided an excellent range of data collection methods in order to triangulate my research results (LeCompte and Schensul 2010, 180). Except for a few interesting areas of inconsistency that will be discussed later, these data sources corroborated one another and together provided a rich picture of the religious identity, beliefs, and practices of the members of the three congregations.

Outline of the Chapters

THE NEXT CHAPTER provides a brief introduction to the Pentecostal tradition, which is especially important for readers who lack familiarity with the movement. Here I offer a functional definition of Pentecostalism, briefly outline the origins of Pentecostalism in the United States and Canada, and, in the final section of the chapter, develop ideal types of traditional Canadian Pentecostal identity, belief, and practice. Before it is possible to determine whether the religious identity and experience expressed by participants adhere to or depart from traditional Pentecostalism, we must first establish static, historical types for these categories that can then be used as a rule against which to measure changes that might exist within Pentecostalism both over time and between different geographical locations.

Chapter 3 is where the reader first becomes acquainted with the voices of the participants through some of the ethnographic material collected during the course of this study. Here I present brief vignettes of the three congregations and also provide short life histories of the senior pastors of each of the churches.

Chapters 4, 5, and 6 are the core of this study. They provide the raw data necessary to demonstrate my hypothesis. In chapter 4, I describe the preponderance of a generically evangelical religious identity among the members of the three congregations. Because it is necessary to first understand what generic evangelicalism is before it is possible to determine whether or not the members of the three congregations exhibit any of the features of this subculture, I begin by providing a definition of the term and describe its main characteristics, namely its tendency towards homogenization and alignment with the culture of therapeutic individualism. I then propose a continuum of religious identity composed of (1) traditional denominational identifiers, (2) latent denominational identifiers, and (3) non-denominational identifiers. This continuum can be used to categorize and understand the ways that various Pentecostals, and possibly members of other religious traditions, choose to describe their religious affiliations. The 86 percent of interview participants who used a generically evangelical or Christian term rather than the term "Pentecostal" to describe their religious affiliation provides evidence to support my hypothesis that Canadian Pentecostal identity is transforming from traditionally Pentecostal to generically evangelical categories.

Chapter 5 describes how the beliefs and practices of the individual members of the three congregations regarding the baptism of the Holy Spirit and speaking in tongues—Pentecostalism's two most distinctive characteristics—do not conform to traditional Pentecostal types. I argue that those elements of Spirit baptism and glossolalia that are either absent or present among participants are those that either oppose or reinforce, respectively, a largely therapeutic understanding of these experiences, which is a core component of the generic evangelical subculture.

In chapter 6, I detail participants' experiences of divine healing, miracles, and other supernatural phenomena such as angels, demons, and the practice of exorcism. Unlike the previous chapter, chapter 6 demonstrates how many of the individuals with whom I spoke expressed commitment to some important traditional Pentecostal experiences. I argue, however, that these individuals do not conform to traditional Pentecostal types regarding divine healing, miracles, and other supernatural phenomena because of any special commitment to the Pentecostal tradition. Rather, I demonstrate that these commitments were expressed at such high rates because the idea that God wishes to relieve suffering through healing, protection, and deliverance already fit into the modern, therapeutic understanding of religion predominant within these generically evangelical congregations.

2

The Pentecostal Tradition

Defining Pentecostalism

Before I introduce the Pentecostal tradition through the discussion of Pentecostal origination, identity, theology, and practice, it is important to first explain how it is that I understand and use the term "Pentecostal." I discern four major approaches to defining Pentecostalism commonly used within the academic study of the tradition: (1) social scientific, (2) theological, (3) historical, and (4) phenomenological. Although definitions are always imperfect because the objects that they define are often in flux, a phenomenological definition of Pentecostalism avoids many of the problems often associated with most social scientific, theological, and historical definitions of the tradition.[7] The pioneering scholar of global Pentecostalism Walter J. Hollenweger explained the rationale for a phenomenological definition of Pentecostalism when he wrote, "Worldwide there is so much variety that about all one can say is that a Pentecostal is a Christian who calls himself a Pentecostal. . . . It's not a strictly theological definition but a phenomenological one" (1998).

Some may rightly wonder how it is that I can adopt such a definition of Pentecostalism given that I have already indicated that most of the participants I spoke with explicitly did not identify themselves as Pentecostal. While most of the participants did not describe themselves as Pentecostal, they did, nonetheless, regularly attend churches that were affiliated with an explicitly Pentecostal denomination. A scholar of religion would not question that an individual who regularly attended a Hindu temple to pray and give offerings, but with whom the amorphous term "Hindu" did not resonate, was, from a strictly phenomenological point of view, what Westerners call a Hindu. I simply applied the same phenomenological principle to participants in the present study. If individuals either called themselves Pentecostals or regularly attended Pentecostal churches (whether or not they were aware of the fact that the churches they attended were Pentecostal), I considered them to be Pentecostals.

Scholars who adopt a phenomenological definition of Pentecostalism recognize the inherent danger in establishing narrow social, theological, or historical criteria—such as the necessity of glossolalia, Spirit baptism, or specific historical relationships—in order to define who is and who is not a Pentecostal. Such narrow definitions will necessarily exclude large numbers of individuals who do not neatly fit into these criteria, but who share, as Allan Anderson explains, "a family resemblance that emphasizes the working of the Holy Spirit" (2010, 15).

In order to address this problem, a number of scholars have developed broad, phenomenological typologies that attempt to account for the diversity found within the global Pentecostal tradition (Anderson 2010, 16–20; Burgess and van der Maas 2002, xvii–xxiii; Hollenweger 1997, 1; Miller and Yamamori 2007, 25–31; Stewart 2012a, 4–5). While there exists little consensus regarding the number and names of the various types, most scholars agree that there exist at least three major branches within the global Pentecostal movement. First are classical Pentecostals, who attend churches sharing historical roots with the Holiness, Reformed, or Oneness Pentecostal denominations formed in North America during the first few decades of the twentieth century. Second are Charismatics, who are members of non-Pentecostal denominations and include, for example, Anglicans, Baptists, Eastern Orthodox, Lutherans, Methodists, Presbyterians, and Roman Catholics who, beginning in the 1950s, adopted Pentecostal theology, practices, and spirituality but decided to intentionally remain within and "renew" their existing denominations. Third are Neo-Pentecostals (also sometimes called Neo-Charismatics, Independent Charismatics, or Proto-Pentecostals), which include non-denominational and independent Christians all over the world who have adopted some aspects of Pentecostal theology, practice, and spirituality but who are not affiliated with either classical Pentecostal or traditional Christian denominational bodies. Some scholars use the term "Renewalists" to refer to all three of these groups of Christians. In this book, however, I simply use the term "Pentecostal" to refer to all three of these groups as a whole, while the terms "classical Pentecostal," "Charismatic," and "Neo-Pentecostal" are used to identify the individual segments of the larger, global Pentecostal movement.

Pentecostal Beginnings

THE ORIGINS OF PENTECOSTALISM are traditionally traced to two important revivals that occurred at the turn of the twentieth century in the United States. The first began in Topeka, Kansas, on 1 January 1901, under the leadership of Charles F. Parham (1873–1929) and the second in Los Angeles, California, on 9 April 1906, under the auspices of William J. Seymour (1870–1922). While Pentecostalism emerged as a discernable religious movement in the first decade of the twentieth century, it did not simply appear out of thin air as traditional narratives of Pentecostal origination often claim. Rather, the beginning of Pentecostalism was the result of the adoption and adaptation of a number of important religious currents already well under way within the broader spectrum of late-nineteenth- and early-twentieth-century Anglo-American radical evangelicalism.

Two of the most important of these influences were the Keswick and the healing home movements. The first emphasized the renewing power that the "infilling" of the Holy Spirit offered Christians in order to live a "higher life" of victory over the power of temptation and sin (Bundy 1975, 1993; Marsden 2006, 72–101). The second represented a burgeoning industry of independent homes and missions, established all over the world, that aimed to provide prayer and guidance for those seeking divine physical healing (Curtis 2007; Opp 2005). While both of these movements played an important role in the development of early Pentecostal theology and spirituality, it was the Methodist Holiness movement that was perhaps most responsible for giving shape to the emerging Pentecostal movement. The Pentecostal historian William W. Menzies writes that the Holiness movement was "the cradle in which the Pentecostal revival was rocked" (Menzies 1975, 97). Additionally, Vinson Synan believes that "what made Pentecostals different from their predecessors was the teaching that the charismata, especially the gift of tongues, was the sign of receiving the subsequent 'second blessing.' . . . Pentecostalism was basically a modified 'second blessing' Methodist spirituality that was pioneered by John Wesley and passed down to his followers in the holiness movement, out of which came the modern Pentecostal movement" (1997, xi).

Here Menzies and Synan argue that Pentecostals are really Methodists who simply added speaking in tongues to the Holiness doctrine of entire sanctification (a second spiritual experience following justification) as a means of verifying the authenticity of the experience (Dayton 1987, 176-78). This is, as both scholars duly acknowledge, an oversimplification; however, the relationship between the Holiness movement and Pentecostalism runs deep. Donald W. Dayton goes so far as to write that "Pentecostalism cannot be understood apart from its deep roots in the Methodism experience" (2009, 171).

The individual who perhaps most articulately explains the relationship between the Holiness movement and Pentecostalism is the historian Donald W. Dayton. In his important book *Theological Roots of Pentecostalism* (1987), Dayton explains that the theological ideas of John Wesley (1703-91)—the founder of Methodism—underwent an elaborate process of revision that laid the necessary groundwork needed to make Pentecostalism a possibility. John Wesley taught that there existed two works of grace leading to salvation that took the form of distinct religious experiences in the life of the believer: justification and sanctification. Justification is the spiritual process that occurs at the time of conversion when one makes a profession of faith, during which God forgives the various sinful acts (or "actual sin") that an individual has committed over the course of his or her life. Sanctification, Wesley and future Methodists believed, is a second spiritual process that occurs sometime after justification, whereby God cleanses the individual from the effects that all humans suffer due to existing in a perpetual state of sin resulting from the fall of Adam and Eve in the Garden of Eden (or "original sin"); this cleansing removes, or at least seriously mitigates, an individual's desire to sin.

Wesley understood sanctification as both a crisis (an event that happens at a distinct moment in an individual's life) and a process (the gradual increase in holiness over the entire span of one's life). Wesley's thoughts on sanctification were augmented by those of John Fletcher, who described the second blessing of entire sanctification as the "baptism of the Holy Spirit" and preferred to think of it as an event that occurred at a fixed point in one's life, which differed from Wesley's preference for both the event and process motifs (Dayton 1987, 35–60; 2009).

It was not until after the American Civil War (1861–65) that the Holiness movement, which Dayton refers to as "the middle term between Methodism and Pentecostalism," gained serious traction within Methodism (2009, 178). Postbellum Holiness adherents followed in the tradition of Fletcher in two important ways. First, they placed much more emphasis on the experience of sanctification as a distinct event as opposed to a gradual process, which they preferred to call "entire sanctification." This was thought to complete the process of salvation initiated in conversion and to make it possible to live a perfect life of holiness without sin. Second, they also commonly referred to entire sanctification as "the baptism of the Holy Spirit," which denoted that, in addition to holiness or perfection from sin, this second work of grace also provided power for Christian service.

In time, a more radical faction within the larger Holiness movement decided to separate this single, second work of grace held to within Methodism and the mainstream Holiness movement into two distinct works: entire sanctification, which came to refer exclusively to the attainment of or growth in holiness, and the baptism of the Holy Spirit, which became solely used to designate the acquisition of supernatural power. Thus, members of the radical Holiness movement, such as the Canadian R. C. Horner and the American Asa Mahan, proposed three separate works of grace leading to salvation: (1) justification (at the time of conversion), (2) entire sanctification (providing holiness), and (3) the baptism of the Holy Spirit (giving power) (Anderson 2004, 19–38; Dayton 1987, 35–114; Synan 1997, 22–67).

These three-work advocates were thought of by most members of the Holiness movement as heretics, and most Methodist and Holiness denominations banned this three-work theology from their official church teachings, instead retaining only justification and sanctification as the two necessary experiences leading to salvation. The importance of this theological innovation in preparing the way for the development of Pentecostalism is difficult to overstate. The three-works-of-grace paradigm established the experience of the baptism of the Holy Spirit as a distinct spiritual event in the life of the believer, which then required only the adoption of speaking in tongues (a not uncommon occurrence within Holiness circles) as a definitive sign or evidence of the authenticity of this experience in order to mark Pentecostalism as a theological tradition distinct from both Methodism and the Holiness movement. In other words, as Donald Dayton writes, "One need only to add the practice of 'speaking in tongues' to have full-blown Pentecostalism" (2009, 184).

It is important to realize that the concepts of a third work of grace or "third blessing," the baptism of the Holy Spirit, and speaking in tongues each on their own added nothing new to late-nineteenth- and early-twentieth-century evangelical revivalism; they were each adhered to and practised by numerous evangelicals. What was truly novel about Pentecostalism, however, was the specific arrangement of these three concepts that required speaking in tongues as a necessary evidence of the third blessing baptism of the Holy Spirit, which proved to be one of the most important combinations of religious concepts developed in the twentieth century. As Donald Dayton again explains, "Popular Evangelicalism was indeed at the time but a hairsbreadth from Pentecostalism. That hairsbreadth of difference was the experience of speaking in tongues as the evidence of having received the baptism with the Holy Spirit" (1987, 176).

The individual who, beginning in 1901, was responsible for putting these varied pieces together into a coherent Pentecostal theological system by advocating tongues speech as the evidence of Spirit baptism, thus earning himself the title of "the founder of Pentecostal theology," was Charles F. Parham (Jacobsen 2003, 18). The pioneering work of Parham was more broadly popularized by one of his students, the African-American pastor William J. Seymour, who was the leader of the Apostolic Faith Mission in Los Angeles, California, that became the site of the now famous 1906–9 Azusa Street Revival so often, though erroneously, described as the isolated source of the global Pentecostal tradition (Stewart 2012b; Stewart 2014).

Early Pentecostals eventually augmented the three blessings pioneered by the radical Holiness movement with the additional beliefs of divine healing and the second coming of Jesus Christ in order to form the full gospel, the beliefs in Jesus Christ as (1) saviour, (2) sanctifier, (3) baptizer in the Holy Spirit, (4) healer, and (5) soon-coming king. Eventually, Dayton explains, those Pentecostals who came from a Reformed theological background and many members influenced by the largely Reformed Keswick movement, lacking any kind of loyalty to Wesley or the doctrine of sanctification, dropped sanctification as a key Pentecostal experience in favour of a fourfold or foursquare gospel: Jesus Christ as (1) saviour, (2) baptizer in the Holy Spirit, (3) healer, and (4) coming king (Dayton 1987, 17-28).

These developments resulted in two major divisions within the early Pentecostal movement: the Holiness (sometimes called Wesleyan), fivefold Pentecostals; and the Reformed (sometimes called Baptistic), fourfold Pentecostals. The Holiness wing of Pentecostalism advocated two works of grace—justification and sanctification—and a third blessing, baptism of the Holy Spirit, that is not tied to the order of salvation. It possessed a significant African-American constituency, thrived in the southern United States where the Holiness movement was most strong, and is today represented by denominations such as the Church of God in Christ, the Church of God (Cleveland, Tennessee), and the Pentecostal Holiness Church. The Reformed wing of Pentecostalism conflated the two works of grace held within Holiness Pentecostalism into a single "finished work" of grace (justification simultaneously including sanctification) that occurred entirely at the time of conversion, and it viewed the baptism of the Holy Spirit as a second blessing unrelated to salvation. It contained a predominantly white constituency, was initially more successful in the northern and western United States and Canada, and now includes the Assemblies of God, the International Church of the Foursquare Gospel, the PAOC, and the Pentecostal Assemblies of Newfoundland and Labrador. The Reformed Pentecostal paradigm represents the predominant theological position among Canadian Pentecostals.

The early Pentecostal movement would undergo another theologically significant innovation when Australian Frank Ewart and American Glen Cook re-baptized each other in the name of Jesus in response to a sermon they heard by Canadian Pentecostal Robert E. McAlister at a camp meeting in

Arroyo Seco, California, in 1913. In his sermon, McAlister, who had previously received the baptism of the Holy Spirit at Azusa Street in 1906, was reflecting on the differences between Jesus's instructions to baptize "in the name of the Father and of the Son and of the Holy Spirit"[8] and the practice of the apostles, who only baptized in the name of Jesus.[9] He concluded that by using the names "Father, Son, and Holy Spirit" in the book of Matthew, Jesus was speaking parabolically about himself and that the apostolic baptismal formula found in Acts was, in fact, more reflective of the singular nature of God. The theological reflection that Ewart, Franklin Small, Andrew Urshan, and the highly influential African-American Garfield T. Haywood subsequently devoted to this concept, resulted in a third major stream within the Pentecostal movement, which was known as Oneness Pentecostalism. Oneness, Apostolic, or Jesus Only Pentecostals, as they are variously referred to, reject the doctrine of the Trinity and require that members be baptized in the name of Jesus Christ alone. The majority of Oneness Pentecostals derive historically and theologically from the Reformed, fourfold Pentecostal stream and today include denominations such as the Pentecostal Assemblies of the World and the United Pentecostal Church (Dayton 1987, 18–19; Reed 2008).

The two early epicentres of Canadian Pentecostalism were the ministries of James and Ellen Hebden in Toronto, Ontario, which "turned" Pentecostal on 18 November 1906, and that of Andrew H. Argue in Winnipeg, Manitoba, which began on 2 May 1907 (Miller 1994, 76; Stewart 2010a). The first historically confirmed individual to experience the Pentecostal Spirit baptism in Canada was Ellen Hebden on 17 November 1906, which appeared to occur independently of the Azusa Street Revival in Los Angeles (Stewart 2010a; Stewart 2014). From this experience emerged the first Canadian Pentecostal congregation, the East End Mission or Hebden Mission, led by Ellen and her husband, James, in the city of Toronto.

Given that the Hebdens retired in 1921, and that Ellen, the mission's primary leader, died on 11 May 1923, the influence of the Hebden Mission on the development of Canadian Pentecostalism, while significant, was also relatively brief. Additionally, the already existing infrastructure of the North American Holiness movement networks meant that the Canadian–American border did little to impede the news of what was happening at the various centres of the Pentecostal revival in the United States, most notably, at Azusa Street. While

Canadian Pentecostalism may not owe its origins to the revival in Los Angeles, the work of Seymour at Azusa Street still exerted a considerable influence upon the development of early Pentecostalism in Canada. Michael Di Giacomo explains:

> While it can be strongly argued that the Hebden Mission influenced the development of Pentecostalism in Canada, the point should not be exaggerated. All early influential Canadian Pentecostal leaders probably came into contact with the Hebden Mission, and therefore its influence in the development of early Canadian Pentecostalism should certainly be recognized as significant. However, the US contribution, especially the Azusa Street Mission, is undeniable and must also be given due credit in the beginning and development of Pentecostalism in Canada. . . . The stamp of Azusa Street on Canadian Pentecostalism is indelible. (2009, 18-19)

Thirteen years after the beginning of the Pentecostal revival in Canada, a number of Canadian Pentecostal leaders, mostly from eastern Canada, organized the PAOC, which received its charter from the government of Canada on 17 May 1919. The PAOC remains the largest and most influential Pentecostal denomination in Canada, currently accounting for approximately 60 percent of all Pentecostals in Canada, the remaining 40 percent being distributed among approximately twelve smaller Pentecostal denominations and numerous independent churches. In that same year, Pentecostals in Alberta and Saskatchewan decided to join the American Pentecostal denomination, the Assemblies of God. In 1920, the PAOC itself also joined the Assemblies of God, which further attests to the co-operation common between Canadian and American Pentecostals in the earliest decades of the movement.

In 1925, the PAOC left the Assemblies of God, which meant that it now included Pentecostals from all nine of the Canadian provinces (Newfoundland was at that time still a part of Great Britain). In 1930, Pentecostals in Newfoundland formed the Pentecostal Assemblies of Newfoundland (now the Pentecostal Assemblies of Newfoundland and Labrador), which remains a distinct denomination but co-operates with the PAOC, allowing its members and ministers to move freely between the two organizations. Over the course of the following decades, both the PAOC and the Pentecostal Assemblies of Newfoundland and Labrador continued to add new churches and members to their rosters (Atter 1965; Hewett 2002; Janes 1996; Kulbeck 1958; Kydd 2002a, 2002b; Miller 1994).

Traditional Canadian Pentecostal Identity, Belief, and Practice

WHILE RONALD KYDD was certainly correct to point out that "Canadian Pentecostals have qualified as evangelicals from the outset" (1997, 295), it is equally true that early Canadian Pentecostals were not completely accepted by the broader evangelical movement, nor did they understand themselves primarily by the same quadrilateral of evangelical ideology (conversionism, activism, biblicism, and crucicentrism) as did other evangelicals.[10] Rather, as I have already mentioned, early Canadian Pentecostals defined themselves according to the fourfold Christological construct that saw Jesus Christ as saviour, Spirit baptizer, healer, and coming king. While the first, fourth, and often even the third, of these emphases were shared by many other evangelicals at the beginning of the twentieth century, the second component of the fourfold gospel—Spirit baptism evidenced by speaking in another language— certainly was not, and it served to distinguish early Pentecostals from other evangelicals. As a result, Kydd explains, "the relationship between the two groups has not always been harmonious, and this tension has frequently been palpable as evangelicals have decried Pentecostalism's emotional excesses, while Pentecostals have scorned a lack of real power in evangelicalism" (1997, 300). Until recent decades, then, there existed very little ambiguity surrounding whether or not someone was a Pentecostal. John Steinbeck's portrayal of the Pentecostal Reverend Jim Casy in his Pulitzer Prize-winning novel (later adapted into an Academy Award-winning film), *The Grapes of Wrath* (1939); James Baldwin's African-American Pentecostal character Gabriel Grimes in his acclaimed novel, *Go Tell It on the Mountain* (1952); Martin Scorsese's vision of Pentecostal murderer and rapist Max Cady (played by Robert De Niro) in his 1991 remake of the 1962 film *Cape Fear*; Robert Duvall's rendering of Pentecostal preacher Euliss "Sonny" Dewey in his 1997 film, *The Apostle*; and Heidi Ewing and Rachel Grady's depiction of Pentecostal children's pastor Becky

Fischer in their 2006 film, *Jesus Camp*: each clearly demonstrates that Pentecostals have routinely been characterized as largely indigent, illiterate, sex-crazed maniacs for much of the last hundred years (Wacker 2001a).

Even earlier in the movement's history, Pentecostals were subjected to ridicule in the popular media, experienced restricted access to employment and education, and suffered the burning of their churches by other Christians. David Barrett's claim that Pentecostals "are more harassed, persecuted, suffering, and martyred than perhaps any other Christian tradition in recent history" (1988, 119) may be an exaggeration. Nonetheless, until recent decades, Pentecostals were often the victims of discrimination. One participant in this study, for instance, recounted to me that when he applied to work as a firefighter in the city of Kitchener in the 1970s, he did not identify himself as a Pentecostal out of fear of not being hired. Also, two other individuals told me that they were denied admission to doctoral programs—one at the University of Toronto and the other at the University of Waterloo—because they were Pentecostal. In an admissions interview, the applicant to the University of Waterloo, who also happened to be a Pentecostal minister at the time, was asked condescendingly by a faculty member whether he wanted to pursue doctoral studies simply to find interesting sermon illustrations. As a result, both of these individuals went on to earn doctorates at other universities. The historically inaccurate, but widely popular, caricature of Pentecostals "as a crude movement of hillbillies and country bumpkins, attracting the lowly or 'disinherited' who sought compensation for their poor lot on earth in a theology of divine reward," meant that there was little ambiguity surrounding the question of whether or not one identified oneself as part of this largely despised religious tradition (Griffith 1998, 222).

In addition to the often high social costs of Pentecostal membership, the doctrinal and ritual requirements of the Pentecostal tradition (namely speaking in tongues as evidence of Spirit baptism) further served to solidify Pentecostal identity until the proliferation of the Charismatic movement in the later decades of the twentieth century made these beliefs and practices more widely accepted within mainline Christianity (Blumhofer, Spittler, and Wacker 1999). Central to Pentecostal identity in the decades before the 1990s, and even in some congregations to this day, was the necessity of having received the Pentecostal experience of Spirit baptism with the evidence of speaking in tongues.

Because of the obviously visible nature of this experience, it was difficult for adherents to avoid this doctrinal and ritual requirement for much of Canadian Pentecostal history.

In short, either you believed and acted a certain way, and so were considered Pentecostal, or you were often excluded from the fold. This practice was a symptom of Pentecostalism's configuration as a sect during at least the first half of its history. William Sims Bainbridge defines a sect as "a deviant religious organization with traditional beliefs and practices," deviant meaning a "departure from the norms of a culture in such a way as to incur the imposition of extraordinary costs from those who maintain the culture" (1997, 24). In other words, Pentecostalism's emergence from the controversial Holiness and Keswick movements of the late nineteenth and early twentieth centuries, in addition to Pentecostalism's recovery of traditional, although no less controversial, ecstatic Christian practices, meant a somewhat strained relationship with society and an easily defined membership. This resulted in a clearly demarcated religious identity within the broader spectrum of North American Christianity for most of its history.

Historian Douglas Jacobsen has argued that "the years 1930 to 1955 form a distinct period in the history of Pentecostal theology" (1999, 90). He elaborates: "These were the years of second-generation Pentecostalism, and the theology produced during them was decisively shaped by the particular needs of this generation and the predilections of its leaders. The most prominent characteristics of the Pentecostal theology written during this era . . . were its logical organization and systematic completeness. Never before had Pentecostals arranged their beliefs with such a degree of logic" (1999, 90). Jacobsen goes on to characterize this period of Pentecostal theological history as the age of "Pentecostal scholasticism" (1999, 90). These were the decades when Pentecostal doctrine was codified into formal systematic theologies, which both guided the movement and served as a touchstone for what it meant to be, believe, and act as a Pentecostal for the next several decades.

While Jacobsen's analysis focuses on the PAOC's sister denomination in the United States, the Assemblies of God, his premise holds true in Canada as well. The two primary textual descriptions of distinctly Canadian Pentecostal forms of both orthodoxy and orthopraxy were developed between 1928 and 1954, largely paralleling the period of American Pentecostal scholasticism identified by Jacobsen. The first of these sources is the PAOC's *Statement of Fundamental and Essential Truths* (PAOC 1994), which is the denomination's official rule of faith. Initially, the PAOC did not adopt a doctrinal statement because the leadership of the denomination believed that such a statement would promote disunity in what was at the time an extremely diverse theological and practical tradition (Miller 1994, 116). When the leaders of the denomination did eventually decide in 1926 that an official rule of faith was needed, they largely adopted the statement earlier developed by the Assemblies of God. It was not until 1928 that the PAOC constructed its own distinct doctrinal statement, entitled *Statement of Fundamental Truths* (Miller 1994, 120). While there have been numerous changes made to both the format and the wording of the statement over the last number of decades, the theology of the current *Statement of Fundamental and Essential Truths* is virtually unchanged from the 1928 original in matters of distinctly Pentecostal content.

The second source documenting traditional Canadian Pentecostal belief and practice is the collective writings of James Eustace Purdie, whom Peter Althouse calls "arguably the most influential person in the formation and development of PAOC doctrine" (Althouse 1996, 3). In addition to playing a significant role in the leadership and the development of the curriculum within the denomination's first college, Purdie also contributed to the codification of traditional Canadian Pentecostal theology and ritual in two other important ways. First, during the 1950s, Purdie sat on the committee that oversaw changes made to the denomination's *Statement of Fundamental and Essential Truths*. Second, Purdie authored two texts published and distributed by the PAOC that served as official explanations of traditional belief and practice within the denomination. The first text, published in 1951, is a 567-question catechism entitled *Concerning the Faith*; the second, published in 1954, is a much shorter thirty-two-page summary of Pentecostal doctrine entitled *What We Believe*. In addition to many of the broadly shared evangelical beliefs and practices such as the authority of the Bible, the virgin birth, the atonement, the bodily resurrection and ascension of Jesus, salvation, evangelism, heaven and hell, and the second coming, Purdie also discusses the Pentecostal themes of the baptism of the Holy Spirit, speaking in tongues, and divine healing, the three most important traditional Canadian Pentecostal beliefs and practices. In what follows, I briefly outline how the *Statement of Fundamental and Essential*

Truths and the two texts written by Purdie explain these three central doctrines and rituals, which, I argue, can be used to help construct ideal types of traditional Canadian Pentecostal identity, belief, and practice.

The preamble to the *Statement of Fundamental and Essential Truths* explains that the PAOC "emphasizes Christ as Saviour and coming King. It also presents Christ as Healer and it adopts the distinctive position that speaking in tongues is the initial evidence when Christ baptizes in the Holy Spirit" (PAOC 1994, 2). Here, in a nutshell, can be found a commitment to Dayton's common fourfold pattern within early Pentecostalism, the beliefs in Christ as saviour, baptizer in the Holy Spirit (accompanied by speaking in tongues), healer, and coming king (Dayton 1987, 15-28). When salvation and the second coming are removed, given that they are widely shared doctrines among most evangelicals, one is left with the same three distinctly Pentecostal beliefs and practices emphasized by Purdie in his writings: Spirit baptism, tongues, and healing.

While healing was indeed a pivotal doctrine and practice among early Pentecostals, it was the baptism of the Holy Spirit and speaking in tongues that were the most important markers of identity and religious experiences within early Pentecostalism. As Grant Wacker writes, "When early Pentecostals wanted to explain themselves to the outside world—indeed when they wanted to explain themselves to each other—they usually started with the experience of Holy Ghost baptism signified by speaking in tongues" (2001b, 35). Regarding the baptism of the Holy Spirit and speaking in tongues, the *Statement of Fundamental and Essential Truths* states: "The baptism in the Holy Spirit is an experience in which the believer yields control of himself to the Holy Spirit. Through this he comes to know Christ in a more intimate way, and receives power to witness and grow spiritually. Believers should earnestly seek the baptism in the Holy Spirit according to the command of our Lord Jesus Christ. The initial evidence of the baptism in the Holy Spirit is speaking in other tongues as the Spirit gives utterance. This experience is distinct from, and subsequent to, the experience of the new birth" (PAOC 1994, 4). This statement makes reference to the believer's "yielding control" of himself or herself, suggesting that the person of the Holy Spirit takes control of the individual, which results in a type of spiritual or mystical union with the Godhead, and particularly with the person of Christ, resulting in a greater degree of power in order to both evangelize and grow spiritually (Warrington 2008, 95-130).

Additionally, the statement explains that the "initial evidence" of this experience is glossolalia, or speaking in tongues, which takes place "subsequent to" conversion. These two theological subtleties have an important place in the history of Pentecostal theology. Gary McGee explains that the term "initial" was first used in relation to the baptism of the Holy Spirit in the Assemblies of God's *Statement of Fundamental Truths* in 1916 (1991, 103). Before long, a debate between two American Pentecostals—Daniel Kerr and Fred Bosworth—developed, in which Bosworth argued that not only tongues but any charismatic gift could indicate the baptism of the Holy Spirit. Kerr argued that tongues alone indicated the experience and won the majority of the support within the denomination, thus securing his position as the doctrinal and ritual norm within both American and Canadian Pentecostalism (McGee 1991, 110).

Peter Althouse explains that it was not until 1927 that the word "evidence" began to be used by Pentecostals in relation to Spirit baptism, and it was as late as 1977 before the two terms were used together as "initial evidence," after which time the question of whether or not one experienced speaking in tongues as the initial evidence of the baptism of the Holy Spirit became a common measure of Pentecostal orthodoxy and orthopraxy as well as a requirement for ministerial credentials (2010, 69). It should be remembered from our discussion of Pentecostal origins that one of the tenets that created space for Pentecostalism as a discrete theological tradition was the idea that the baptism of the Holy Spirit is a distinct spiritual experience that occurs sometime after conversion. The reason for this was that Holiness and Keswick Christians also advocated a baptism of the Holy Spirit, but they believed that it occurred either at the time of conversion or at the time of sanctification. "Subsequence," then, is a term used by traditional Pentecostals in order to argue for the baptism of the Holy Spirit as a distinctly Pentecostal experience and, for some, legitimates the continued existence of Pentecostalism apart from the Methodist and Holiness traditions (see, for instance, Menzies and Menzies 2000, 109-19).

Turning to the writings of Purdie, we see that questions 253 and 255 in *Concerning the Faith* ask, respectively, "What is the Infilling of the Holy Spirit?" and "What is the purpose of the Infilling of the Holy Spirit?" To these questions Purdie replies, "The Infilling of the Holy Spirit means that the believer, who already has a measure of the Spirit, is now filled and empowered for service, according to Acts 1:8 and 2:4.... It means that God gives us additional power and liberty for service enabling us to freely and efficiently witness for Christ—Acts 1:8" (1951, 44). Similarly, Purdie writes in *What We Believe*, "the purpose of the infilling is to give us additional power in order that we may be more useful to the Lord and bring greater glory to His name" (1954, 22).

Regarding the evidences of Spirit baptism, the answer to question 256 in *Concerning the Faith* reads: "They are: 1. The physical evidence of speaking in other tongues—Acts 2:4; 10:44–46; 11:15; 19:6. 2. Following this supernatural evidence of the Infilling of the Holy Spirit, there are practical evidences, such as power for witnessing—Acts 4:33; passion for souls; and a greater love for the Word of God, and towards all true Christian people" (1951, 44). In *What We Believe*, Purdie also explains, "The Biblical evidence that one is filled with the Spirit is that he speaks supernaturally in a tongue he has never learned (Acts 2:4).... A further evidence of the Infilling of the Holy Spirit is that one receives power for witnessing, which every believer needs (Acts 4:33); a much greater passion for souls; a greater reverence for the Word of God, and a greater love toward all true Christian people, as well as a deepening of the prayer life" (1954, 22–23).

One will immediately notice that Purdie does not refer to the Pentecostal second blessing as the "baptism" of the Holy Spirit, but instead as an "infilling" of the Holy Spirit. Purdie preferred the term "infilling" to "baptism" in most of his writings for a few important reasons. First, Purdie, like the Anglican faculty who educated him at Wycliffe College in Toronto, was deeply influenced by the theology and language of the Keswick movement, which preferred the term "infilling" over "baptism" when referring to this spiritual experience. Purdie appears to have followed the Keswick theologians in his use of terminology. Second, even though Purdie was a major figure within the Pentecostal movement in Canada, he remained a committed Anglican priest his entire life and avoided the use of the term "baptism" in relation to the second blessing so as not to disregard the historic Christian belief that there exists only "one baptism."[11] Third, implicit within the term "baptism of the Holy Spirit" was the Wesleyan idea that this experience formed a second work of grace that contributed to one's salvation. Purdie, however, located himself firmly in the Reformed tradition within the Anglican Church and did not subscribe to the idea that there were additional works of grace following justification. The use of the term "infilling of the Holy Spirit," then, allowed Purdie to accept the empowerment that this second blessing offered but did not require him to assent to the Wesleyan notions of a second-work baptism (Althouse 1996, 13-18).

It is also interesting to note that, unlike the *Statement of Fundamental and Essential Truths*, Purdie offers several evidences of Spirit baptism, and even makes a distinction between the physical evidence of speaking in tongues and the practical evidences of empowerment for service, including greater love for the Word of God and other Christians and a deeper prayer life. The understanding of love as an evidence of Spirit baptism is something that Purdie shared with William Seymour. After Charles Parham's thwarted attempt to take over the Apostolic Faith Mission from Seymour in 1906, Seymour's position regarding the evidence of Spirit baptism began to migrate away from the evidentiary tongues view pioneered by Parham to the theme of divine love.

An article from 1907 in Seymour's periodical, *The Apostolic Faith*, explains: "Tongues are one of the signs that go with every baptized person, but it is not the real evidence of the baptism in the every day life. Your life must measure with the fruits of the Spirit. If you get angry, or speak evil, or backbite, I care not how many tongues you may have, you have not the baptism with the Holy Spirit. You have lost your salvation. You need the Blood in your soul" ("To the Baptized Saints," 2).

The anonymous author of this passage—likely either Seymour or the journal's editor, Clara Lum—views tongues as one of many possible "signs" of Spirit baptism and love as its true evidence. Another article from *The Apostolic Faith* dated a year later is even more direct. It asks the question, "What is the real evidence that a man or woman has received the baptism with the Holy Spirit?" to which it unequivocally answers, "Divine love, which is charity" ("Questions Answered," 2). We can clearly see, then, a theological tradition within both American and Canadian Pentecostalism that allows for multiple signs or evidences of Spirit baptism other than glossolalia. It should be said, however, that Canadian Pentecostal theology has maintained a stronger stance on tongues being the necessary and primary evidence than has its American counterpart, while love and other attributes are always considered secondary evidences.

Neither the *Statement of Fundamental and Essential Truths* nor Purdie's writings discuss the gift of speaking in tongues and the interpretation of tongues also mentioned in the New Testament.[12] When studying Pentecostalism, it is essential to recognize that the term "speaking in tongues" is often used in three distinct contexts. First is the previously mentioned evidence of the baptism of the Holy Spirit, which is usually understood as a unique and singular event. Second is the gift of tongues and interpretation, which, Pentecostals generally believe, happens at more regular intervals, but does not involve Spirit baptism. Third is what is called "praying in the Spirit" or sometimes "singing in the Spirit," the practice of praying or singing in tongues as part of an individual's personal prayer life or worship experience, where no interpretation is expected. Thus, tongues can be an evidence of Spirit baptism, a spiritual gift normally expecting an interpretation, or an entirely private religious experience without the necessity of a corporate component. It is also important to note that Pentecostals generally believe that the second and third senses of tongues speech—the gift of tongues and praying or singing in tongues—are limited to those individuals who have first experienced the rite of Spirit baptism. Spirit baptism, then, is often understood as an initiatory rite that opens the door to other religious experiences.

Douglas Jacobsen explains that early Pentecostals "recognized that the experience of tongues differed from individual to individual. Some received the ability to speak in tongues at the time of their baptism and continued to exercise that gift for the rest of their lives. Other recipients of the baptism of the Spirit spoke in tongues at the moment of their baptism and then never spoke a word in tongues again" (2003, 75). Pentecostal theologian Keith Warrington defines the gift of tongues this way:

> The gift of tongues is best understood as an extemporaneous or spontaneous manifestation in a form that is a quasi-language. The speaker is in control of her/his speech and the forming of sounds; the Spirit does not manipulate or coerce the speaker into a particular speech pattern. It is possible that the sounds themselves already existed in the mind and experience of the speaker, being reconstituted in the form of the tongues s/he employs though it is also possible that they are previously unimagined phonetic forms. Most

Pentecostals have concluded that speaking in tongues is a phenomenon that has divine and human elements in that the Spirit inspires the manifestation but the person articulates the sounds. (2008, 87)

That our two primary sources of traditional Canadian Pentecostal belief and practice fail to mention not only the gift of tongues but also any of the other gifts of the Spirit mentioned in the New Testament (wisdom, knowledge, faith, miracles, prophecy, discernment) except healing is quite interesting. Warrington explains, however, that "Pentecostals have spent minimal time exploring the actual science or theology of tongues" (2008, 84) and it is likely that both the *Statement of Fundamental and Essential Truths* and Purdie imply the normalcy of the gift of tongues, and perhaps the practice of praying or singing in tongues, in their discussions of its evidentiary role in the baptism of the Holy Spirit.

The *Statement of Fundamental and Essential Truths* only includes a brief article on healing: "Divine healing provided in the atonement of Christ is the privilege of all believers. Prayer for the sick and gifts of healing are encouraged and practised" (PAOC 1994, 5). The mention of healing in relation to the atonement is not incidental; rather, it refers to the traditional Pentecostal belief (also shared by many other evangelicals) that Christ's death on the cross does not merely provide, but actually guarantees, healing to all Christians who ask for it. This is, to say the least, a problematic theology, as it has often created a scenario within Pentecostal churches where those suffering with serious illnesses can be perceived to have a lack of faith, and even their salvation can be questioned, if they are not healed (Warrington 2008, 271–79).

Purdie, on the other hand, has a great deal more to say about healing than what is contained in the *Statement of Fundamental and Essential Truths*. Question 290 in his catechism asks, "What is Divine Healing?" He answers, "It is the direct power of God operating upon the human body in response to the prayer of faith." Question 291 addresses what divine healing is not, to which he provides two components: "1. Divine Healing is not Christian Science, which claims to heal by exercising the power of mind over matter. 2. Divine Healing is not Medical Science. Medical Science may be termed God's second best while Divine Healing is God's best" (1951, 49).

This passage is reminiscent of the tension that Pentecostals have had with medical science since the inception of the tradition. Some Pentecostals believe that seeking medical attention, as well as, for instance, owning any form of insurance, demonstrates a lack of faith on the part of the believer, and that instead those suffering from illness should seek only divine healing (Synan 1997, 192; Wacker 2001b, 191–92). This position is much less common than the one outlined by Purdie, who acknowledges the appropriateness of both divine healing and medical healing. Keith Warrington explains that, generally, Pentecostals recognize "that medicine and natural curative properties of the body are examples of the world of a creative God" (2008, 280). It should still be noted that Purdie and other traditional Pentecostals would often consider medical science as a second or last resort after seeking the possibility of divine physical healing.

Purdie also asks, in question 292, "What is the Ground of Healing?" He responds, "The Ground of Healing is the work of Christ completed on the cross of Calvary" (1951, 49). Here Purdie's commitment to the view that divine physical healing is provided in the atoning work of Jesus Christ on the cross, and that it is to be preferred over medical intervention, is very clear. Traditionally, Canadian Pentecostals prayed for the divine healing of not only themselves, but also their family members, friends, and even people from outside their church community. They believed that it is possible to receive prayer for divine healing on behalf of someone who is not in attendance at the service or even someone who is not a Christian. Opportunity to receive prayer for divine healing would be made in almost every traditional Pentecostal church service, in addition to home prayer meetings and Bible studies organized throughout the week.

The most important moment in traditional Pentecostal healing liturgy occurs after the communion service, which is typically held only one Sunday morning each month. Pentecostal theologian Veli-Matti Kärkkäinen explains that, much like the Roman Catholic theology of Eucharistic healing, "Pentecostal piety and church life is open to the idea of connection between healing and the celebration of the Lord's Supper" (2008, 126–27). What usually happens is that, following communion, the pastor will invite all those seeking prayer for healing to proceed to the altar at the front of the church, where the pastors, deacons, and often anyone who feels "led by the Spirit" can pray for those gathered to receive healing. The pastor and sometimes lay leaders typically anoint those seeking healing with oil according to the injunction found in the New Testament, which the pastor may also read at the initiation of the healing liturgy: "Are any among you suffering? They should pray. Are any cheerful? They should sing songs of praise. Are any among you sick? They should call for the elders of the church and have them pray over them, anointing them with oil in the name of the Lord. The prayer of faith will save the sick, and the Lord will raise them up; and anyone who has committed sins will be forgiven. Therefore confess your sins to one another, and pray for one another, so that you may be healed. The prayer of the righteous is powerful and effective."[13]

Purdie was particularly adamant about the rite of anointing with oil those being prayed over for healing. He writes that "it is definitely clear that anointing the sick is part of the Christian ministry. Any Ministers who keep exempt from the practice of a healing ministry are themselves very great losers as also the Church they represent" (1954, 28). The Pentecostal healing liturgy can take as little as a few minutes to as much as several hours of intense and loud prayer accompanied with messages in tongues and interpretations intended to beseech God and encourage the ill. Given that this specific liturgy is performed after communion, which is typically, though certainly not always, the last component of a Pentecostal communion service, the conclusion of the healing liturgy generally concludes the meeting.

Conclusion

THIS BRIEF ANALYSIS of the PAOC's *Statement of Fundamental and Essential Truths* and the foundational writings of Purdie have helped me to demonstrate two important things. First, the high social costs as well as the theological and ritual requirements of Pentecostal affiliation meant that there existed little ambiguity regarding the question of religious identity for most Canadian Pentecostals during much of the twentieth century. Put simply, prior to recent decades, if you were a Pentecostal, you knew it. Second, a close examination of the authoritative sources of traditional Canadian Pentecostal orthodoxy and orthopraxy reveals that the three most important beliefs and practices within the tradition were Spirit baptism, speaking in tongues, and divine healing. It is these four elements—the notion of a discrete Pentecostal identity, commitment to Spirit baptism, speaking in tongues, and divine healing—that define traditional Canadian Pentecostalism. It is also true that the idea of the imminent return of Christ was a central belief among early Canadian Pentecostals (Althouse 2003). This belief, however, was very widely shared among other evangelicals of the era—even more so than that of divine healing—and, as a result, was not as important a characteristic in defining early adherents of the movement as Spirit baptism, glossolalia, and divine healing were. The aim of chapters 4, 5, and 6 will be to demonstrate to what degree the members of Freedom in Christ, Elmira Pentecostal Assembly, and Elevation demonstrate these elements of the tradition. We now turn our attention to meeting these congregations and the pastors who lead them. ❥

3

The Churches and Their Pastors

Freedom in Christ

THE FIRST TIME that I attended Freedom in Christ I remember thinking that I was given the wrong address. At 1643 Bleams Road, located in the southwest end of the city of Kitchener, stood what I thought was a warehouse, or at best an agricultural equipment retailer. Built with cinder blocks and adorned with commercial-grade brown bricks and aluminium siding, the only thing that distinguished this building as sacred space was a small, white steeple rising up from the centre of the roof. Even this single cosmic pillar was eradicated a few years later when water damage necessitated that the rotten wood structure be removed.

As you pull into the driveway at Freedom in Christ, you cannot help but notice a large, refurbished farmhouse to the immediate left. The main level of this building was used to hold Sunday school classes, mid-week Bible studies, board meetings, community events, and sessions for a local Christian counselling agency. On the second floor was an apartment that the church rented out in order to provide additional income. To the right of this same driveway, exactly parallel to the farmhouse, was a large steel shed that was used for storage. Next to the shed were two lit beach volleyball courts and a soccer field. At the back of the property sat a large, derelict blue barn, a softball diamond, and a few acres of manicured turf adorned with apple trees, remnants of the horse farm that preceded the church.

During the spring, summer, and fall, Freedom in Christ's ten-acre property was used seven days a week, day and night. Most of these patrons had no connection whatsoever with the religious activities of the church. They, nonetheless, found the grounds of the church to be a convenient oasis in the midst of the surrounding suburban sprawl. There were many nights, during the summer months especially, when there were more cars in the parking lot and more people on the various sports fields than there ever were in attendance inside the church on a Sunday morning. A foreign observer could be forgiven for concluding that the purpose of this property was recreational rather than religious. I met numerous visitors to the property who told me that they thought 1643 Bleams Road was city property and were surprised to hear that it was in fact owned by a church.

Through the main doors and past the vestibule of the church is a small lobby with a welcome centre. To the immediate right of the lobby is the church's main office with a door leading into the senior pastor's office. On the left side of the lobby is another small office and Sunday school classroom. There are two small hallways that emerge from the lobby. The one to the right of the lobby leads to member mailboxes, two other small offices, the fellowship hall, and the kitchen. The one on the left directs visitors to the washrooms, the nursery, a wall of coat racks, and a side exit.

A set of double doors leads visitors from the lobby into the church's sanctuary, or main meeting space. The room that Freedom in Christ uses for its sanctuary was originally intended to serve as the church's gymnasium. The plan was always to build a larger, more traditional sanctuary when the church grew to the appropriate size and had secured the necessary finances. These conditions have not yet been met. In the back of the sanctuary is an audiovisual booth where the church's sound system, video projector, and stage lights are controlled. The walls of the sanctuary are composed of equal parts cinder blocks and multicoloured bricks. Instead of pews, the sanctuary contains two hundred interlocking chairs arranged in two equal sections, each section containing one hundred chairs arranged in ten rows of ten, with a centre aisle leading from the audiovisual booth to the platform.

At the front of the sanctuary is a small table used once a month to hold the elements for communion. Behind this table is a large platform that runs the entire width of the room and is approximately ten feet deep. Three stairs lead up to the platform, on which can be found a drum kit, a few guitar amplifiers, an electric keyboard, microphone stands, music stands, a few chairs, and, at the centre of the platform, a simple music stand that is used to hold the preacher's notes. The room is lit by several chandeliers but is devoid of natural light due to the lack of windows. The sanctuary at Freedom in Christ is completely bereft of religious iconography of any kind: no Bibles or hymn books, no banners with Scripture verses, not even the simple wooden cross that is standard operating equipment in most traditional Canadian Pentecostal churches. While the room's features make it ideal for multimedia presentations, it more closely resembles a hotel conference room than sacred space.

The members of Freedom in Christ did not always meet at the charmless building on Bleams Road. The congregation was founded in 1939 as Doon Full Gospel Mission and occupied a quaint, traditional, white church building in Doon Village, in the southeast end of the city of Kitchener. In 1988, however, the ten-acre horse farm was purchased on Bleams Road, and the present building was constructed with the hopes of growing the congregation. The original building in Doon was sold and is now used as a wedding chapel. When the congregation from Doon relocated to Bleams Road, their new church was surrounded by farmland and lay on the outskirts of the city. Before long, real estate developers purchased much of the surrounding farmland and transformed it into a tight network of sprawling subdivisions and shopping complexes. As a result, Freedom in Christ is no longer a rural church, but finds itself in the middle of an ever-expanding suburban development. Much of the congregation's original membership has left the church and has been replaced by other families who often have few or no ties to Pentecostalism.

The worship at Freedom in Christ is little different from what one would experience in the dozens of other evangelical congregations in the Region of Waterloo. Most practitioners arrive at the church ten to fifteen minutes before the service begins, at which time they talk with fellow members and perhaps enjoy a cup of coffee available at the welcome centre in the lobby. The service begins with the worship leader and worship team playing a high-energy song intended to signal the transition from this informal greeting time to the worship component of the service. After the first song, one of the pastors will address those present by giving a call to worship, providing some explanation for why it is that they worship God through music. After another three or four songs come the announcements and the collection or offering, which are both usually directed by the senior pastor of the congregation. The offering is followed by one or two more subdued worship songs, intended to prepare the worshipers for the sermon. On most Sunday mornings the senior pastor delivers the sermon. Occasionally, however, the assistant pastor or a lay leader within the congregation preaches instead. If it happens to be the first Sunday of the month, the congregation will celebrate communion, which usually follows the sermon, the senior pastor officiating with the assistance of lay leaders. Many Sunday services are concluded with a closing song, but they can also end with a simple prayer of benediction at the conclusion of the sermon or with a question-and-answer period intended to engage listeners with the content of the sermon. The entire service from beginning to end usually lasts ninety minutes, from ten o'clock to eleven thirty, or sometimes slightly longer on a communion Sunday.

The attendance counts at Freedom in Christ during my study period fluctuated to a much greater degree than they did at either Elmira Pentecostal Assembly or Elevation. Some Sundays I counted fewer than 100 adults and children in attendance at Freedom in Christ, while on other Sundays there could be as many as 180 people in attendance. The average attendance that I recorded during my period of study, however, was approximately 150 people, including roughly 125 adults and 25 children. Freedom in Christ holds a Sunday morning worship service at ten o'clock, a mid-week program on Wednesday evenings beginning at six thirty, a program for mothers and young children on Thursday mornings at nine thirty, and a youth program on Friday nights at seven o'clock.

Until the summer of 2010, Freedom in Christ employed a senior pastor, an assistant pastor, a youth pastor, a children's pastor, and a secretary—all full-time positions. In the spring of 2010, however, the leadership of the church decided to terminate the positions of youth pastor and children's pastor due to decreased financial giving at the church. It simply became impossible for a congregation of this size to financially support five full-time staff members. This transition left the senior pastor, his daughter—the assistant pastor, and his wife—the church secretary. The fact that all of the church's full-time staff are currently members of the senior pastor's immediate family resulted in accusations of nepotism by some members of the congregation and was also accompanied by a dramatic decline in church attendance, perhaps by as much as 50 percent.

The senior pastor at Freedom in Christ is fifty-eight-year-old Del Wells. Del is an athletic man who enjoys running year-round and has played a variety of sports throughout his lifetime. He and his wife have a daughter and son who are both married and attend Freedom in Christ. Despite his limited formal education, Del reads widely and tries to stay current in the areas of church leadership and changes within contemporary society.

Del was raised in a Pentecostal pastor's home in Ontario and witnessed the personal and professional challenges of being a pastor from a young age. After he graduated from high school, being a pastor was not something that rose to the top of Del's list of potential career options. Instead, Del married, worked as a real estate agent, and was an active lay leader within his local congregation. Over the next number of years, Del felt increasingly pulled towards a life in full-time pastoral ministry and decided to leave the real estate profession and pursue this calling. At the age of twenty-eight, he enrolled in a ministerial diploma correspondence program offered by the PAOC for individuals who were either working full-time or lived in remote locations and could not attend one of the residential denominational colleges. In 1980, after only a few months of study, Del was asked to become the assistant pastor in his home church, Hamilton Southmont Gospel Temple. Del worked in this capacity for one and a half years while he completed his education through the correspondence program.

In 1982, at the age of twenty-nine, Del left his home church to become the senior pastor of Thedford Bethel Church, where he worked for five years and witnessed the congregation experience growth. In 1987, Del moved to Petrolia, Ontario, to pastor Petrolia New Life Assembly for fifteen years, where again the congregation experienced significant growth. From Petrolia, Del moved to Owen Sound, Ontario, where he assumed leadership of Rockcliffe Gospel Temple in 2001. This pastoral charge, he explained, "was an assignment from God for clarity for my wife and I to sort out what we were to do next. We had a real sense at that time that we wanted to finish our ministry strong and we wanted to leave a legacy. So we ended up here at Freedom." Before becoming the senior pastor of Freedom in Christ in 2005, Del first worked as the associate pastor within the congregation from 2003 to 2005. At the time of this writing, Del has worked at Freedom in Christ for a total of twelve years—two as associate pastor and ten as senior pastor.

Freedom in Christ's mission statement is "To equip people to live a Christ-centered life through daily transformation." The congregation's vision statement is described as "Transformed lives impacting our world." The membership of Freedom in Christ strives to accomplish this vision by focusing on three core values: "Connecting: building authentic relationships—Training: learning to think and act like Jesus—Impacting: positively influencing the world for Jesus." What immediately strikes one about the mission statement, vision statement, and core values at Freedom in Christ is that there is nothing about them that is overtly Pentecostal. Equipping people, transforming lives, impacting the world, connecting, and training are emphases that could be rallied around by the members of almost any evangelical congregation. There is no mention, for instance, of wanting to help believers experience divine physical healing or the baptism of the Holy Spirit. Not a single one of the most central concerns within traditional Pentecostalism is even so much as alluded to in these three congregational directives.

While the mission statement, vision statement, and core values at Freedom in Christ are bereft of any distinctive Pentecostal content, the congregation's statement of faith did mention some of these traditional Pentecostal concerns. When I began my fieldwork in the fall of 2009, Freedom in Christ's statement of faith read this way:

> We believe the Holy Scriptures to be divinely inbreathed, infallible, inerrant, and the authoritative Word of God. We believe that there is one God, eternally existent in the persons of the Holy Trinity. We believe in the virgin birth of the Lord Jesus Christ, His unqualified deity, His sinless humanity and perfect life, the eternal all-sufficiency of His atoning death, His bodily resurrection, His ascension to the Father's right hand, and His personal coming to His second advent. We believe in holy living, the present day reality of the baptism in the Holy Spirit according to Acts 2:4, the gifts of the Holy Spirit, and

the Lord's supernatural healing of the human body. We believe in Christ's Lordship of the Church, the observance of the ordinances of Christian baptism by immersion for all believers and the Lord's Supper. We believe in the eternal blessedness of the redeemed in heaven and the eternal doom of the unregenerate in the lake of fire.

In addition to all of the mainstays of generically evangelical belief (inerrancy, the Trinity, the virgin birth, the atonement, Jesus's bodily resurrection and ascension, the second coming, the two Protestant ordinances, and the existence of heaven and hell), this statement also includes mention of a number of distinctly Pentecostal elements. These include: holy living (a major emphasis within the early Pentecostal movement), the baptism of the Holy Spirit with special mention of Acts 2:4 (a passage traditionally used by Pentecostals to argue that this experience happens in addition and subsequent to conversion), the gifts of the Holy Spirit, and divine physical healing (two additional emphases that the Pentecostal movement was largely responsible for reviving within twentieth-century Christianity).

This statement of faith initially caused me to question whether or not Freedom in Christ was a more traditional Pentecostal congregation than I had initially imagined. Within a matter of months, however, I noticed that the leadership at Freedom in Christ had changed the wording of this earlier statement of faith. Most of the main elements found in the original statement were retained minus explicit mention of the ordinances, heaven and hell, holy living, the baptism of the Holy Spirit, the gifts of the Spirit, and divine physical healing—all of the previously included Pentecostal content.

The section on the Holy Spirit in the revised statement, for instance, reads: "The Holy Spirit was sent from heaven by the Father and Son to live in every believer in Jesus Christ as a helper, teacher and guide. The Holy Spirit empowers believers to be witnesses of Christ and gives gifts of grace for ministry and worship. The Holy Spirit convicts the world of sin and leads people to faith in Jesus." In addition to the role that the Holy Spirit plays as a "helper, teacher and guide," the statement also mentions that the Holy Spirit "empowers believers" and gives them "gifts of grace for ministry and worship." The wording of the new statement is much more ambiguous than the previous one, and the belief that the Holy Spirit empowers believers and provides gifts for ministry and worship are certainly not distinctly Pentecostal convictions. Additionally, holy living and, more importantly, physical healing—one of the most important components of traditional Pentecostal belief and practice—are not even mentioned in the revised statement. The changes that the leadership of Freedom in Christ made to the congregation's statement of faith are an intimation of the congregation's gradual drift away from traditionally Pentecostal to generically evangelical modes of identity and experience.

During the course of my participant observation and other methods of congregational analysis, it became clear to me that the organizational thrust of Freedom in Christ was the incorporation of new members. This was the one activity around which all others were centred and by which they were evaluated. This emphasis was not simply the result of the personal aims of the senior pastor; rather, it was an active concern from the time the congregation relocated from Doon to Bleams Road in the late 1980s for the primary purpose of building a larger church. The explication of Freedom in Christ's core value, "Impacting: positively influencing the world for Jesus," makes this congregational objective abundantly clear. It reads: "As followers of Christ, we are His advertisements, strategically placed as His representatives in our world. We encourage our people to be positive influences in their neighborhoods, workplaces, schools and places of recreation." The members at Freedom in Christ are unapologetically instructed to advertise or market themselves to the members of their communities for the purpose of incorporating new members into the congregation.

Elmira Pentecostal Assembly

THIRTY KILOMETRES—or approximately a thirty-minute drive—north of Freedom in Christ at 290 Arthur Street South in Elmira, Ontario, is Elmira Pentecostal Assembly. Elmira Pentecostal Assembly is by far the oldest of the three churches that I studied. The congregation was originally founded after members from Kitchener Pentecostal Tabernacle (now Kitchener Gospel Temple), led by the early Canadian Pentecostal pioneer Reuben E. Sternall, held evangelistic tent meetings at the Elmira Fairgrounds in the summer of 1921. At the close of the summer, enough members had gathered together to warrant the purchase of an old theatre on Church Street, where they began to hold services as Elmira Pentecostal Tabernacle. The congregation occupied various locations until they built their own church on Memorial Street in 1946; they remained there until 1989, at which time they purchased the current building on Arthur Street South from Woodside Bible Fellowship and changed their name to Elmira Pentecostal Assembly. Originally a Brethren church, the current building boasts an attractive brick exterior, a columned entrance, and a white steeple—much more representative of the region's post-Second World War conservative Protestant churches than the commercial architecture found at Freedom in Christ. Elmira Pentecostal Assembly does not sit on nearly as large a piece of land, nor does it house the same variety of sports facilities, as does Freedom in Christ. It does, however, sit on a few acres of land that would make future expansion of the church possible.

The first time that I visited Elmira Pentecostal Assembly on a Sunday morning, I was immediately and warmly greeted as I entered the vestibule of the church. In the vestibule one finds coat racks, the church's main office, and a hallway leading to the pastors' offices. Through the vestibule is the church's main lobby, about the same size as the one at Freedom in Christ, which similarly contains a welcome centre. The lobby offers access to a hallway on the left leading to the washrooms, fellowship hall, kitchen, a meeting room, and the stairs leading to the church's basement. Behind a large wall of windows are two sets of glass double doors that lead into the sanctuary. The basement of the church houses a large, central meeting room connected to several classrooms that are used for Sunday school.

The two sets of double doors leading into the sanctuary create two aisles which lead to the platform of the sanctuary and divide the space into three sections of wooden pews. One's attention is quickly taken from the plain drywall interior of the sanctuary to its vaulted, wooden ceiling and its simple, yet attractive, stained glass windows, which allow an element of natural light in addition to the sanctuary's array of chandeliers. In the back right-hand corner of the sanctuary is an audiovisual booth, but, unlike the one at Freedom in Christ, it is enclosed with a window overlooking the sanctuary so as to demarcate these technical operations from the sacred activities otherwise designated for the sanctuary.

At the front of the sanctuary sits a table that is used for holding the elements for communion. Unlike at Freedom in Christ, however, the table in Elmira is very large and made out of hardwood, with the words "Do this in remembrance of me" taken from Jesus's injunction in Luke 22:19 (also found in 1 Corinthians 11:24) inscribed in large letters on the front. A few steps up on a platform one also finds a drum kit, a few guitar amplifiers, a baby grand piano, microphone stands, music stands, and a large wooden pulpit that matches the communion table in significance. At the back of the platform, behind the projector screen, is a baptismal tank. In contrast, the one time that I witnessed baptisms being performed at Freedom in Christ, the senior pastor used a rented hot tub.

Another notable difference between the platforms of the two churches is that at Elmira there are a few chairs on the platform; this is where the senior pastor and assistant pastor sit during the worship component of the service, a common practice in more traditional Canadian Pentecostal churches. Here the assistant pastor would remain seated on the platform while the senior pastor would preach, or vice versa. At Freedom, however, all of the pastors sit in the same seats as the rest of the congregation. Compared with Freedom in Christ, religious iconography abounds at Elmira Pentecostal Assembly. In addition to the inscription on the communion table and the presence of hymnals in the pews, there is a large wooden cross adorning the wall behind the pulpit that is difficult to ignore. Unlike at Freedom in Christ, one has little doubt that one is approaching sacred space when entering the sanctuary at Elmira Pentecostal Assembly.

The worship at Elmira Pentecostal Assembly follows a format that is nearly identical to that at Freedom in Christ: greeting, high-energy opening song, call to worship, three or four additional songs, announcements and offering, one or two slower songs, sermon, and conclusion of the service. While the Sunday morning service begins at ten thirty—a half-hour later than at Freedom—it usually lasts the same ninety minutes, ending around noon. The songs sung at Elmira Pentecostal Assembly are of the same general character—and many are exactly the same songs—as those sung at Freedom in Christ.

The average weekly attendance during my fieldwork period at Elmira Pentecostal Assembly was approximately 120 people, about 90 adults and 30 children, making it the smallest of the three congregations. Elmira is a small town of approximately 12,000 residents, surrounded by farms and Mennonite homesteads, just twelve kilometres north of the city of Waterloo. While not exactly a "rural" church, Elmira Pentecostal Assembly is about as rural as Pentecostal churches come in the Region of Waterloo. This is due to the fact that all of the churches belonging to the PAOC in the region are located in either incorporated towns or cities. One of the first things I noticed about this congregation was the relatively high proportion of elderly members and young families with children. While Freedom in Christ has a number of families with young children, it has far fewer older members and more middle-aged couples whose children no longer live at home.

On Sundays, Elmira Pentecostal Assembly conducts Sunday school for both children and adults beginning at nine thirty, followed by the Sunday morning worship service at ten thirty; it also sometimes offers different types of devotional studies on Sunday evenings beginning at six thirty. The church also offers a family night on Wednesdays at seven o'clock, with programs for people of all ages, and on Thursdays both a women's Bible study at ten o'clock in the morning and a senior-high-school ministry at seven thirty in the evening. The staff at Elmira includes a full-time senior pastor, an assistant/youth pastor, a part-time children's pastor, and a full-time secretary.

The senior pastor at Elmira Pentecostal Assembly is thirty-eight-year-old Hansley Armoogan. Hansley is a physically fit man of average height and possesses the ability to make those with whom he is speaking feel that they have his full attention. It is clear that his past ministry in a large urban and in two small rural Pentecostal churches serves as a potent combination of experiences for the task of leading the church in Elmira, which straddles both rural and urban modes of life.

Hansley was born into a West Indian family in Trinidad, where his father converted to Christianity as a young adult and attended Bible college before engaging in evangelistic ministry throughout the island. In the early 1970s, Hansley's father decided to emigrate to Canada, motivated by, as Hansley explained, "the aspirations of his children, and to provide them with more opportunity than what seemed to be present in Trinidad." Initially, Hansley's father moved to Montreal, and nine months later, in 1973, Hansley (aged two), his older brother, and his mother joined his father in Montreal.

After a few years, the Armoogans moved to Waterloo and began attending Waterloo Pentecostal Assembly, which is affiliated with the PAOC. Hansley was raised in this conservative Protestant West Indian context and felt the call to ministry during high school. Hansley graduated from Waterloo Collegiate Institute in 1990 and immediately pursued a bachelor of theology degree from Eastern Pentecostal Bible College (now Master's College and Seminary) in Peterborough, Ontario. The school in Peterborough is the designated training institute for the denomination in eastern Canada. Within the PAOC, the minimum educational requirement for ordination is a three-year ministerial diploma, although since the mid-1980s many students have chosen to pursue a four-year bachelor of theology degree. Because of the continued emphasis on pragmatism within the denomination, the educational standards for ordination within the PAOC are significantly lower than the standard bachelor's degree and master of divinity degree that are required for ordination within many other Canadian denominations.

It was while attending Eastern that Hansley met his wife. In the fall following their graduation in 1994, Hansley was hired to lead the youth ministry in a Pentecostal church in Perth, Ontario. The church in Perth was quite small, with Hansley and the senior pastor being the only pastors on staff. The church could not afford to pay Hansley a full-time salary even though he was working full-time hours. Nonetheless, the Armoogans enjoyed their time in Perth, and, over the course of thirteen months, they saw the size of the youth ministry grow from about seven to forty young people. A year later in 1995, Hansley was asked to interview for a position in the youth and young adult department at Kennedy Road Tabernacle, a large Pentecostal church in Brampton, Ontario. The situation at Kennedy Road Tabernacle was radically different from the church in Perth. The youth and young adult department alone had four full-time pastoral staff and a budget twice the size of the entire church in Perth. After accepting the position, Hansley soon became the head of the department, which ministered to approximately 400 youth and young adults. Hansley stayed at Kennedy Road Tabernacle for seven years, sometimes contributing as many as 110 hours per week to the busy ministry.

With the birth of the Armoogans' first two children in Brampton, it became increasingly apparent that it would be impossible to both maintain a healthy family life and fulfill the expectations of the position at Kennedy

Road Tabernacle. As a result, Hansley began investigating other ministry opportunities and in 2001 took a position as the senior pastor of a rural Pentecostal church in Sturgeon Falls, Ontario, located just west of the city of North Bay. Pastoring this rural northern Ontario congregation allowed Hansley to spend the kind of time with his family that he desired as well as to broaden his ministry experiences beyond the confines of a youth and young adult ministry. Hansley stayed in Sturgeon Falls for four years, and in 2005 a denominational representative suggested his name to the pastoral search committee at Elmira Pentecostal Assembly. Hansley was at the same time also thinking about the possibility of moving on to another congregation. In the middle of all this, and just three weeks after the birth of his youngest son, Hansley was unexpectedly diagnosed with non-Hodgkin's lymphoma and within ten days of the diagnosis began undergoing chemotherapy. Even with Hansley's recent cancer diagnosis, the church in Elmira, which Hansley refers to as "incredibly gracious," waited for him to be well enough to interview for the position of senior pastor; he began in this role in the last week of August 2005.

There is no doubt that Elmira Pentecostal Assembly is the most traditional of the three churches that I studied. Its members are slightly older than those of the other two congregations, a greater number of traditional choruses and hymns are sung in Elmira, and the more rural location of the church contributes to a slower pace of congregational life. A simple but telling indication of its more traditional nature is the fact that Elmira Pentecostal Assembly has retained the word "Pentecostal" in its name. This is a practice—as I explained in chapter 1—that is becoming increasingly less common among Canadian Pentecostal churches. Interestingly, the legal name of Freedom in Christ is actually "Freedom in Christ Pentecostal Assembly"; however, this name does not appear on the church's sign, website, or any other advertisement, and I seriously doubt if anyone other than the leadership of the congregation is aware of it.

While traditional Pentecostal identification and experience were higher at Elmira Pentecostal Assembly than in the other two congregations, the majority of members in the Elmira church were overwhelmingly generically evangelical in their commitments. Very closely mirroring the congregational culture at Freedom in Christ, the focus of the leadership and membership at Elmira Pentecostal Assembly is on developing an extensive roster of church programs for all ages in an attempt to attract as many new members as possible from a broad spectrum of religious backgrounds. This is done while at the same time remaining committed to core evangelical theological commitments. These emphases are accurately captured in Elmira Pentecostal Assembly's vision statement: "Reach with Love (Matthew 25:35–36): We will reach out to all people of every race, nationality and culture, both young and old, with the love and compassion of Jesus Christ. . . . Teach the Truth (Colossians 3:16): We are committed to teach people to know God and His Word, and to care for each other through His grace. . . . Send in Power (Luke 10:2): We are raising up people of God to send out into our township, our province, our nation and all over the world with the power of the Holy Spirit to spread the gospel."

Elmira Pentecostal Assembly's vision statement mentions sending its members with evangelistic intent replete "with the power of the Holy Spirit," which is tempting to interpret as referring to the baptism or infilling of the Holy Spirit, a central doctrinal and ritual component within traditional Pentecostalism. Without specifically mentioning the terms "baptism" or "infilling," however, this statement amounts to little more than the universal Christian affirmation of the power given to all believers to fulfill Jesus's great commission at the time of their conversion.

One notices a striking similarity between the vision statement at Elmira Pentecostal Assembly—"reach with love, teach the truth, send in power"—and the core values at Freedom in Christ—"connecting, training, and impacting." Both propose a cyclical formula for community building and church growth that focuses on evangelization (reaching, connecting), followed by education (teaching, training), and finally (re)evangelization (sending, impacting). Like Freedom in Christ's mission statement, vision statement, and core values, nothing about Elmira Pentecostal Assembly's vision statement stands out as overtly Pentecostal.

Much like its vision statement, Elmira Pentecostal Assembly's statement of faith also contains a number of generically evangelical emphases. When I first started my fieldwork in Elmira, the statement of faith found on the church website read this way:

> In a nutshell, here's what we believe: God is bigger and better and closer than we can imagine. The Bible is God's perfect guidebook for living. Through His Holy Spirit, God lives in and through us now.

Nothing in creation "just happened." God made it all. Grace is the only way to have a relationship with God. Faith is the only way to grow in our relationship with God. God has allowed evil to provide us with a choice, God can bring good even out of evil events, and God promises victory over evil to those who choose Him. Heaven and hell are real places. Death is a beginning, not the end. The church is supposed to serve people like Jesus served people. JESUS IS COMING AGAIN!

This statement outlines a commitment to the supremacy of God, the inerrancy of Scripture, the existence of the Trinity, creation, salvation by faith through grace, relationship with the person of Jesus Christ, an Arminian emphasis on free will, the existence of evil as well as heaven and hell, the possibility of eternal life, the priority of Christian service, and the second return of Jesus Christ. One element that is interesting about this statement is its lack of biblical references, which is likely an attempt to display a more informal approach; more traditional statements of faith adopt a propositional format and are often riddled with biblical references supporting various theological claims. One will also notice that in the summary of its core theological beliefs, this Pentecostal church does not mention a single distinctive Pentecostal belief or practice. There is absolutely no mention of the baptism of the Holy Spirit, speaking in tongues as evidence of this experience, the spiritual gifts, or the possibility of divine physical healing. Given that the website is one of the church's first points of contact for many potential visitors, the fact that none of these distinctive Pentecostal beliefs and practices is included is quite significant and indicates that these elements are not central to the life of the congregation.

Coincidentally, as at Freedom in Christ, the leadership at Elmira Pentecostal Assembly also changed the statement of faith found on their website during the course of my fieldwork. What is most interesting about the change made to the statement at Elmira Pentecostal Assembly, however, is that the change was not from a more traditional Pentecostal direction to a more ambiguous, generically evangelical one, as was the case at Freedom in Christ, but rather in the completely opposite direction. The new statement at Elmira Pentecostal Assembly significantly expanded its discussion of each of the previously included areas of faith, and it also contained several new sections, each with extensive biblical citations hyperlinked to the full text of these passages. Interestingly, when I accessed these hyperlinks to read the biblical passages cited within the statement, I was brought to the website of Woodvale Pentecostal Church located in Ottawa, Ontario. I then discovered that Elmira's updated statement of faith had been copied in its entirety from Woodvale Pentecostal Church's website.

It is entirely possible that this change to Elmira's statement of faith was completely coincidental to my involvement with the congregation. It is also possible that the selection of a new statement of faith was the result of my constant probing of the leadership and members at Elmira Pentecostal Assembly regarding the transformation of Pentecostal identity and experience within the congregation. I did notice that some members of both the leadership and laity at the church in Elmira were somewhat unsettled by the general migration from traditionally Pentecostal to generically evangelical modes of identity and experience that my involvement in their congregation uncovered. I remember distinctly sensing that these individuals were not so much concerned that these changes were occurring as they were that the changes had been exposed. It is possible, then, that the leadership of the congregation decided to replace the earlier, more ambiguous statement of faith with a more traditionally Pentecostal statement in an attempt to reassert their commitment to the Pentecostal tradition and/or the PAOC.

Regardless of the rationale behind the change to Elmira Pentecostal Assembly's statement of faith, the new statement not only expands on the previously discussed topics but also includes sections outlining the previously unmentioned distinctively Pentecostal areas of belief and practice. Most notably, the revised statement includes the declaration, "We also believe . . . in the infilling of the Holy Spirit, with the initial physical evidence of speaking with other tongues, which gives power for service, and is manifested in the fruit and gifts of the Spirit [and] . . . that divine healing for the body is provided by Christ's death." Additionally, the statement includes sections under the headings "Why we have speaking in tongues and interpretation of those tongues," "Why we prophesy," "Why we receive tithes and offerings," and "Why we publicly invite people to the altar."

Elmira Pentecostal Assembly's revised statement of faith describes a congregation that does not exist. Despite what the statement suggests, and the fact that commitment to traditional modes of Pentecostal identity and experience were higher in Elmira than at the other two congregations, my close observation of Elmira Pentecostal Assembly and the interviewing and surveying of its members revealed that the majority of the members within this congregation adhered to generically evangelical forms of identity and experience. During the twelve months that I spent at Elmira Pentecostal Assembly, it became clear that the congregation was in the midst of an identity crisis and was attempting to decide whether or not it was a distinctly Pentecostal church or just another evangelical church among many others. The congregation, and particularly the church's senior pastor, was straddling the fence that separated distinctly Pentecostal and generically evangelical emphases.

Elevation

APPROXIMATELY HALFWAY between Freedom in Christ and Elmira Pentecostal Assembly at 101 Father David Bauer Drive in Waterloo, Ontario, is Elevation, the last of the three congregations that I studied. Unlike both Freedom in Christ and Elmira Pentecostal Assembly, at the time that I conducted my fieldwork Elevation did not own its own building. Instead, it met in a rented space in the Waterloo Memorial Recreation Complex, just a short walk from Uptown Waterloo and the campuses of the University of Waterloo and Wilfrid Laurier University. Built in 1993, Waterloo Memorial Recreation Complex houses an Olympic-size ice surface, an indoor running track, a large swimming pool, a banquet hall, and a variety of meeting rooms used for conferences and community programs. By comparison, the facilities used by Elevation made Freedom in Christ look like St. Paul's Cathedral. There was nothing that appeared sacred at all about the conference room that constituted Elevation's sanctuary and the several small meeting rooms used for its Sunday school classes.

This, however, was not simply pragmatism at work, the result of the best available space for the best available price. Instead, the decision to use a recreation complex in the middle of the city was an intentional theological decision. Both the leadership and the laity at Elevation attempted to develop an ecclesiology that deliberately challenged more traditional concepts of the divide between the sacred and the profane. Unlike Freedom in Christ, where the warehouse-style facility was the result of pragmatism and utility, Elevation's decision to meet in a recreation complex every Sunday morning represented a conscious decision to conduct church where everyday life takes place. Instead of a space specifically designed to be separate from the rest of the world, the members of Elevation brought their congregation into the daily experience of hundreds of people playing hockey, swimming lanes, and running the track.[14]

The first time that I attended Elevation on a Sunday morning, I had no idea what to expect from this experimental form of church. After parking I walked into the main lobby of the recreation complex alongside parents carrying their children's hockey bags and one little girl skipping up the concrete steps on the way to her swimming lesson. On entering the lobby I was unable to find any directions to Elevation. I approached a recreation complex staff member sitting behind a Plexiglas enclosure and asked her where Elevation met. She directed me to two flights of stairs to my right leading to a landing overlooking the large swimming pool complex below. Standing at a glass door next to an elevator was an eager-looking young man who asked me if I was looking for Elevation. He handed me a bulletin and directed me up yet another flight of stairs. Here was a small vestibule that housed a few bulletin boards sitting on tripods advertising various church programs, a table with more bulletins, some books for sale, and a large wooden box for members to give their offerings. Through the vestibule was a room to the left with several round tables and chairs where some people were sitting, talking, and drinking coffee. Next was a much larger room that constituted the congregation's main meeting room, which I still find difficult to describe as a sanctuary.

To the immediate right of the narthex, as I passed through the entrance to the sanctuary—which was really just a slightly ajar folding partition wall—was the audio booth, from which a series of large, bundled cables ran to the front of the sanctuary. The sanctuary itself was a very simple room, the cinder-block walls, fluorescent lighting, and panelled ceiling signalling that this space was designed as a generic, multi-purpose room and not a place of Christian worship. As strange as it may sound to many Canadians who attend more traditional places of worship, these radically non-Christian surroundings are a major point of attraction for many North Americans who no longer trust traditional religious institutions (Miller 1997, 1). I at once noticed the large windows at the left side of the room, which open onto the ice surface and running track. This point of contact between the worship service and the hockey games and Sunday morning runners seemed appropriate given Elevation's mission as a church that aims to take place where everyday life happens.

The sanctuary contained three unequal sections of approximately 350 interlocking chairs arranged to maximize the available seating space rather than for aesthetics. These were divided by two aisles leading from the back of the sanctuary to the platform at the front of the sanctuary. At the front of the sanctuary were a video projector on a trolley and a music stand that was used to hold the preacher's notes. Behind this was a platform on which sat a drum kit, keyboard, guitar amplifiers, microphone stands, and music stands. Because Elevation did not own its own facility, all of this equipment, chairs included, were set up very early every Sunday morning and torn down and stored at the recreation complex every Sunday afternoon following the service. It took a tremendous amount of work and a committed team of volunteers to pull off each Sunday morning service at Elevation.

Worship at Elevation diverged in a few significant ways from that at both Freedom in Christ and Elmira Pentecostal Assembly. First, the music at Elevation was of a near-professional quality. The worship leader, vocalists, and musicians provided a highly polished musical experience. While worship at Freedom in Christ and Elmira Pentecostal Assembly was contemporary and utilized a wide range of instruments and styles, the leadership allowed novices and individuals with lesser degrees of talent or training to participate in leading the worship experience. Second, the worship service at Elevation contained more variety than those at the other two congregations. While the service at Elevation was about the same length and often followed the same general format as at the other two churches, it often contained elements of experimentation and improvisation, which served to indicate that something different and significant was taking place.

During most services that I attended at Elevation, for instance, someone from the congregation would be included in the service in some significant way by either sharing a spiritual insight, giving a report from a recent missions trip, or reading a portion of Scripture purely as an act of public worship. These types of experimentation with the normal liturgy certainly occurred at Freedom in Christ and Elmira Pentecostal Assembly, but they were much less common and usually reserved for special occasions and services. Finally, and most significantly, every worship service at Elevation concluded with the members of the congregation exiting the sanctuary and sitting in small groups around the tables in the adjacent room in order to discuss the sermon. Opportunity was almost always provided for the members to ask the preacher specific questions about the sermon. A dialogical component of this degree was absent at Freedom in Christ and Elmira Pentecostal Assembly.

Elevation held two Sunday morning services, at nine thirty or nine fifteen (the time of the service changed from the former to the latter partway through my fieldwork) and eleven o'clock from the fall to the spring. Because church attendance drops in many congregations in the area during the summer, which is compounded at Elevation by the fact that many of its members are university students, in the summer months the congregation moved to a single Sunday morning service beginning at ten o'clock. The average attendance at Elevation was approximately 350 people at the two services combined. On some Sundays, however, and particularly when university students returned to the city in the fall, Elevation could have more than 400 people in attendance at just one of its services, requiring overflow seating. Comparatively, Freedom in Christ and Elmira Pentecostal Assembly typically looked about half or—on a particularly busy Sunday—two-thirds full. Because Elevation did not own its own facility, the congregation did not hold additional meetings throughout the week where the whole church community could gather together, as was done in the other two congregations. Rather, Elevation held "Affinity+" and "Focus Groups," which were small group gatherings held in various locations and times throughout the week, usually in the homes of members. Some of Elevation's Focus Groups included a mother's group, a women's study group, a newlywed group, an early morning men's group, and a monthly "creative communion" service called "The Table on Tuesdays." Elevation employed four full-time staff members: a senior pastor, an associate pastor, a worship leader (who also provided administrative support), and an administrative assistant.

The history of Elevation is deeply intertwined with the life story of its founder and senior pastor, thirty-two-year-old Brandon Malo. Brandon was baptized in the Lutheran Church and attended St. John's Lutheran Church in Waterloo as a child. After his confirmation during junior high school, Brandon stopped attending church. He explained that it became clear to him that being confirmed meant that he was now responsible for his own faith: "I would decide whether I had to go to church or not. So after my confirmation I didn't go to church anymore. I just kind of slept in and that was kind of the end of that." Also contributing to his lack of involvement in the Lutheran Church was the fact that, he claimed, the church did not do a very good job of engaging its younger members: "I had a really tight-knit group of friends at the church, but the church didn't really respond well to where we were at in our interests or needs and they didn't really know how to. I think a lot of us just decided to leave and not really be engaged anymore." As a result, Brandon began to spend more time with his friends from high school and did not attend church for the next few years.

At the end of grade ten, Brandon began dating a girl (now his wife) from high school who attended Waterloo Pentecostal Assembly, and he began attending the church with his new love interest. The Pentecostal church, he explained, "was pretty bizarre for me at the time. I had never heard people pray out loud. I had never seen people worship in that kind of a format. In the Lutheran Church it was always singing a hymn with a pipe organ. I had never even seen anything other than that, so it was kind of an interesting experience and I would go because I was interested in her."

Not long after Brandon began attending Waterloo Pentecostal Assembly, the church hosted a production of *Heaven's Gates and Hell's Flames*, a touring evangelistic drama that aims to induce viewers to make a profession of faith in Jesus Christ by frightening them with images of hell and eternal suffering. Brandon explained that it was after attending this production that he became a committed Christian: "I look at it now and I think there is so much wrong with that production, but for me at the time, I didn't need to hear the message it had, I just needed to hear the part where they said that God loves you, accepts you where you are, and wants you to commit your life to following him. And when I heard that I was like, 'For real? I can do this?' So, I did. I made a commitment to do that and it took quite a while for me to understand what that meant. I had a lot of lifestyle changes to make, but I did it."

Brandon made the decision to commit his life to following God in 1992 at the age of fifteen. He spent the remaining years of high school becoming increasingly involved in leadership at Waterloo Pentecostal Assembly. Upon graduation from high school in 1995, Brandon enrolled in a bachelor's degree in business administration at Wilfrid Laurier University. After two years of study, however, Brandon and his now fiancée felt a calling to pastoral ministry. In May of 1997, when Brandon was driving home from a co-op interview in Mississauga, Ontario, he experienced an important event in his life:

> I was kind of listening to this tape in the car and a song on the tape really challenged me. The lyrics were along the lines of "Deep in your heart there is a tug of war, trying to figure out what your life is for" and I really felt that God was saying this isn't what I want you to do with your life. Rather, I felt like God was telling me, "I've called you and it's time for you to respond." When I was in early high school I knew I wanted to go into business. I knew I wanted to get an MBA and that was what I wanted to do with my life. I knew for years, however, I really felt God saying to me that I have to drop that dream. You have to give it up and I'll give you something else. Everything that I've been involved with and who I am is the result of that decision.

After receiving this call to a life devoted to pastoral ministry, Brandon dropped out of his business program at Wilfrid Laurier the day before his wedding and subsequently enrolled in the requisite ministerial diploma program required to receive ministerial credentials with the PAOC. Brandon was able to get about a year's worth of academic credits transferred from his two years of study at Wilfrid Laurier and completed the remaining two years of coursework by correspondence in just twelve months. Over the course of the following year of reading, writing, and studying to complete his program via correspondence, Brandon was essentially alone in his apartment while his wife worked during the day. He explained:

> I started missing the campus and thinking about my friends who were there and hadn't left. I just started thinking, how are they going to find out about Christ? When I was at university I didn't know any

Christians when I was there. I know that there were Christians, but I didn't know any. None of my peers at university were Christians. I was the "church guy" in all of my circles and I started wondering who would connect with these people. I'm out of their lives now. I may have been one of the only people following Christ who was in their lives for all I knew. So I started really thinking about that a lot and God really began to impress on me that I needed to respond to that need. As I began to think about it and pray about it, this concept of starting a church for university students came to me.

Brandon had tried inviting friends to Waterloo Pentecostal Assembly, but because it was replete with regular demonstrations of ecstatic religious practices it proved to be ineffective in recruiting these friends and others of the same age cohort. He explained: "So I started having these thoughts that maybe the thing to do is just to have a church that is just for students that would address their stage of life, speak to their issues, speak their language, connect in ways that would make sense and be significant to them. So I started thinking about things and toying with things and I had this name 'The Embassy' sticking in my mind. I would draw little logos and come up with little slogans, but all in my mind. I wouldn't talk to anyone about it."

Brandon remembers two events in particular that he considers to be the breakthrough points for the beginning of the Embassy, the predecessor and sister congregation of Elevation. The first was a youth leadership conference. The speaker at the conference was mentioning that the majority of Christian young adults abandon their faith during the course of their university education. The speaker then proposed that the solution to this problem was to, in Brandon's words, "get people so fired up for God that when they go to university they won't lose their faith." Brandon believed that this was a horrible strategy for campus ministry: "I was thinking, that's not the answer at all. The answer is to be there, to actually have someone who is in their lives. Who cares how fired-up someone gets? I've been there. I spent two years there and knew what it was like. It's hard to live your faith out on a university campus."

The second event was a conversation that Brandon and his wife had with a couple that were close friends of theirs. The husband was just about to finish his bachelor of theology degree from the denominational college and was offered a staff position in the church that he had interned with during his final year of studies. He mentioned that he might as well take the position because it seemed to be the most practical decision. Brandon, however, who was wrestling with this idea of starting a totally new ministry venture, reacted strongly—he admits maybe a bit too strongly—to his friend's willingness to simply take the first available position that came up. He explained: "When they left, my wife asked what was the matter with me. So I just spilled it out and said this is what God has put in my heart and this is what I want to do. And she said, 'Let's do it.'"

Brandon then shared his vision for a church specifically designed for university students with the senior pastor of his church, who was extremely supportive of the idea. They assembled a small group of about four other leaders and launched the first Embassy meeting in September 1998 in the Humanities Theatre at the University of Waterloo. The venture was, Brandon explains, "just this big, giant question mark. We had no clue what to expect and that was where the Embassy began." Before the Embassy's first service Brandon remembers "practically begging God to draw 50 people out because we had this massive cavernous theatre. It seated 360 people in the lower level and another 300 in the balcony, but, as it turned out, we actually had 85 people in our first night and that was just way more than we ever could have expected."

The Embassy did not experience much growth during its first year of operation, its numbers hovering around what they were at the opening night. In the fall of 1999, however, they averaged about 140 people. In the summer of 2000, attendance increased again to an average of about 200, and in the fall of 2000 attendance jumped to over 400 people. By the fall of 2001, the Embassy was drawing an average of more than 800 students—and on some particularly busy nights, well over a thousand—to its weekly services. This significant increase in attendance required that they move to two services and switch venues to Federation Hall. This was quite a contrast to the ministry operated by a chaplain at Wilfrid Laurier University, whose group averaged around twelve students per week and who had initially told Brandon that the type of ministry that he had envisioned was not needed in Waterloo.

It was not long before the necessary work of operating and promoting this large student ministry began to take its toll on the small group of mostly volunteers who ran the Embassy each week. Sensing the spiritual fatigue of his volunteers, Brandon started a ministry called "Embassy Unplugged" in 2000. Embassy Unplugged was intended to be a small, low-key worship service exclusively for the leaders of the Embassy, where they would not have to worry about planning and carrying out a high-energy event but could simply unwind and experience a worship time of their own.

Initially, Embassy Unplugged had an attendance of only about fifteen to twenty people. Brandon explains: "The Embassy was always about putting together an essentially kick-butt presentation meant to demonstrate the potential of the Christian life and we put a lot of effort into the details. So when we started Embassy Unplugged, we essentially wanted to put no effort into anything. So we would just rotate whoever would teach. Someone would come up and share some thoughts. We would share a meal together. Someone would just get up on a guitar or whatever and sing a song. It was just totally low-key, the exact opposite of what the Embassy was."

A year later, in September 2001, Brandon founded Elevation, which essentially grew out of and replaced Embassy Unplugged. The reason for this new ministry was, as Brandon explains, "people started having babies and getting married and we kind of thought that we had to start thinking about what we were doing long-term here." Basically what happened was that some of the original members of the Embassy had graduated from university and started careers and families. The large-scale, high-energy experience offered by the Embassy was no longer what families with small children were looking for. Brandon explained:

> We figured our options were either: First, change the Embassy in order to include these young families. From day one we had a very focused target audience of eighteen- to twenty-five-year-olds, primarily students, and secondarily young adults in the community. Parents with kids were not part of that. Second, we could basically say to these young families, "Thanks for coming out, but find another church." Or, third, we could start another church. So we kind of voted for the third option. It's the only one that really made sense to us. And, you know, for the first couple of years, to say we didn't care about Elevation might not be exactly accurate, but it's pretty darn close. It was kind of like a younger sibling. The Embassy was huge.

It was big. It was everything. Everyone knew about the Embassy. It was just "the thing." And Elevation, we just didn't want it to be that. We just wanted it to be a place for us to get together and talk about faith and not have to go through the whole gamut of stuff. But, of course, people came and it began to grow quite slowly and take on a character of its own. And we focused on things that the Embassy intentionally did not focus on.

The weekly attendance at Elevation began at about 50 people and slowly grew to an average of about 350 people. Brandon led both the Embassy and Elevation for four years, but in August 2005 decided that he needed to hire someone to take over the Embassy so that he could devote his time and energy to the maturing community at Elevation. In January 2005, the Embassy and Elevation changed their venues from Federation Hall at the University of Waterloo to the Waterloo Memorial Recreation Complex due to a complex series of disputes between university officials and the leadership at the Embassy and Elevation. Leaving the university campus has not affected attendance at Elevation in any significant way. The departure from the university campus, however, has dealt a serious blow to both attendance and the vision at the Embassy. It has been difficult for a church intended specifically for university students to not be on a university campus. The Embassy, however, managed to bring some closure to their dispute with the administration at the University of Waterloo and began meeting again in the Humanities Theatre once a month in September 2009.

There is another pastor who has also played a crucial—although more recent—role in the development of Elevation. Steve Tulloch is the fifty-two-year-old associate pastor of Elevation who oversees pastoral care, coaching of ministry teams, and outreach. Steve was born in Sault Ste. Marie, Ontario, and was raised in a devout Christian Brethren (Plymouth Brethren in the United States) home. When Steve was finishing high school, his family moved to Richards Landing on St. Joseph Island, a small community about one hour southeast of Sault Ste. Marie. Here Steve's family and a number of their friends planted a Brethren church named Island Bible Chapel. After graduating from high school, Steve attended a Brethren college in Edmonton, Alberta—Mount

Carmel Bible School. It was here that Steve met his future wife, and the two were married in 1979.

After college, Steve and his new bride returned to Richards Landing. He worked at Algoma Steel from 1979 to 1981 while also working towards a bachelor of arts degree in religious studies at Algoma University in Sault Ste. Marie, which was then a satellite campus of Laurentian University in Sudbury, Ontario. In 1981, Steve was also asked by the leadership of the church in Richards Landing to begin serving as their full-time worker (Christian Brethren churches do not traditionally use the term "pastor"). Steve accepted the offer and was responsible for about a third of the preaching, as well as overseeing the children and youth programs. After graduating with a bachelor of arts in 1983, Steve moved with his family to Dallas, Texas, where they lived from 1983 to 1985 so that he could pursue graduate studies at Dallas Theological Seminary. Steve completed all of the requirements for a four-year master's degree in just two years, while his church continued to financially support him and his family. With the exception of the time they were in Dallas, Steve and his wife led the church in Richards Landing in addition to running a children's summer camp each year and teaching at Kawartha Lakes Bible College, a Brethren college in Peterborough, Ontario. By 2001, it became clear that managing these various responsibilities was exacting too high an emotional price from Steve and his family. In 2002, they agreed to become the leaders of the Christian Brethren congregation New Hope Community Church, located in Waterloo.

Once in Waterloo, Steve heard about Elevation and became friends with Brandon. Both Steve and Brandon felt that their two congregations shared a great deal in common, and they even held a joint service together in 2003. Under Steve's leadership New Hope had experienced significant growth and eventually outgrew its rented space in Westvale Public School in Waterloo. Neither the school nor the members of the community wanted New Hope to leave, because the congregation was extremely active in the neighbourhood. The space, however, was simply no longer adequate for New Hope's changing needs. It tried meeting in other churches, but found that meeting in another congregation's space on a regular basis made it extremely difficult to maintain a distinct congregational identity. New Hope also met at the Bricker Academic Building on the Wilfrid Laurier University campus, which was only ever intended as a short-term solution. With these changes in venue, New Hope began to experience declining attendance and a loss of overall congregational identity. Steve explained:

> [Eventually,] New Hope found a potential facility down on King Street that had a kind of missional space and more office space than we needed. We thought that it was worth buying, but we didn't need all the office space. The question came to mind, "Would Elevation?" I called Brandon and he and I met and talked about it. In either our first or second conversation I said to him, "You may consider this a completely whacked idea, but would you consider the possibility that maybe we should just join up, that we might be better together? What would you think about that?" That was where the discussion went. That happened in probably March of 2008. A year and a half ago that first discussion happened and we merged four or five months later.

After the merger in September of 2008, Brandon continued as the senior pastor of Elevation, while Steve assumed the role of associate pastor. It is difficult to accurately convey the significance of Elevation's decision to merge their congregation with New Hope. Canadian Pentecostalism is traditionally a highly sectarian religious tradition and has historically perceived other Christian denominations with a great deal of suspicion. The mistrust of other denominations is perhaps exaggerated within Pentecostalism because of the tradition's insistence that only those who have experienced the baptism of the Holy Spirit with the evidence of speaking in tongues are living in the fullness of the Christian life. The PAOC does allow congregations from other denominations to join their ranks as long as they agree to support the tenets and conventions of the PAOC. The members of New Hope, however, were permitted to merge with Elevation without any such conditions. In fact, a number of the members that I interviewed from New Hope were not even aware that they were attending a Pentecostal church until this was revealed during the course of the interview. The fact that Elevation sought to merge with a Brethren congregation that did not support traditional Pentecostal positions, and that the leadership within the PAOC allowed this, confirms both the lack of commitment to traditional Pentecostal norms among the members of Elevation and the casualness with which the denominational hierarchy regarded the maintenance of distinctly Pentecostal identity and experience within its congregations.

The ambiguity surrounding Pentecostal identity and experience at Elevation is even further illustrated by the fact that Steve—the associate pastor of the congregation—does not hold any ministerial credentials with the PAOC. Rather, he continues to operate under his commendation within the Christian Brethren tradition granted by Missionary Service Committee Canada. When I asked Steve if he ever intends to seek ordination with the PAOC he replied, "You know what, probably not, although I am open to that. Brandon and I actually had a little conversation about that just yesterday. So I still haven't learned enough to know whether that is something I should do or not. There hasn't been any rush to."

When I asked Steve whether or not the fact that Elevation was a Pentecostal congregation was important to him he simply replied, "No." When I tried to probe a bit deeper into Steve's religious identity, I was expecting to find that it would be defined by traditionally Brethren concerns; however, this was not the case at all. Steve continued:

> New Hope was not very classic Brethren. As a result, New Hope held many of the really important distinctives of Brethren churches down through the years with an open hand or had either actually dismissed or reapplied them a little bit. So we weren't really classic Brethren. For example, I was called a pastor, which is not done in the Brethren tradition. Women were much more involved in leadership roles than they would be in most Brethren churches. We were really open to the idea of partnering with different people and, as a result, were not very exclusive; we didn't stay to ourselves. So those things were important in the way we related to other churches, one of which was Elevation.

I discovered that Steve was probably not a typical Brethren church leader and that from an early point in his life he had been gradually shifting from traditionally Brethren to generically evangelical modes of identity and experience. This transformation had perhaps come to fruition in his role orchestrating the merger between New Hope and Elevation and his current leadership in a Pentecostal church. Steve explained:

> I always thought that the exclusivism within the Brethren Church was elitist and arrogant and prideful. I grew up thinking that we were a little more "New Testament" than anybody else was and I couldn't quite buy that. I thought pretty early on we probably have some good distinctives that we can value and I don't want to drop those, but I'm pretty sure that other people must have some good distinctives too. So to partner with other people—even from an early age—was important to me. I can remember as a grade twelve and thirteen student, influential Christian teens in Sault Ste. Marie getting together every Sunday night for a singalong with the people from First Baptist, Elim Pentecostal, and People's Pentecostal.

Even though Steve explained that he and New Hope were not the classic versions of a Brethren leader or congregation, the fact that Elevation allows him to operate as their pastor with credentials from a non-Pentecostal denomination is an important indication of the low level of commitment to the Pentecostal tradition that the leadership and members of Elevation possess.

While my fieldwork at Elevation definitely confirmed that the majority of the members within the congregation were overwhelmingly generically evangelical in their commitments, it also revealed that this congregation did not follow many of the same patterns held in common between Freedom in Christ and Elmira Pentecostal Assembly. For instance, Elevation's four key values, "Life Together, Journey Mentality, Shared Responsibility, and Spirit-Centered Living," while remaining generically evangelical in their emphases, do not fit the evangelization–education–(re)evangelization pattern shared by Freedom in Christ and Elmira Pentecostal Assembly. Rather than this common seeker-sensitive model, Elevation's core values are strongly evocative of the emphases typically expressed within the emerging church movement, and they deeply resonate with four of Eddie Gibbs and Ryan Bolger's nine key practices of emerging churches (Gibbs and Bolger 2005, 45). Life Together, Journey Mentality, Shared Responsibility, and Spirit-Centred Living correlate with Gibbs and Bolger's key practices three (living highly communal lives), four (welcoming the stranger), eight (leading as a body), and nine (taking part in spiritual activities) (2005, 45, 121).

Unlike Freedom in Christ and Elmira Pentecostal Assembly, which use seeker-sensitive evangelization techniques with a proven track record among baby boomers, who respond to more blatant attempts to shape religious content according to consumer demand (Sargeant 2000), Elevation is primarily interested in recruiting the young, urban professionals who work in the thriving technology, education, and finance sectors in the Region of Waterloo. These young adults, Robert Wuthnow tells us, are looking for things in churches that the boomer-oriented seeker churches typically do not offer. Some of these include an authentic sense of community; high-quality music that is both traditional and contemporary (i.e., hymns and modern choruses); the inclusion of the fine arts in the liturgy; opportunities for young adults to meet potential mates instead of only "family programs"; an openness towards gays and lesbians, single-parent families, and inter-religious families; and opportunities for both local and international ministry and service (Wuthnow 2007, 223–32).

On the one hand, Elevation's key values—in addition to my observations and interviews—suggest that both the leadership and the laity at Elevation have shaped a religious community that addresses many of the needs and desires commonly expressed by young adults, a community that could accurately be labelled as an "emerging church." Elevation's focus on this particular demographic might partly explain why they have had much more success attracting and integrating young adults and achieving a more consistent overall attendance than either of the other two congregations. On the other hand, the religious culture found at Freedom in Christ and Elmira Pentecostal Assembly more closely resembles that of older, seeker-sensitive churches, which, Wuthnow notes, many contemporary observers believe "are now passé" (2007, 224). Freedom in Christ and Elmira Pentecostal Assembly's focus on attracting families with children (who are the most likely demographic to already be attending a church elsewhere) may also explain why these churches have had a more difficult time recruiting young adults and achieving their desired Sunday morning attendance goals.

Conclusion

IN THIS CHAPTER I have attempted to provide a snapshot of the three congregations that form the basis for this study. There is much more that could be said and I am sure that others would have chosen to emphasize elements I have merely skimmed over or even ignored altogether. Nonetheless, the time that I spent at these three churches convinced me that knowing a little about the physical characteristics, activities, attendance, senior pastors, and stated values of each of the congregations would provide the most important background necessary for understanding the following three chapters, which draw almost exclusively on interview data gathered from individual members of the three congregations.

While the relatively low levels of commitment to traditional Pentecostal identity, belief, and practice make Freedom in Christ, Elmira Pentecostal Assembly, and Elevation generically evangelical congregations, they also possess a number of unique characteristics that serve to distinguish them from one another. In addition to their suburban, rural, and urban locations and constituencies, each of the three churches are currently facing their own unique challenges.

Freedom in Christ is struggling with the question of how to reorient their previously rural congregation to meet the needs of the tens of thousands of unchurched residents that now surround the church amidst the growing suburban developments of southwest Kitchener. The leadership of Freedom in Christ has adopted a largely seeker-sensitive approach in its attempt to incorporate the throngs of potential new members across the street, a strategy which has, thus far, yielded few results. The leadership at Elmira Pentecostal Assembly has also promoted a pared-down, seeker-sensitive version of the Pentecostal tradition. Unlike Freedom in Christ, however, the leadership at Elmira Pentecostal Assembly not only is interested in incorporating new members, it is also attempting to use the shift towards generically evangelical themes and forms as a way to update the overall style of a congregation that has been focused on meeting the needs of its previously predominant farming constituency.

The leaders and members at Elevation tend to view the flagrant, consumer-oriented, seeker-sensitive approach implemented at churches like Freedom in

Christ and Elmira Pentecostal Assembly as both outmoded and distasteful. From their very inception the objectives of the Embassy and Elevation were to provide an expression of Christian community for young people who no longer connected with either traditional Pentecostalism or the seeker-sensitive churches created for their baby boomer parents. The typical member at Elevation appears to be searching for a church that is less institutional and less consumer-focused. They are interested in something that they would describe as more "authentic" and that focuses more on the "journey" of the Christian life rather than the cyclical process of evangelization–education–(re)evangelization commonly espoused within seeker churches.

What the leadership and members of Elevation may be unaware of, however, is that this very autonomous, anti-consumerist form of evangelicalism has become its own unique "brand" within the local religious environment (Ellingson 2007, 105). Elevation—either consciously or unconsciously—has institutionalized and commoditized its very aversion to institutionalization and commoditization. Elevation's unconventional setting and structure and its denunciation of mega-church and seeker church techniques are the very way that it distinguishes itself in the local religious environment. Several individuals that I spoke with at Elevation were proud that they attended a congregation that did not pander to consumer demand, as many of the churches they had attended in the past so often had done. What the members at Elevation may fail to recognize is that they themselves are paying allegiance to just another segment of the religious marketplace. Much like the person who wishes to demonstrate his or her nonconformist ideals by buying "alternative" clothing or music that is, in fact, marketed by multinational corporations and purchased by millions of other consumers, some members at Elevation feel that they have found a unique religious community that refuses to commoditize the Christian tradition, when, in actuality, they themselves have been the victims of a very successful niche marketing campaign.

4

Generically Evangelical Religious Identity

As I explained in chapter 1, when I began my fieldwork in September 2009 one of the first things that I did was talk informally with the members of Freedom in Christ, Elmira Pentecostal Assembly, and Elevation in order to gauge participants' commitment to traditional modes of Pentecostal identity and experience (Bernard 2006, 211; Fetterman 2010, 41-42; Murchison 2010, 101-5). One of the ways that I did this was by asking questions such as, "Is it important to you that Freedom in Christ is a Pentecostal church?" In addition to providing the basis for the central hypothesis of this study, the responses elicited during these and other informal conversations anticipated what I found in both the personal interviews and the congregational surveys.

Of the forty-two people that I interviewed, only six (approximately 14 percent) explicitly chose the term "Pentecostal" to describe their religious affiliation (see table 3). Furthermore, the results of the congregational surveys revealed that just 36 percent of respondents answered "yes" to the question "Is it important to you that this is a Pentecostal church?" Only 7 percent of respondents said that if they were to move and needed to find a new church that they would only look for a Pentecostal church. And only 61 percent of respondents either completely agreed or generally agreed that the term "Pentecostal" accurately described their religious views; this was tied with the term "Charismatic," compared with 79 percent for "Protestant," 84 percent for "evangelical," 89 percent for "born-again," and 100 percent for "Christian."

It is important to note that I strongly suspect that for many of the 61 percent of survey respondents who agreed that the term "Pentecostal" accurately described their religious views (as well as those who responded similarly regarding the term "Charismatic"), this likely indicated their commitments

TABLE 3. Highlights from the congregational surveys on religious identity

	Freedom in Christ (%)	Elmira Pentecostal Assembly (%)	Elevation (%)
Attended a Pentecostal church most frequently as a child	64.6	41.7	14.3
Attended a Pentecostal church most frequently before coming to their present congregation	79.2	58.3	19.0
Indicated that it was important to them that their current church was Pentecostal	60.9	64.5	4.8
Indicated that if they had to find a new church they would only look for a Pentecostal church	8.7	19.4	0.0
Completely agreed that the term "Pentecostal" accurately described their religious views	52.2	61.3	5.0
Completely agreed that the term "Christian" accurately described their religious views	95.7	87.1	87.3

to Charismatic or supernatural beliefs and practices more than it did their commitment to traditional Pentecostal identity, belief, and practice. This is suggested by the fact that just 36 percent of respondents thought that it was important that their church was Pentecostal and just 7 percent would only look for a Pentecostal church if they moved. While I am not suggesting that these terms are mutually exclusive, the responses from the interviews and surveys do clearly indicate that participants felt that the label "Pentecostal" did not describe their religious self-identities as accurately as a variety of more generic terms and suggests a situation quite different from the Pentecostalism of generations past when this degree of ambiguity would not have existed.

My objectives in this chapter are simple. I aim to demonstrate that the vast majority of the individuals I interviewed at Freedom in Christ, Elmira Pentecostal Assembly, and Elevation did not adhere to traditionally Pentecostal modes of religious identity. Rather, most of the members of these congregations espoused a generically evangelical religious identity with loose, if any, traditional or denominational linkages. In this chapter I also develop a simple typology of religious identity derived from interviews, survey data, and observations that allows us to compare the ways that individuals religiously self-identify within other Pentecostal congregations in Canada and the United States. The fact that an overwhelming majority of participants used a generically evangelical or Christian term to describe their religious affiliation provides strong evidence for my hypothesis that Canadian Pentecostal identity is being transformed from traditionally Pentecostal to generically evangelical forms. Before I discuss the generically evangelical religious identities of participants in any detail, it is first necessary to briefly explain what it is that I mean by the term "generic evangelicalism."

Generic Evangelicalism

CANADIAN SOCIOLOGIST SAM REIMER is responsible for developing the use of the term "generic evangelicalism" in the sense that it is most commonly used by sociologists of religion at the present time.[15] The central aim of much of Reimer's research has been to identify the similarities and differences between American and Canadian evangelicals (1995; 2000, 228; 2003, 4–5). In order to compare and contrast evangelicals across national boundaries, Reimer had to first develop an appropriate definition of evangelicalism. To do this he differentiated between two basic definitional strategies that are alternatively based on either (1) belonging or (2) belief and behaviour (2000, 228–29).

Perhaps the best-known example of a belief-and-behaviour-based definition of evangelicalism is the one proposed by the British historian David Bebbington. Bebbington argued that evangelicals are best understood as those Christians who are highly committed to a quadrilateral of traditionally significant evangelical beliefs and behaviours, namely conversionism, activism, biblicism, and crucicentrism (1989, 1–19). While Reimer recognizes that such belief-and-behaviour-based definitions have their place in specific applications, he prefers to define evangelicalism according to belonging, and more specifically, as a particular subculture shared across various conservative Protestant denominations. He explains:

> I focus on evangelicalism as a *subculture*, limiting the term to those who participate in conservative Protestant denominations. Since I study the effect of the evangelical subculture on individual evangelicals, it is necessary to study those who actively participate in the subculture. Alternatively, one could study evangelicalism as a *movement*, which would include all those who meet a certain set of evangelical believing and/or behaving criteria, regardless of their denominational affiliation or religious identity. In other words, belief and behaving definitions will include conservative mainline Protestants and Roman Catholics in the evangelical category. These conservatives meet evangelical criteria but are not embedded in the evangelical subculture. (2000, 229; emphasis original; see also Reimer 2003, 6–7)

Reimer examined the characteristics of Christians belonging to this evangelical subculture from various denominations in both Canada and the United States. He discovered that, except for (1) a larger disparity among American versus Canadian evangelicals regarding what they say they do and what they actually do, (2) the predisposition of American evangelicals to view national history and politics through a moral and religious lens, (3) the increased tendency towards political conservatism and extremism among

American evangelicals, and (4) higher proportions of irenicism among Canadian evangelicals, evangelicals in Canada and the United States were nearly identical, particularly in terms of belief and practice (1995; 2000, 235-36; 2003, 118-51).

Reimer demonstrated that "in areas of religious experience, belief, morals, practice, and commitment, differences are minimal" (2003, 142). This observation led him to posit the existence of a "transnational generic evangelicalism" in Canada and the United States (2000, 242; 2003, 15, 39). While this "transdenominational transnational evangelical subculture" (Reimer 2003, 21) allows for national and even regional differences—especially in areas of a political or social nature (Reimer 1995)—it represents a remarkably homogeneous, shared religious culture that unites evangelicals in both Canada and the United States through a vast network of clergy, colleges and seminaries, conferences, curricula, institutions, professional associations, literature, music, movies, television, and a whole host of new media platforms including blogs, social media, software, and websites.

Reimer's recognition of the existence of a generic evangelicalism has been corroborated and expanded in terms of its denominational reach by American sociologist Stephen Ellingson. Ellingson found significant evidence of a generically evangelical religious subculture in several Evangelical Lutheran churches in the San Francisco Bay area. He defined those churches that adopted the generic evangelical paradigm as individualistic, emotive, pragmatic or utilitarian, technique driven, needs focused, contemporary in music and technology, homogeneous, therapeutic, moralistic, marketing savvy, passive in participatory orientation, and obsessed with church growth (2007, 111-13). He writes, "worship in the evangelical tradition appeals to emotion and experience rather than intellect and doctrine and will experiment extensively with any technique or technology to create an environment conducive to conversion" (2007, 113). Ellingson perceived the emergence of generic evangelicalism within the congregations that he studied as a largely regrettable process of the evangelical "colonization" and homogenization of American Lutheranism (2007, 179-85).

I believe that the phenomenon within conservative Protestantism identified by Reimer and Ellingson is the same trend that Donald E. Miller caught only a glimpse of in California and labelled as "new paradigm churches" (1997,

1) and what Margaret Poloma and John Green describe within the Assemblies of God as "alternative congregations" (2010, 25). The promotion of a generically evangelical orthodoxy, and the adoption of a similar form or way of doing church, represents a common and significant transformation in late-twentieth- and early-twenty-first-century North American Christianity. Generic evangelicalism is certainly not a completely coherent religious movement. It is better described as a prevailing cultural trend that scholars have detected in many different contexts across Canada and the United States. That being said, it is difficult for individuals who have engaged in fieldwork within these types of congregations to deny that, as Richard Kyle explains, "Denominational lines have broken down, theology has been diluted, religious traditions have gone by the way side, and the parachurches have become increasingly important. Consequently, a generic evangelicalism has come to the forefront" (2006, 312).

There exists a tremendous degree of congregational variety within the vast swath of generically evangelical congregations present throughout Canada and the United States. While generically evangelical congregations all promote a markedly similar "kit" of conservative Protestant identity, beliefs, and practices, this kit can be assembled in substantially different ways, resulting in a range of options for how congregations choose to package this religious culture. Two of the largest and most important approaches to packaging generic evangelicalism are what are often described as seeker-sensitive churches and emerging churches (Poloma and Green 2010, 38).

Seeker-sensitive churches (or simply, seeker churches) emerged in the 1970s and 1980s, particularly with the founding of Bill Hybels's Willow Creek Community Church in South Barrington, Illinois, in 1975 and Rick Warren's Saddleback Valley Community Church in Orange County, California, in 1980. These congregations and others like them were built with the intention of attracting largely baby boomer religious seekers by packaging conservative Protestant belief and practice "in an innovative, contemporary form" (Sargeant 2000, 1). "A seeker church," according to Kimon Howland Sargeant, "is one that tailors its programs and services to attract people who are not church attenders" (Sargeant 2000, 2). This often involves a rock band playing contemporary music; the use of drama and multimedia presentations; a practical and encouraging message; and an overall casual, upbeat, and welcoming experience with little pressure for commitment.

Seeker churches share a number of other common characteristics. They include churches that (1) are markedly anti-institutional and non-denominational in emphasis, if not in actuality; (2) have historically drawn the majority of their members from the baby boomer generation; (3) value clergy who are pragmatic over those with formal theological education; (4) emphasize contemporary, soft-rock worship; (5) usually include some kind of small-group ministry; (6) encourage (and, in some cases, even require) informal dress; (7) prioritize tolerance and individualism, and, as a result, de-emphasize potentially offensive religious symbols such as crosses and controversial topics such as the crucifixion, hell, and judgment; (8) stress technique and method over liturgy; (9) embrace a corporate culture and intentionally utilize current marketing practices to help increase attendance; and (10) above all else, focus on the incorporation of religiously inactive seekers by being sensitive to their felt needs.

Emerging churches are a more recent development on the North American religious landscape.[16] In the 1990s, a number of conservative Protestant clergy in Canada and the United States began to feel that the seeker church approach was too blatantly consumerist and failed to connect with the "Gen X" and "Millennial" cohorts who no longer identified with the modern, rationalistic, and propositional form of evangelicalism favoured by their baby boomer parents or grandparents (Belcher 2009, 9, 35–36; Marti 2005, 36; Poloma and Hood 2008, 12). *A New Kind of Christian: A Tale of Two Friends on a Spiritual Journey* (2001), written by former English professor and non-denominational pastor Brian McLaren, marked a kind of beginning for the emerging church movement. McLaren's book is a fictional dialogue between Dan Poole, a conservative Protestant pastor who is experiencing a crisis of faith, and Neil Everett Oliver, a former pastor and now high-school science teacher. Poole stands as a type for disaffected evangelicals everywhere, while Neil (who prefers to be called Neo) stands as a type for "a new kind of Christian."

Through his conversations with Neo, Dan gradually comes to realize that Christianity is not simply about traditional ecclesial structures and correct doctrine, but more about an ongoing spiritual "relationship" and "journey" (two key words within the emerging church). This new kind of Christian is someone who attempts to mould a wholly new vision of the Christian faith that is more attentive to postmodern conceptualizations of epistemology and ontology. Theologian Ray Anderson explains that emerging churches promote "second-order change," which "produces a new system and new way of behaving rather than a new behaviour within the same system" (2006, 21). In practical terms, this means that emerging churches are often not simply the retooling of an existing conservative Protestant church, but, like Brian McLaren's own church, are totally new communities intentionally designed from the ground up.

The emerging church is notoriously difficult to define, as one of its main, self-described emphases has been the avoidance of the modern tendency to erect foundational categories and definitions. Nonetheless, Eddie Gibbs and Ryan Bolger identify three core and six derivative practices that they believe define the emerging church: (1) identifying with the life of Jesus, (2) transforming the secular realm, (3) living highly communal lives, (4) welcoming the stranger, (5) serving with generosity, (6) participating as producers, (7) creating as created beings, (8) leading as a body, and (9) taking part in spiritual activities (2005, 43-45). This oft-cited definition of emerging churches is so ambiguous that it could refer to almost any Christian congregation on the planet, and while certainly pointing to some of the themes commonly emphasized within the emerging church, it does not work as an adequate definition of the movement.

Many evangelicals do not fully understand or accept the emerging church movement. Scot McKnight began an article in *Christianity Today* by summarizing the caricature that many outsiders have drawn of the emerging church:

> It is said that emerging Christians confess their faith like mainliners—meaning they say things publicly they don't really believe. They drink like Southern Baptists—meaning, to adapt some words from Mark Twain, they are teetotalers when it is judicious. They talk like Catholics—meaning they cuss and use naughty words. They evangelize and theologize like the Reformed—meaning they rarely evangelize, yet theologize all the time. They worship like charismatics—meaning with their whole bodies, some parts tattooed. They vote like Episcopalians—meaning they eat, drink, and sleep on their left side. And, they deny the truth—meaning they've got a latte-soaked copy of Derrida in their smoke- and beer-stained backpacks. (2007)

Much like the positive definition suggested by Gibbs and Bolger, negative stereotypes of the emerging church described by McKnight, while containing an element of accuracy, are equally unhelpful in trying to identify the movement (for another example see DeYoung and Kluck 2008, 20–22).

At its most basic and popular level, the emerging church movement is a type of protest, first beginning within conservative Protestantism and now found throughout much of North American Christianity, against traditional forms of Christian doctrine and church leadership (Belcher 2009, 40–43). At the congregational level, emerging churches are those that, in my own estimation, often feature (1) contemporary music and alternative forms of artistic expression; (2) dialogical and discussion-oriented messages rather than expository preaching or propositional teaching; (3) an outward-looking, social-justice orientation; (4) an emphasis on orthopraxy over orthodoxy, given that adherents often purport that truth is positioned, and, thus, elusive; (5) engagement with popular culture; and (6) political liberalism.

Generic evangelicalism shows a remarkable similarity with many of the most distinct developments that occurred within North American religion during the latter half of the twentieth century. Some of these include the domestication of religion from a transcendental reality to a component of the human consciousness, or what some call "psychological polytheism" (Berger 1965, 41; Hillman 1989, 38–45; Moore 1992, 66–67; Wuthnow 1998, 160–61); the rise of a pervasive therapeutic, individualistic culture (Bellah et al. 2008, 47; Campbell 1987; Rieff 1966; Turner 2011, 71); the increasing popularity of non-denominationalism (Carroll and Roof 1993; Roof and McKinney 1987; Wuthnow 1988); and the development of a "spiritual quest culture" or "spirituality of seeking" (Roof 1999, 59; Wuthnow 1998, 3–4). Generically evangelical churches can best be defined as churches that, above all else, filter their religious content through a therapeutic, individualistic lens, which encourages the purging of traditional, denominational features in favour of a kind of lowest-common-denominator, homogeneous version of evangelical identity, belief, and practice.

Commenting on the discernable presence of this therapeutic individualism within North American evangelical literature, theologian George Lindbeck writes, "Acceptance of Christ as one's personal savior is still the touchstone or shibboleth of piety in this evangelical literature, but the Jesus one accepts is no longer chiefly the forgiver and redeemer from sin. He is rather 'the friend who helps one find happiness and self-fulfillment'" (1986, 369-70). The recasting of the image of God from the creator and sustainer of the universe who is to be feared and honoured to that of a kind of master therapist who is instead consulted and recommended was a consistently encountered theme during my fieldwork.

The generically evangelical conviction that religion should be both personally fulfilling (therapeutic) and negotiable (individualistic) has resulted in a religious culture in many congregations where it is acceptable for nearly all traditional, denominational aspects of a religious tradition to be, borrowing a term from Wuthnow, "tinkered" with, in order to provide the most personally "rewarding" and "relevant" religious experience possible. With particular reference to young adults,[17] who now constitute the single largest demographic of North Americans, Wuthnow elaborates: "Spiritual tinkering was not just a form of restlessness that characterized baby boomers and then could easily be reversed among their offspring. Spiritual tinkering is a reflection of the pluralistic religious society in which we live, the freedom we permit ourselves in making choices about faith, and the necessity of making those choices in the face of uprootedness and change" (2007, 135). As we will now observe, religious identity is an area of religious life that has been significantly affected by this culture of religious adaptation.

Traditional Denominational Identifiers

OVER THE COURSE OF CONDUCTING PERSONAL INTERVIEWS with the members of the three congregations, a discernable pattern emerged regarding the way that interview participants described their religious identities. All of the interview participants fell into one of three main groupings, ranging from those with a high degree to those with a low degree of denominational affinity, with a significant number somewhere in between these two extremes. I labelled the first group of participants within this typology "traditional denominational identifiers." This meant two things. First, when asked the question, "What term would you use to describe your religious views?" their first answer was "Pentecostal." Second, when asked, "Do you consider yourself to be a Pentecostal?" they explicitly answered "Yes." To my surprise, this category included just six, or 14 percent, of the forty-two interview participants.

Consider, for instance, the response of Gordon, a twenty-seven-year-old student from Elmira Pentecostal Assembly.

>**Author:** What term would you use to describe your religious views?
>**Gordon:** I would say that I am a Pentecostal. Maybe not an extreme Pentecostal, but a Pentecostal.
>**Author:** But you wouldn't be opposed to using the label Pentecostal to describe yourself?
>**Gordon:** No, never.
>**Author:** Is it important to you that this is a Pentecostal church?
>**Gordon:** Yes, it is important to me.
>**Author:** Why?
>**Gordon:** That's a good question. I wouldn't be opposed to going to a non-Pentecostal church, but it's important to me because I really believe in the working of the Holy Spirit and that he still works in people's lives today. I think that this is an important aspect of the Church. That would be my main reason why it's important to me that this is a Pentecostal church. Not so much that we stick to the historical roots of Pentecostalism, but stick to the belief that the Holy Spirit does work in people's lives today in the many different ways that he does.
>**Author:** Do you consider yourself to be a Pentecostal?
>**Gordon:** I do, yeah.

Ruth, a middle-aged woman also from Elmira Pentecostal Assembly, was another traditional denominational identifier.

>**Author:** What term would you use to describe your religious views?
>**Ruth:** Well, I would just tell people that I am a Pentecostal.
>**Author:** Would you?
>**Ruth:** Yes. I'm not ashamed of that. I'm more proud of it now than when I was a kid. When I was a kid going to school, well, Pentecostals were labelled as "funny." They thought that we were

the "Holy Rollers" and I didn't want anybody to know that I attended a church that was being made fun of. Well, you probably heard all of those kinds of stories? Did you? That we swung from the chandeliers?

Author: Yes, I have.

Ruth: I had people tell me that they saw people in my church swinging from the chandeliers. I said that this was impossible because the windows were too high and they were stained glass. They said that we acted weird and rolled around the aisles. Oh, you name it, it was said. Nobody says that anymore. They don't label us the same way. Maybe we were kind of strange to them then because we spoke in tongues, so they thought something funny was going on in there.

Thomas from Freedom in Christ shared this same commitment to traditional Pentecostal identity, but with an interesting nuance.

Author: What term would you use to describe your religious beliefs?

Thomas: Because I am a more technically minded person, I would just tell them the name of my denomination—that I belong to the Pentecostal Assemblies of Canada—which makes them ask the question "What is that?" This, then, allows me to explain exactly what my religion is. I believe that if I just say "Pentecostal" that they might think they know what this means, but because the word "Pentecostal" has such a broad definition, their understanding might not accurately reflect what I believe. I would rather give them a thirty-second blurb of who I am and of my religion.

Author: Do you consider yourself to be a Pentecostal?

Thomas: I'm a fully pledged Pentecostal. That is the church that I chose to participate in 100 percent.

Where Thomas differed from Gordon and Ruth is that he was raised in New Brunswick, which boasts one of the largest populations of Oneness, or non-Trinitarian, Pentecostals in Canada. As someone brought up in a congregation belonging to the PAOC in New Brunswick, it was necessary for Thomas to express denominational specificity if he wished to clearly differentiate himself from the much-maligned Oneness Pentecostals. Thomas rightly feared that if he simply told other New Brunswickers that he was a Pentecostal, that they might assume that he was a Oneness Pentecostal. When Thomas moved to Ontario he continued using the same degree of denominational specificity when describing his religion because he was unaware that Oneness Pentecostals were a much smaller minority in Ontario.

To document the responses of the three remaining interview participants who also maintained traditional denominational identities would be redundant, as there is not much in the way of distinction or gradation that can be made among this group of respondents. The objective here is simply to observe that there were a few individuals that I interviewed who remained committed to traditional Pentecostal identity, as well as to provide a point of contrast for the other interview participants. As one might expect, given my description of the three congregations in the previous chapter, four of the six traditional denominational identifiers that I interviewed came from Elmira Pentecostal Assembly (the most traditional of the three congregations), two came from Freedom in Christ, and I did not encounter any traditional denominational identifiers at Elevation (the least traditional of the three congregations).

Latent Denominational Identifiers

I LABELLED THE SECOND GROUP of interview participants in my typology of religious identification—moving from those with the greatest to those with the least degree of denominational affinity—"latent denominational identifiers." Unlike traditional denominational identifiers, who held a firm sense of Pentecostal identity, when I asked this second group of participants the question "What term would you use to describe your religious views?" they provided either a generically evangelical or a generically Christian response such as "evangelical," "born-again," or "Christian." However, when I asked participants in this group, "Do you consider yourself to be a Pentecostal?" they, often after much consideration, answered "Yes." This category included fourteen people or approximately 33 percent of participants. The reason that I call this group "latent denominational identifiers" is because their first instinct was to *not* identify as Pentecostal and many only hesitantly acquiesced to considering themselves Pentecostal, often with very specific nuances or qualifications.

Consider, for instance, Arthur, a twenty-six-year-old construction foreman who attended Freedom in Christ. Arthur was raised in a devout Christian Reformed home and attended a Christian Reformed church in Kitchener until he went to college. Arthur's wife was raised in a Baptist family, and, after the two were married, they attended Immanuel Pentecostal Church in Kitchener for approximately three years before beginning to attend Freedom in Christ in 2007. Arthur and his wife chose to attend a Pentecostal church after they were married as a compromise between the Christian Reformed and Baptist traditions. Even though Arthur did not choose the term Pentecostal to describe his religious identity and maintained a commitment to Reformed theology that sometimes clashes with the largely Arminian theology predominant within the Canadian Pentecostal tradition, he still, in an interesting way, considered himself to be a Pentecostal.

> **Author:** What led you to initially come to Freedom?
> **Arthur:** Our decision to switch churches was led mostly by the availability of programs for our children at Freedom.
> **Author:** If you had to choose a term to describe your religious views, what would you use?
> **Arthur:** A term to describe my religious views?
> **Author:** Yes. Or, if someone you just met for the first time asked you what your religion was, what would you tell them?
> **Arthur:** Christian.
> **Author:** Is it important to you that Freedom is a Pentecostal church?
> **Arthur:** No.
> **Author:** Do you consider yourself to be a Pentecostal?
> **Arthur:** Well, we're attending a Pentecostal church, so, yes.
> **Author:** You believe that attending Freedom makes you a Pentecostal?
> **Arthur:** My denominational views are—I'm a non-denominational kind of person in that sense. I believe that what's important is the teaching rather than the umbrella that you are under. So, yes. If someone asked me the question I would tell them that I'm

a Pentecostal because I attend a Pentecostal church, but not so much because of my belief and practice.

Alice, a twenty-nine-year-old member of Freedom in Christ since 2000 who attended Lutheran and Mennonite Brethren churches as a child, also preferred a generic religious self-descriptor, but, like Arthur, expressed some vague sense of Pentecostal identity.

Author: What term would you use to describe your religious views?
[*long pause*]
Author: If someone you just met for the first time asked you what your religion was, what would you tell them?
Alice: Well, I would say that I am a Christian and that I go to a Pentecostal church. I don't feel restricted to denominations, personally. To me it's more where I fit in and where the church meets the needs that I have and if I fit into what is going on at the church at the time. That's kind of how I look at it.
Author: What led you—and keeps you coming back—to this church?
Alice: Friends. I met someone from this church at work. She said, "Hey, you should come out to our young adults group." So I came out with her. The associate pastor said, "You should come check out a Sunday service" because I was still kind of between churches. So I thought, "Well, okay, I'll come check it out." So I came and enjoyed it, then I just decided that I liked it here and I gave it a couple of months. People were very welcoming and I thought, "OK, I fit in here, it's a good fit for me" and here I am.
Author: Is it important to you that this is a Pentecostal church?
Alice: No.
Author: Do you consider yourself to be a Pentecostal?
Alice: I would think now I do because I've been going to a Pentecostal church and now that I understand, well, sort of understand, what it means to be part of a Pentecostal church. But, like I said, to me, when I was growing up denominations were never something that was like "You have to be Lutheran, or you have to be this." I just kind of always went wherever I felt that I fit in.

Author: So, what do you think it means to be a Pentecostal?
Alice: I guess I don't necessarily know what it means.

It is interesting that both Arthur and Alice described their religious affiliation simply as Christian and indicated that it was not important to them that Freedom in Christ was a Pentecostal church, but at the same time they considered themselves to be Pentecostals. It is clear from their responses, however, that this latent form of denominational identity had absolutely nothing to do with a sense of belonging to the Pentecostal tradition as, later on in the interviews, it became apparent that they knew little or nothing about Pentecostalism.

Arthur and Alice represented a segment of the participants that I spoke with, most of whom were raised in non-Pentecostal traditions and who chose to join a Pentecostal church as adults out of personal preference. To many of these participants, the fact that the church that they attended was Pentecostal was incidental. Arthur, for instance, initially chose to attend Immanuel Pentecostal Church as a compromise between his and his wife's religious traditions and chose to attend Freedom because of "the availability of programs for our children." Alice decided to initially attend Freedom in Christ because a friend invited her. She later made the decision to regularly attend the church because she felt that she "fit in" and that the church, in her words, met "the needs that I have."

These participants were simply attending churches where they felt welcome, had success making friends, and found the programs that best met their needs. These same participants, however, were deeply committed members of their congregations and were not opposed to telling people that they attended Pentecostal churches, or by extension, that they were Pentecostal as a result of their attendance. It would, however, be a mistake to confuse this latent form of denominational identification as an indication of their commitment to the Pentecostal tradition. Rather, these participants indicated that they considered themselves to be Pentecostal as a means of demonstrating their sense of belonging and commitment to their specific congregations, not out of a sense of denominational belonging or identity. In other words, they felt that if their churches were Pentecostal and if they were contributing and committed members of their congregations then, ipso facto, they must also be Pentecostal.

Also under the umbrella of latent denominational identifiers are those participants who were raised in the Pentecostal tradition but who, like Arthur and Alice, identified their religious affiliation using a generic evangelical or Christian term. While they also maintained a latent sense of denominational identity, members of this group understood the doctrines, rituals, and stereotypes that they were clearly distancing themselves from by adopting a more generic religious self-descriptor. Rather than a means of demonstrating congregational commitment, these participants expressed a certain degree of denominational identification because many of them continued to maintain core Pentecostal theological and ritual commitments. While these individuals refused to identify their religious affiliation as "Pentecostal," there were elements of the tradition that they either still practised or at least continued to feel a sense of affinity towards and so eventually acquiesced to a latent form of Pentecostal identity.

Edward, for instance, was a thirty-eight-year-old office administrator who has spent most of his life attending Pentecostal churches and has attended Elevation since 2001. While he preferred not to describe his religious affiliation as Pentecostal, he did consider himself to be a Pentecostal and associated this sense of identity with traditional Pentecostal theology and ritual.

> **Author:** What term would you use to describe your religious beliefs?
> **Edward:** My Facebook profile says "conservative-ish Christian."
> **Author:** What would you say to someone from your workplace, for instance, who asked you what religion you practised?
> **Edward:** I would say Christian without hesitation. But Christian is a broad term in many senses. Okay, you're Christian, but are you Catholic, Baptist, Pentecostal, Methodist? They're all Christians, right? It's funny because I identify with the Pentecostal Church and doctrine, but if I was at the office today, for example, and somebody asked me what my religion was, I'm not really sure how I would answer, because although I personally don't have a problem with most of the stuff that goes on in a Pentecostal church, there is a huge perception in our culture that Pentecostals are a bunch of Holy Rollin', freaky, speaking in tongues, dancing around the church type of people. And that

is not something that I want to be identified with. I don't have a problem being identified as having a passionate faith, whether or not people would think that of me, who knows. I don't have a problem with many forms of worship and that type of thing. Like with any church there are extremes, right. There are Pentecostal churches that are dry and dead and kind of boring. There are others that are just crazy, yelling and jumping around and that kind of stuff, and I don't like either. So, if someone asked me what church I went to I would say "Elevation," which would mean absolutely nothing to them. And if they asked "What kind of religion or denomination is that?" I would tell them that it was Pentecostal. And I might follow that up with some kind of light-hearted joke "But not like the rollin' around in the aisles kind of Pentecostal" or something. You know what I mean?

Author: Yes.

Edward: It's interesting how people get an image of what anything is, whether it is, you know, what is a Catholic? A Catholic is someone who stands there with their arms folded and kneels five times and hums some Latin songs that they don't know, right? That's not the case in a lot of Catholic churches. A lot of my friends are Catholic, and that's totally not them. That's just the stereotype. My view, anyway, is that Pentecostals are labelled as kind of the freaky, Charismatic weirdos. And in movies—I haven't seen this movie, but I've heard about it, *Jesus Camp*.

Author: Oh, yeah. I have seen that.

Edward: Have you?

Author: Yes.

Edward: Well, I haven't seen it, so I don't know all about it, but I've seen trailers and excerpts on newscasts. Is that a Pentecostal camp?

Author: Yes. The pastor featured in the film is a Pentecostal, but I do not know which denomination that they are associated with or if they are an independent church.

Edward: Even as a Pentecostal, that type of thing bugs me when I see that. I'm Pentecostal, but I'm not that. There are all kinds of other denominations that probably have the same problem with stereotyping. It's just that, it's stereotyping, whether it's true or not. [*long pause*]

So, I'm Christian. [*laughter*]

Author: After all that, you're just a Christian.

Edward: [*laughter*]

Author: Is it important to you that Elevation is a Pentecostal church?

Edward: My short answer is yes. Probably because for the better part of my intellectual life that is what I've been a part of. That's what I've been taught, so to speak. I subscribe to the doctrines and beliefs of the Pentecostal movement. Again, not the extreme stuff. Some of the things that people do, like speaking in tongues, are big Pentecostal things, right? I don't disagree with it. I don't think it's a bad thing. As a matter of fact, I think it is true or valuable. However, if people are just, like, flapping off all the time and it just gets out of hand, then that bothers me. But, yeah, I subscribe basically to the Pentecostal view and teaching. So in that sense, yeah, it's important to me that Elevation is a Pentecostal church.

Author: Do you consider yourself to be a Pentecostal?

Edward: I would consider myself a Pentecostal, I guess. I mean I consider myself a citizen of the world, I guess, do you know what I mean? [*laughter*] To me that question is almost like "What are you versus everyone else?" I am not saying that is how you asked it, but that is how I interpret it. It would be the same as saying that if someone were a Catholic that everything about them is Catholic and everything not Catholic is not for them. That is not the type of Pentecostal I am.

Author: Would you consider referring to yourself as Pentecostal, never mind all of the other implications?

Edward: Yes. That being said, one of the things that I've really learned, especially at Elevation and through our discussions and personal development at Elevation, is that even though I would identify myself as a Pentecostal, it's not for me to say that because I'm Pentecostal I disagree with every other denomination. It's just that, you know what, this denomination is the one that I have the least problems with. [*laughter*]

Shane, who was twenty-seven years old and had been attending Elmira Pentecostal Assembly for two and a half years, is another example of someone who spent most of his life attending Pentecostal churches, but who espoused a latent rather than a traditional form of denominational identity.

Author: What term would you use to describe your religious views?
Shane: I would use the term "Christian" because it describes a lot more than just a denomination. Obviously, we are associated with the Pentecostal Assemblies of Canada here and I have been a part of that denomination for my entire life. That's what I have been raised in and that's what I know. But at the same time, there are other denominations and other people that, really, we share the same beliefs and the same systems with. The Christian faith has some fairly strict guidelines and understandings and a big one is that we realize that Christ died for our sins and rose again and that we have salvation in him through that. There are some things like that that really are not negotiable in our faith. There are some other things that I think Scripture leaves us to discover for ourselves. A lot of those can be deep theological arguments or debates that people go through. But I think it's finding a place where you are comfortable and finding a place where you are at home. For me, I've grown up in the Pentecostal Church and what the Pentecostal Assemblies of Canada says to be true is stuff that, through life experiences and different things, I have not been left with too many doubts about whether or not it is true.
Author: Is it important to you that this is a Pentecostal church?
Shane: I would say that it is. I think more for me in a personal sense because I've been raised Pentecostal. I have, however, attended a church from another denomination at one point, and that's not to say that one church is right and another is wrong. Rather, it's just something that I'm familiar with. I guess it is important to me that I understand what happens. No matter whether you are

attending a contemporary or a classical—more traditional—Pentecostal church you kind of know what to expect. So I think it's definitely a comfort level for me to some extent. That's why it matters to me. It's not the name associated with it or tagged on to it, but more so due to familiarity, I think.

Author: Do you consider yourself to be a Pentecostal?
Shane: Yes.

Finally, Harold from Freedom in Christ also fit into this second tier of latent denominational identifiers.

Author: What term would you use to label your religious views?
Harold: What are my choices?
Author: Whatever you want.
[*very long pause*]
Harold: I would say—and this is going to sound strange and you may have not had anyone answer it this way—grace-centred. The older I get, the more I describe myself as grace-centred. When I was younger it was this and that. And there are still some things that are black and white. There are no issues or concerns about that. But more and more—I'm not perfect at it—I'm just trying to err on the side of—if you can say that—the grace-centred thing. Offer people the same kind of grace I would want offered to me if I was in their situation or whatever the case is.
Author: Is it important to you that Freedom is a Pentecostal church?
Harold: Specifically there, no.
Author: But say you were to go to another church, would that be something that you would look for?
Harold: It would be something that we would look for up front, yes. There's no question about it. I'm not going to say that it would be the determining factor, because, in all honesty, there are non-denominational churches out there that I find that are more "Pentecostal" than some Pentecostal churches are.
Author: Do you consider yourself to be Pentecostal?
Harold: I do.

Edward, Shane, and Harold typified a second major grouping within the latent denominational identifier category. Unlike the first group, who indicated that they considered themselves to be Pentecostal as a means of identifying with their congregations, these individuals were committed to at least some traditional elements of Pentecostalism that served to anchor their religious identities. These individuals were at the same time different from traditional denominational identifiers who exhibited no hesitation when describing their affiliation with Pentecostalism. Here we see a sort of second-order form of Pentecostal identification that would not show up in regular conversations with their neighbours and co-workers or perhaps even in a census questionnaire, but does emerge after some probing and sustained reflection on their religious identities.

Edward, like many of the participants I interviewed, was clearly leery of the negative stereotyping that Pentecostals often receive in both popular culture and in society at large. This significantly contributed to his hesitancy to openly self-identify as a Pentecostal. Both Edward and Shane very carefully bracketed their religious identities, stressing commitment to a more ecumenical understanding of Christianity as opposed to the sectarian understanding of Pentecostalism common to their childhood experiences. While participants like Edward, Shane, and Harold exercised caution in explicitly identifying themselves as Pentecostals due to a sense of embarrassment regarding how others often perceive the tradition, some elements of Pentecostal doctrine and practice remained important to them. A latent sense of denominational identity helped them to sustain this aspect of their religious identities.

The degree of loyalty that Edward, Shane, and Harold expressed towards the PAOC, however, remains unclear. Edward, for instance, explained that, ultimately, he attended a Pentecostal church not because he completely agreed with everything within the Pentecostal tradition but because "this denomination is the one that I have the least problems with." Similarly, Shane explained that attending a Pentecostal church had most to do with the fact that it is the tradition that he was "raised in" and where he felt "comfortable" and "at home." Likewise, Harold mentioned that he would have absolutely no problem attending a church that belonged to a denomination other than the PAOC as long as it possessed the characteristics that are most important to him and his family.

This suggests, then, that participants like Edward, Shane, and Harold, who were raised in the Pentecostal tradition and used generic labels in order to identify their religious identities, much like the previous group of latent denominational identifiers, may continue to participate within a Pentecostal congregation only as long as they continue to feel welcome and their needs are met. If they were to move or leave their present congregation due to a conflict and were unable to find a Pentecostal church that also happened to meet the above criteria, then they would likely begin experimenting with churches belonging to other denominations that better met their needs.

Non-denominational Identifiers

THE FINAL CATEGORY OF RELIGIOUS IDENTITY that I observed among the participants at Freedom in Christ, Elmira Pentecostal Assembly, and Elevation is composed of those individuals that I call "non-denominational identifiers." Like latent denominational identifiers, when asked the question "What term would you use to describe your religious views?" this third group of participants also provided either a generically evangelical or generically Christian response. Unlike both traditional denominational and latent denominational identifiers, however, when asked, "Do you consider yourself to be a Pentecostal?" non-denominational identifiers universally answered with a negative response. Non-denominational identifiers were the single largest group, accounting for twenty-two, or 52 percent, of the forty-two interview participants.

Non-denominational identifiers were composed of two roughly equal groups. In one group were those participants who did not mind that people knew that they attended a Pentecostal church and for whom being part of an organized denomination provided them with a sense of confidence in the doctrinal soundness of their congregations. These individuals did not openly identify as Pentecostal and did not personally consider themselves to be Pentecostal, but they were relaxed about others labelling them that way or using the term "Pentecostal" simply to describe the church that they attended as opposed to describing their own religious identities, beliefs, and practices. In the other group were those participants who very consciously avoided reference to the term "Pentecostal" altogether. Some of these individuals, much like Edward, had a heightened sense of the negative connotations often associated with the term and so avoided using it, sometimes even when identifying their churches. Others simply felt that there was nothing about their religious identities or experiences that could be accurately described as Pentecostal.

Elsie was a twenty-nine-year-old homemaker who grew up in a conservative Pentecostal church in Listowel, Ontario, and attended Elmira Pentecostal Assembly. While she had no problem telling people that she attended a Pentecostal church, she had very serious reservations about labelling herself as a Pentecostal.

> **Author:** What term would you use to define your religious views?
> **Elsie:** Born-again Christian.
> **Author:** Is it important to you that this is a Pentecostal church?
> **Elsie:** I would say yes, I guess. Because that is what led us to first attend this church. So, yeah, I guess it would be important to us.
> **Author:** That is what led you to check it out?
> **Elsie:** Yeah, for sure. It's not like it had to be Pentecostal or we would not go. It's not like that. But that was what led us there because we both grew up in a Pentecostal church and we are both familiar with it.
> **Author:** Do you consider yourself to be a Pentecostal?
> **Elsie:** Like, as a label?
> **Author:** If someone asked you if you were a Pentecostal would you say "yes?" Are you comfortable using that term?
> **Elsie:** I go to the Pentecostal church, but I don't know if I would say "I am Pentecostal." I'm a born-again Christian. That's how I would label myself, but not as a Pentecostal.

Jane, a forty-four-year-old accountant who has attended Freedom in Christ since 2002, echoed Elsie's convictions.

> **Author:** What term would you use, Jane, to describe your religious views? In other words, if someone were to ask you, maybe from your workplace, someone that you didn't know that well, what your religion was, what would you tell them?

Jane: Evangelical.

Author: You would use that term?

Jane: Evangelical? Yeah. That's probably what I would say.

Author: Is it important to you that Freedom in Christ is a Pentecostal church?

Jane: Well, I don't know that it is. I think if I left here and found a church that offered the same values. Like, we used to attend Wilmot Missionary Church, and if you walked into Wilmot Missionary today—if it had the same feel as it did when we were going there—it's probably way more Pentecostal than Freedom is. So, if that's what you're asking, probably not. I don't think that I'm—I don't want to say that I'm Pentecostal. I didn't even understand what those things were when I was starting going to church, so no.

Author: Do you consider yourself to be a Pentecostal?

Jane: If somebody asks me what church I go to, I don't have a problem saying that I go to Freedom Pentecostal Church. But I don't know that I need to be labelled that way; I hate labels. So, I don't think that I want to be labelled a Pentecostal. I don't even know what that means. So, for me, it's okay that there are lots of churches that have the same values and beliefs but are not Pentecostal. So, I don't even understand, you know, why we have to label it Pentecostal.

Author: So the label is not an important part of your identity?

Jane: No.

Derek, thirty-four, has been a member of Embassy and Elevation since their inception. He was raised in the Pentecostal tradition and is a graduate of a denominational Bible college, but he also hesitated to identify with Pentecostalism.

Author: Is it important to you that Elevation is a Pentecostal church?

Derek: No. [*laughter*] Though I am not opposed to it. I don't want to say that I am opposed to it, but it is not important to me.

Author: It's not on the top of your list of priorities.

Derek: Yeah.

> **Author:** Would you describe yourself as a Pentecostal?
> **Derek:** I would not, but I wouldn't be opposed to being called that. [*laughter*]
> **Author:** You wouldn't self-identity that way?
> **Derek:** No I wouldn't, no I wouldn't.

Finally, Henry, who was thirty-two years old and has been attending Freedom in Christ since 2004, also explained that for him the only important aspect of denominational belonging was the sense of doctrinal assurance that it provides.

> **Author:** What term would you use to label your religious views? What would you say to someone who asked you what your religion was?
> **Henry:** I would tell them that I am a Christian.
> **Author:** Is it important to you that Freedom is a Pentecostal church?
> **Henry:** It is in the sense that it's important that biblical truths are being preached and taught. I mean if it were some kind of a Satan-worshipping cult, we certainly wouldn't attend. But the actual denomination itself was not a deciding factor on our joining the church.
> **Author:** Do you consider yourself to be a Pentecostal?
> **Henry:** I honestly don't know what it would even take to consider oneself a Pentecostal. [*laughter*]

There was a segment of the non-denominational identifier group, like Elsie, Jane, Derek, and Henry, who were not opposed to the fact that people knew that they attended a Pentecostal church and, like Derek, did not mind if other people labelled or called them Pentecostals. At the same time, however, they were very clear about the fact that they did not believe that the term accurately described their religious views. Also, they did not personally identify or consider themselves to be Pentecostal even if others might cast them in that light. For many of these participants, as we see in Henry's response, the knowledge that their church was part of a larger organization was important to them only in so far as (they believed) it guaranteed their congregation's commitment to Protestant Christian orthodoxy. For these participants, however, the fact that their church was affiliated with a Pentecostal denomination was inconsequential to their religious identities.

At the more extreme end of the spectrum of the non-denominational identifier group was Trevor, a thirty-six-year-old college professor attending Freedom in Christ, who not only avoided the use of the term "Pentecostal" but also that of "evangelical" in describing his religious commitments.

> **Author:** If you had to pick a specific term to label your religious views, what would you use?
> **Trevor:** Yeah, I don't know. I wrote on your sheet "non-denominational Christian" because that is how I used to identify. You know, four years ago when I got married, on my wedding licence, I wrote, Lutheran. But I haven't attended a Lutheran church in years except when I go to visit my family. So—[*laughter*]
> **Author:** A lot of people find themselves in a similar situation.
> **Trevor:** Yeah. So, I mean—I know it's a trend now too—that people call themselves non-denominational Christians and there are non-denominational Bible colleges and all that kind of stuff. You know, my wife, on her wedding licence, wrote Christian. She started Catholic and then her family went Baptist and then they went Pentecostal and then when we moved here we were Baptist again before coming to Freedom. So we're not going to necessarily give ourselves a name. So, okay, I'm a non-denominational Christian, I guess. That's what I mean by it. I still have Lutheran tendencies. I still have some hang-ups. Like I had both of my kids baptized by my brother, who is a Lutheran minister. But not just for family reasons, it just seemed really important to me. I guess I have the attitude, I would rather have it and not need it than need it and not have it.
> **Author:** Is it important to you that this is a Pentecostal church?
> **Trevor:** You know what, no. No. It is not important that it is Pentecostal. In fact, sometimes when I tell people I go to a Pentecostal church I'm concerned about their reaction and how they are going to label me. I guess I'm evangelical, but I don't like to call myself evangelical because when you identify as evangelical

there are sometimes a whole lot of things besides your faith that people assume. They assume that you are politically very conservative. In some ways I am and in some ways I'm not. Suddenly you are categorized. And maybe it's my own bias. Maybe not everyone does think of me that way, but my impression is that if I tell you, "Hey, I'm evangelical," that encompasses a lot more. [*pause*]

Author: That they are assuming things about you that are not necessarily true?

Trevor: Yeah, yeah. And I guess the word "evangelical" does mean that. I mean, a Lutheran doesn't call himself evangelical. So what does evangelical mean? Well, often there are political beliefs, you're socially conservative. What are some of the other characteristics of evangelical? Some of these, I guess, do describe me. Like I'm family-oriented and everything like that. [*pause*]

Author: In the United States, for instance, the term "evangelical" often carries the connotation of being radical or extreme.

Trevor: Yeah. You're almost certainly Republican and you're trying to covert everybody. So, I guess I wouldn't label myself an evangelical. Certainly I would label myself as Christian. I guess I still have a very open mind to some other things, like Orthodoxy has some appeal to me. Even Catholicism—as I've looked into it more—I am realizing that the negative things I previously thought about it were merely what I thought Catholicism was and not exactly what it is. I still don't think of myself as Pentecostal, I guess, because I still have a lot of those Lutheran influences and I still have some hang-ups about speaking in tongues and stuff like that. I believe it's true, it's just not something that I've embraced. But I really enjoy going to the Pentecostal church. Mostly it's the sense of Christian community I get from it.

Sidney, thirty-five, and Elizabeth, twenty-nine, a couple I interviewed together who have attended Elevation for one year, also avoided the labels

"Pentecostal" and "evangelical," and were even hesitant to use the term "Christian" to describe their religious affiliation.

> **Author:** What term would both of you use to describe your religious views? If someone were to ask you what your religion was, what would you tell them?
>
> **Elizabeth:** I don't know. That's a hard one. Usually I would just say "Christian," I think. Yeah, I just love Jesus.
>
> **Sidney:** I think that's it for me too. I don't even like to just say "Christian" because there is a lot of religious trappings with that. When I try to describe my faith or spiritual experience I don't want it to include the religious trappings. The people we bought this house from were flipping it. They were Christians, and our neighbour two doors down is not. The people we bought from made the comment to him, "Oh, a good young Christian family is moving in." And my heart sank when our neighbour said that to me because I thought, I've just got all this baggage added on to me that I would have rather not had.
>
> **Author:** Is it important to you that Elevation is a Pentecostal church?
>
> **Sidney:** No.
>
> **Elizabeth:** No, it's not.
>
> **Author:** Do either of you consider yourselves to be Pentecostal?
>
> **Sidney:** I don't.
>
> **Elizabeth:** No, I don't consider myself to be a Pentecostal.
>
> **Author:** It is very interesting that many people attending the congregations that I am studying are not even aware that they are attending a Pentecostal church.
>
> **Elizabeth:** I didn't know that I attended a Pentecostal church until I was completing your survey. When reading the questions I was like, "I don't know. What is this? I don't know what that is?" Then I found out that Elevation was a Pentecostal church.

Martha, a twenty-five-year-old member of Elevation who has attended both the Embassy and Elevation since 2002, was also hesitant to describe herself as a Christian.

Author: What term would you use to describe your religious views?
Martha: Currently?
Author: Yes.
Martha: I would say that I'm a Christian but don't associate with any particular denomination. Depending on whom I'm having a conversation with, I would be hesitant to say that I'm a Christian. I feel that my beliefs really line up with a Christian identity, but because of negative connotations that some people associate with Christianity I sometimes wouldn't label myself that way.
Author: Is it important to you that Elevation is a Pentecostal church?
Martha: No, it's not important to me that it's a Pentecostal church. In fact, when I first learned that it was a Pentecostal church I was sort of surprised.
Author: Oh, really?
Martha: I always knew it had that affiliation, but it didn't seem strongly apparent to me in the way that the services were run and through Brandon's speaking. And I was just going off of my experiences of attending other Pentecostal churches and some friends and stuff.
Author: Do you consider yourself to be a Pentecostal?
Martha: No. [*laughter*]

The responses of Elsie, Jane, Derek, Henry, Trevor, Sidney, Elizabeth, and Martha represented the dominant mode of religious identity at Freedom in Christ, Elmira Pentecostal Assembly, and Elevation. The fact that the majority of the members of these congregations did not feel any commitment to not only traditional but even latent or vague forms of Pentecostal identification might be evidence of a broader transformation of religious identity currently under way within the Canadian Pentecostal tradition. It is also interesting to note that a number of the non-denominational identifiers that I spoke with (like some latent denominational identifiers such as Edward) very explicitly told me that they were uncomfortable using the term "Pentecostal" (and sometimes even the terms "evangelical" and "Christian") to describe their religious affiliations. These individuals did not want—in fact, were embarrassed—to be associated with popular negative stereotypes of Pentecostals.

For instance, Tracy, the assistant pastor at Freedom in Christ, told me, "If I was standing in the schoolyard talking to one of the other kindergarten moms waiting for our kids to go to school like I was today, I probably wouldn't tell her that I was Pentecostal. I would tell her that I was a Christian and that I went to a Pentecostal church. That's probably how I would define that to someone who had no idea of what Pentecostal is. I would love for someone to come and experience what Pentecostalism is—this definition and expression of it—rather than what people may or may not understand about Pentecostals or what they think they've seen on TV about evangelicals or whatever."

The use of a generic evangelical or Christian label to identify religious affiliation was clearly being used by many of the interview participants as a means of distancing themselves from what they perceived to be embarrassing and inaccurate representations of Pentecostals found within popular culture and broader society in general. It was also interesting to note that this uncomfortableness with labels extended for some individuals to the terms evangelical and even Christian.

Conclusion

THE PURPOSE OF THIS CHAPTER was to demonstrate that a significant proportion of the members of Freedom in Christ, Elmira Pentecostal Assembly, and Elevation displayed generically evangelical rather than traditionally Pentecostal modes of religious identity. Only six participants explicitly identified as Pentecostal when asked to describe their religious views. Another fourteen participants expressed some degree of latent Pentecostal identity, and a further twenty-two participants neither used the term Pentecostal to describe their religion nor considered themselves to be Pentecostal in any way other than to identify the church that they attended. What these numbers reveal is that if these forty-two participants provided similar responses (and I have no reason to suspect that they would not) to question number twenty-two—the religion question—on the Canadian census form, only 14 percent of the interview participants that I spoke with would be recorded as "Pentecostal." The remaining 86 percent of interview participants would have been labelled in the generic "Christian" category.

Notwithstanding the admittedly small case study, the fact that so few of the people that I interviewed described themselves as Pentecostal raises the question of whether or not this phenomenon exists on a wider scale within other congregations affiliated with the PAOC or even within churches belonging to other denominations. If so, this might demonstrate that the number of individuals attending Canadian Pentecostal churches did not decrease at the same rate as an uninformed examination of the 2001 Canadian census data may otherwise suggest. I am not implying that commitment to traditional forms of Pentecostal identity and experience have totally evaporated within Canadian Pentecostal congregations. I observed, quite clearly, that at Freedom in Christ, Elmira Pentecostal Assembly, and Elevation slightly fewer than half of the participants continued to express a form of either traditional or latent Pentecostal identity. However, the fact that a majority of participants did not express any commitment to Pentecostal identity and a significant number of participants intentionally avoided being labelled as Pentecostals suggests the need to examine this trend on a broader, national scale.

5

Spirit Baptism and Speaking in Tongues

So far I have shown that there exists a trend towards religiously self-identifying as generically evangelical rather than traditionally Pentecostal among the members of Freedom in Christ, Elmira Pentecostal Assembly, and Elevation. Another component of my hypothesis is that it is not only the religious identity, but also the religious experience (i.e., belief and practice) of the members of the three congregations that no longer conforms to traditional Pentecostal types. It is not only the way that members religiously self-identify, but also what they believe and the way that they practise their faith that suggests a broader transformation occurring within Canadian Pentecostalism. In this chapter I will demonstrate how the members of the three churches do not display traditional Pentecostal beliefs and practices surrounding the experiences of Spirit baptism and speaking in tongues—Pentecostalism's two most distinctive characteristics. While Spirit baptism and glossolalia, as Margaret Poloma and John Green write, "have become less common" in many North American Pentecostal churches (2010, 47–48), they have not simply been jettisoned as evolutionary understandings of religious development might suggest. Rather, the experiences of the members of these three congregations suggest a reinterpretation or reframing of these two historic doctrines in order to better reflect a largely therapeutic understanding of both the person of God and the nature of religion commonly found within the generic evangelical subculture that permeates these congregations (Ellingson 2007, 88).

More specifically, in this chapter I will show that the traditional Canadian Pentecostal positions on Spirit baptism and glossolalia are neither a priority in the preaching or teaching of the three congregations nor a deeply held conviction of most members, as revealed by the following: (1) several interview participants demonstrated a lack of awareness regarding the baptism of the Holy Spirit, (2) the majority of interview participants did not maintain the traditional Pentecostal belief that Spirit baptism occurs subsequent to conversion, (3) none of the interview participants supported the official denominational position that speaking in tongues is the unique evidence of Spirit baptism, and (4) more than half of the interview participants who valued the baptism of the Holy Spirit as a unique spiritual experience understood its role as offering largely therapeutic and psychic benefits to individual members rather than providing power for evangelism.

Ignorance and Confusion regarding Spirit Baptism

OF THE FORTY-TWO PEOPLE THAT I INTERVIEWED, twenty-six (62 percent) indicated that they believed the baptism of the Holy Spirit was an important spiritual experience. This was almost 20 percent lower than the 81 percent of respondents who answered similarly on the congregational survey (see table 4). The reason for this disparity is, I believe, not an actual difference of opinion between survey and interview participants, but rather the fact that during the interviews I had the opportunity to ask follow-up questions, which allowed me to get a better sense of participants' opinions regarding this experience. This additional probing revealed that a significant number of participants who initially indicated that they believed the baptism of the Holy Spirit was an important spiritual experience did not actually think this way but simply answered affirmatively, either because they had no idea what the term referred to but thought they ought to think that it was important or because they confused it with water baptism. The number of interview participants who

TABLE 4. Highlights from the congregational surveys on Spirit baptism and glossolalia

	Freedom in Christ (%)	Elmira Pentecostal Assembly (%)	Elevation (%)
Completely or generally agreed that Spirit baptism was an important experience	84.4	93.1	72.6
Completely or generally agreed that glossolalia is the evidence of Spirit baptism	64.5	72.4	12.9
Reported never having spoken in tongues in a public church service	81.8	88.9	90.5
Reported praying at least once a year for someone to receive Spirit baptism	34.0	55.5	19.6
Reported having received the baptism of the Holy Spirit	77.3	85.2	38.1

Most of the interview participants conflated Spirit baptism with conversion. Likely that was the case among most survey respondents. Hence, it might be inaccurate to correlate these levels of commitment to Spirit baptism with the traditional Pentecostal view of this experience.

were either ignorant or confused regarding the doctrine and practice of Spirit baptism clearly revealed that this historic Pentecostal experience was not a priority in the preaching or teaching of the three congregations. This finding was also a very clear affirmation of the advantages of using mixed methods research in the study of lived religion.

During my interview with Henry from Freedom in Christ, for example, it became clear that he had very little understanding of what the baptism of the Holy Spirit was, except that, perhaps, it had some connection with the gifts of the Spirit.

Author: Do you think that receiving the baptism of the Holy Spirit after conversion is an important part of the Christian life?

Henry: Now, you might need to elaborate a bit on the baptism of the Holy Spirit. Do you mean like receiving spiritual gifts?

Author: Within traditional Pentecostalism there is this idea that sometime after conversion the believer undergoes a spiritual experience called the baptism of the Holy Spirit, which is usually accompanied by speaking in tongues.

Henry: Then I am going to answer that with a no . . . A lot of that stuff sounds a little bit legalistic, if you will. Like you are not really a Christian if you don't receive the baptism of the Holy Spirit. You know what? I really think we need to get away from all that legalistic stuff because that's what needs to differentiate Christians per se with a "religion." Our main focus is to bring more people to Christ. Being legalistic and saying you're not this or that because you haven't experienced this does not bode well for achieving this objective, in my opinion. So from that standpoint we should get away from all that kind of legalism, if you will.

Author: Have you ever received the baptism of the Holy Spirit?

Henry: I have never spoken in tongues. I believe I've been accepted into Christ's family of believers but haven't received the baptism of the Holy Spirit. To be honest, it's not really all that important to me, so I've never really considered whether I have or have not. I know that I am saved.

The same was true of Elizabeth from Elevation.

Author: Do you think that receiving the baptism of the Holy Spirit after conversion is an important part of the Christian life?

Elizabeth: See, on the survey, I answered yes and then I found out what that actually means.

Author: What did you think it meant?

Elizabeth: I just assumed that it meant that the Spirit came and lived inside of you. I didn't realize it meant that you developed the other stuff, like the gifts of the Spirit.

I found the responses of those individuals who confused the baptism of the Holy Spirit with water baptism to be particularly interesting. One individual who responded this way was Albert from Elevation, a twenty-year-old student at the University of Waterloo.

>**Author:** Do you think that receiving the baptism of the Holy Spirit after conversion is an important part of the Christian life?
>**Albert:** Yes.
>**Author:** You do? Could you tell me a bit more about that?
>**Albert:** It's a tough one. I don't exactly know the specific reason why, but it does say in the Bible that when they mention the steps of conversion, baptism is always one of them. Not to say that, like, if someone on their deathbed accepts Jesus and they didn't get baptized, they would go to hell.
>**Author:** I'm talking about Spirit baptism, not water baptism.
>**Albert:** Ahh. Okay.
>**Author:** In traditional Pentecostalism, there is this idea that after conversion and water baptism there is another spiritual experience where the believer is baptized with the Holy Spirit, like found in the Book of Acts.
>**Albert:** Oh, okay, yeah, yeah, yeah.
>**Author:** This experience is usually "evidenced" or accompanied by speaking in tongues.
>**Albert:** Oh, then, no. I thought you were talking about water baptism.

While Jeremy from Elevation indicated that the baptism of the Holy Spirit was not important to him, he, like Albert, confused the experience with water baptism, and specifically, with adult baptism practised outside of the Reformed tradition in which he was raised.

>**Author:** Do you think that receiving the baptism of the Holy Spirit after conversion is an important part of the Christian life?
>**Jeremy:** No. Because I come from a background where we do infant baptism, so when people are converted we have a thing called "Profession of Faith" where they basically do a class type thing where

they go over the doctrines of the Church and all that. And then they get up in front of the church and confess or profess their faith and then they become full members of the church and are allowed to participate in communion. So it's basically kind of the same thing, I think, as adult baptism, but without the actual baptism.

Author: What I am talking about is actually different. There are obviously infant baptism and adult baptism, but then Pentecostals also have this thing called baptism in the Holy Spirit, which is not water baptism. It is an experience after conversion. So you are converted and baptized, or even baptized as a child and confirmed, and then, within traditional Pentecostalism, you have a subsequent kind of emotional experience that Pentecostals call "baptism of the Holy Spirit." And it's usually "evidenced" by this other thing called "speaking in tongues," which you have probably heard about at least on television or something.

Jeremy: Yes. So, baptism of the Holy Spirit doesn't actually refer to baptism with water?

Author: That's right. Within traditional Pentecostalism you would experience conversion, water baptism, and then baptism in the Holy Spirit.

Jeremy: Okay.

The responses of those interview participants who initially indicated that they believed the baptism of the Holy Spirit was an important spiritual experience but who either had no idea what the baptism of the Holy Spirit was or confused the experience with water baptism illustrate the paucity of teaching on Spirit baptism within the three congregations.

Spirit Baptism and the Question of Subsequence

IF WE TAKE A CLOSER LOOK at interview participants' responses we also see that only seventeen participants, or 40 percent, explicitly indicated that they believed the baptism of the Holy Spirit occurred after conversion (the traditional Pentecostal position), a level of distinction not possible to confirm with the responses to the survey instrument. This means that more than a third of the twenty-six interview participants who affirmed the importance of Spirit baptism viewed this experience as synonymous with the indwelling of the Holy Spirit at the time of conversion. Additionally, it should be noted that the sixteen interview participants who indicated that receiving the baptism of the Holy Spirit was not important to them also equated Spirit baptism with the reception of the Holy Spirit at the time of conversion. What this means is that 60 percent of participants equated Spirit baptism with the experience of conversion.

Receiving the Holy Spirit at the time of conversion is not the traditional Canadian Pentecostal understanding of Spirit baptism. In question 263 of his catechism Purdie asks, "Is the Infilling of the Holy Spirit definite and distinct from the New Birth?" He replies, "Yes. To be regenerated or born again by the Holy Spirit and have a measure of His presence is one thing; to be FILLED with the same Spirit is something additional" (1951, 45; emphasis original). Similarly, the *Statement of Fundamental and Essential Truths* states, "This experience is distinct from, and subsequent to, the experience of the new birth" (PAOC 1994, 5). Clearly, traditional Canadian Pentecostals believed that the baptism of the Holy Spirit is a distinct spiritual experience that occurs subsequent to conversion.

Several interview participants such as Mavis—a fifty-four-year-old mother of two from Freedom in Christ who has attended Pentecostal congregations since childhood—clearly disagreed with this traditional view of subsequence.

> **Author:** Do you think that receiving the baptism of the Holy Spirit after conversion is an important part of the Christian life?
> **Mavis:** It depends what you mean by receiving the Holy Spirit?
> **Author:** Why don't you tell me what you think that it means?
> **Mavis:** My own understanding, today, is that when you become a Christian, the Holy Spirit dwells within you. Whereas speaking in tongues, which is what used to be thought of as the baptism of the Holy Spirit, is a different thing.

Arthur, also from Freedom in Christ, echoed Mavis's sentiments.

Author: Do you think that receiving the baptism of the Holy Spirit after conversion is an important part of the Christian life?

Arthur: No. I believe it's important that we receive the Holy Spirit in our lives. That's incredibly important. My first response to your question is that the traditional view of Spirit baptism—speaking in tongues, yada, yada, yada—I don't think is necessary. I think the Spirit comes into you right off the bat and I think that sometimes you may experience him in a greater way, but for some people it's very visible and for others it is not.

Author: Do you think that speaking in tongues is the initial physical evidence of the baptism of the Holy Spirit?

Arthur: No.

Author: Have you ever received the baptism of the Holy Spirit?

Arthur: Have I ever received the baptism of the Holy Spirit? I would say yes. Have I ever received the baptism of the Holy Spirit in the traditional Pentecostal view? I would say no.

Author: So not with speaking in tongues.

Arthur: Right.

This opinion was by no means unique to the members of Freedom in Christ. Derek from Elevation concurred with Mavis and Arthur.

Author: Do you think that receiving the baptism of the Holy Spirit after conversion is an important part of the Christian life?

Derek: I believe the baptism of the Holy Spirit happens when you are converted.

Author: So you would say no to that?

Derek: Yes. I do not think that it is a second experience.

Martha from Elevation also provided a very typical response to this question.

Author: Do you think that receiving the baptism of the Holy Spirit after conversion is an important part of the Christian life?

Martha: Would someone who has been baptized in the Holy Spirit have to speak in tongues?

Author: Some people believe you do, and some people believe you don't.

Martha: Okay. I guess I'm not familiar enough with what the baptism of the Holy Spirit is. I definitely believe that when someone has invited God into their life, that the Holy Spirit is now with you and guiding you, and whatever gifts that involves for you. But I don't believe that everyone would necessarily have the same gifts of the Spirit and has to speak in tongues and that sort of thing.

While the single greatest proportion of those individuals who affirmed the traditional Pentecostal view of Spirit baptism as occurring after conversion were found at Elmira Pentecostal Assembly (nine), there were still several participants from the Elmira church, such as Elsie, who did not affirm the concept of subsequence.

Author: Do you think that receiving the baptism of the Holy Spirit after conversion is an important part of the Christian life?

Elsie: It's a gift. People can be a Christian without having it. I wouldn't say that it's an important thing. I would say that the most important thing is being a Christian, a born-again Christian. So I would say no, I guess.

Most of the people that I spoke with did not support the traditional Pentecostal view that Spirit baptism occurs sometime after conversion in a usually dramatic and public fashion. Instead, the majority of participants indicated that they believed that the baptism of the Holy Spirit is synonymous with the indwelling of the Holy Spirit that is believed to take place at the time of conversion. This represents a significant departure from traditional Canadian Pentecostal understandings and practices of Spirit baptism.

Speaking in Tongues as Evidence of Spirit Baptism

ALTHOUGH THERE WERE MANY INTERVIEW PARTICIPANTS who did not know what the baptism of the Holy Spirit was, who confused Spirit baptism with water baptism, and/or who did not believe that Spirit baptism happened after conversion, a much greater number of participants did not believe that speaking in tongues was the unique evidence of this experience. These two religious beliefs and practices—particularly as they relate to one another in a kind of procedural, commonsense formulation (i.e., tongues = Spirit baptism = power to witness)—are the two most defining characteristics of traditional Pentecostalism and have historically been used by Pentecostals to differentiate themselves from other evangelicals.

Even while bearing in mind the immense importance of both salvation and divine healing among traditional Pentecostals, Spirit baptism accompanied by speaking in tongues is the *sine qua non* of traditional Pentecostal identity and experience. As Grant Wacker explains of first-generation Pentecostals, "In principle salvation should have come first and sanctification second, but in practice Holy Ghost baptism, signified by speaking in tongues, took priority" (2001b, 40). Likewise, Gary McGee writes, "More than any other factor, including their stalwart belief in faith healing, speaking in tongues distinguished Pentecostals from their radical evangelical parents" (2010, 90).

The importance of glossolalia as the evidentiary assurance of Spirit baptism for traditional Canadian Pentecostals is also confirmed in the writings of Purdie and in the *Statement of Fundamental and Essential Truths*. In *What We Believe*, for instance, Purdie wrote, "The question is often asked, 'What is the evidence that one is filled with the Holy Spirit?' The Biblical evidence that one is filled with the Spirit is that he speaks supernaturally in a tongue he has never learned (Acts 2:4)" (1954, 22). Likewise, the *Statement of Fundamental and Essential Truths* unequivocally states, "The initial evidence of the baptism in the Holy Spirit is speaking in other tongues as the Spirit gives utterance" (PAOC 1994, 5). Few interview participants at Freedom in Christ, Elmira Pentecostal Assembly, and Elevation, however, agreed with this traditional Pentecostal position.

None of the individuals that I interviewed affirmed the belief that speaking in tongues is the *only* evidence of Spirit baptism—the official view promulgated by the PAOC. Instead, participants fell into one of two rather broad categories: first, those who understood glossolalia as one of many evidences of the baptism of the Holy Spirit, and, second, those who did not believe glossolalia to be an evidence of this experience at all. Harold from Freedom in Christ was an example of someone from this first category.

> **Author:** Do you think that speaking in tongues is the initial physical evidence of the baptism of the Holy Spirit?
>
> **Harold:** Yes, I do. I think there are other evidences, however. I just look at the everyday logic of the, you know, whole power to witness thing and tongues and all that kind of stuff, and when I read the Bible, and I read the sequence, it does make sense to me. And yet at the same time, some of the most incredible people I know—sharing their faith, the lives they live—would come from, for instance, a Baptist denomination where they don't believe in the baptism of the Holy Spirit, but they are way better witnesses and have more powerful lives than people who have been in Pentecostal churches and may speak in tongues, but I wouldn't give you two cents for the life they live. But the younger generation looks at that and thinks, "Okay. You say this, but shouldn't that change this over here?" I do believe in tongues being the initial evidence. It's not the only evidence, but some people would argue with me on that.

Emily, also from Freedom in Christ, closely mirrored Harold's response.

> **Author:** Do you think that speaking in tongues is the initial physical evidence of the baptism of the Holy Spirit?
>
> **Emily:** Usually. [*laughter*] Is that a good answer? I was always taught that speaking in tongues was the evidence. It makes sense that it is because how do you know if the experience is authentic if there isn't some certain evidence. And yet I've seen people who seem to be very full of the Holy Spirit that don't speak in tongues. So, that's why I say "usually."

Although Colin from Elmira Pentecostal Assembly initially responded negatively to this question, it became clear that he did not mean that speaking in tongues is not an evidence of Spirit baptism, but rather that it is not the only evidence of Spirit baptism.

> **Author:** Do you think that speaking in tongues is the initial physical evidence of the baptism of the Holy Spirit?
>
> **Colin:** No, I don't. No. I don't think so, just because I know people who have been baptized with the Holy Spirit and they don't speak in tongues. I've heard that's because, you know, they're not taught that speaking in tongues is the evidence. And, you know what, maybe that is true. But I don't see why God wouldn't fill them with speaking in tongues whether they knew about it or not. But I don't believe that you need to be speaking in tongues to be filled with the Holy Spirit. I know for myself, I have the gift of speaking in tongues, however, I was filled with the Holy Spirit before I received that gift and spoke in tongues. So I don't think it's necessarily a sign that you have been filled.

These three participants represented a further division within the first category of respondents who believed that tongues were only one of the evidences of Spirit baptism. First were those like Harold, Emily, and Colin who appeared to support this belief because they were aware of individuals who they believed displayed the characteristics of Spirit baptism but who have not spoken in tongues. Second were a number of participants who supported the idea of multiple evidences because they more explicitly believed that other gifts of the Spirit could serve as evidence of Spirit baptism. James from Elevation, for instance, had previously given this question a considerable amount of thought before he provided me with a particularly articulate response.

> **Author:** Do you think that speaking in tongues is the initial physical evidence of the baptism of the Holy Spirit?
> [*long pause*]
>
> **James:** No. Allow me to qualify that one. I always had a problem with that Pentecostal distinctive. If it was "a" instead of "the"—if it

was an indefinite article—I would be fine with it. But since it is a definite article and it's usually interpreted as "the only" initial evidence, then that's where I have a problem with that. That's why I said "no."

Similarly, Mike from Elmira Pentecostal Assembly made an explicit connection between the mention of numerous gifts of the Spirit in the New Testament and Spirit baptism.

Author: Do you think that speaking in tongues is the initial physical evidence of the baptism of the Holy Spirit?
Mike: Not necessarily.
Author: So, do you think there could be other evidences?
Mike: Yes. The Bible mentions various gifts, so any of those gifts that come along and you start to see that you have them or they are given to you. I would think that's probably also part of the baptism of the Holy Spirit.

Finally, Alice from Freedom in Christ recognized that there could be different evidences for different individuals.

Author: Do you think that speaking in tongues is the initial physical evidence of the baptism of the Holy Spirit?
Alice: I think that it is one of the evidences, but I don't think it is the initial one. I think it is different for everybody. Everybody will have a different type of experience. Me, personally, I spoke in tongues, but other people might not necessarily do that.

There were also a number of participants who simply did not think that speaking in tongues played any role whatsoever in the baptism of the Holy Spirit. Most of these respondents, like Trevor from Freedom in Christ, also believed that the baptism of the Holy Spirit was not subsequent to, but rather synonymous with conversion.

Trevor: One of the Pentecostal teachings is that speaking in tongues is evidence of the baptism of the Holy Spirit. I don't know if I agree with that interpretation. I've talked to my brother who is a Lutheran minister about it and he says, "Yeah, people speak in tongues, but it's something that might be overemphasized." But my brother says that we believe it happens and obviously the Bible says that it happens, but I've never seen it happen in a Lutheran church. At the Pentecostal church in Sudbury that my family and I attended, it seemed to be happening less and less and less. It seemed to be a little more generically evangelical. And a couple of times our pastor would be in the middle of speaking or we'd be singing and somebody in the middle of the song would start speaking in tongues. The pastor would actually chastise them and say, "We are worshipping corporately now and you are speaking out." I thought that was kind of interesting. You're not being moved the way you think you are. [*laughter*]

Author: Do you think that the baptism of the Holy Spirit is an important experience?

Trevor: I guess I don't believe in the baptism of the Holy Spirit manifesting itself through speaking in tongues or something like that. I know that's a pretty core Pentecostal belief.

Derek from Elevation provided a somewhat more complicated response. Unlike Trevor, Derek told me that he had spoken in tongues in the past and continued to speak in tongues and that he viewed this as a highly rewarding spiritual experience. That being said, he thought that speaking in tongues was not an evidence of Spirit baptism, but that one receives a full measure of the Holy Spirit at the time of conversion.

Author: Do you think that speaking in tongues is the initial physical evidence of the baptism of the Holy Spirit?

Derek: No, though I have no problem with speaking in tongues.

Author: But you wouldn't identify it as the evidence?

Derek: No.

Author: Have you ever received the baptism of the Holy Spirit?

Derek: I am a Christian, which I would argue is the baptism of the Holy Spirit. Have I spoken in tongues, I gather is part of that? Yes, I have, though I don't regard that as an evidence of the baptism of the Holy Spirit. I regard that as a gift.

Finally, Thomas from Freedom in Christ provided a rather unusual illustration for explaining his idea that speaking in tongues is not an evidence of the baptism of the Holy Spirit. Rather, he viewed it as a spiritual experience that may help to increase the degree to which the Holy Spirit operates in the life of the believer in more of a quantitative rather than a qualitative way.

Author: Do you think that speaking in tongues is the initial physical evidence of the baptism of the Holy Spirit?
Thomas: No.
Author: Could you tell me more about what you think about that?
Thomas: I haven't really educated myself on this and I know, as a Pentecostal, I should. But I do believe that as soon as I become a Christian that the Holy Spirit is inside of me. Do I have to speak in tongues for the Holy Spirit to be inside of me? No. I think just being a Christian will mean that you have the Holy Spirit in you. Now, does speaking in tongues help you? From what I read, it does. I look at it like a weight trainer. If he eats healthy, he can achieve his results. And a natural way of doing it faster, and it's not illegal, is taking creatine. You're still going to get there. My basic understanding of Pentecostalism is that it's like taking creatine as a supplement for lifting weights. You'll get there faster. But at the end of the day, the guy who took creatine and the guy who didn't are both the same people. They are both equal in the eyes of God, but the guy who took the creatine—or spoke in tongues—might experience spiritual growth a little faster. I guess that's my best way of explaining it.

These responses clearly demonstrate that the individuals with whom I spoke did not support the PAOC's official position stating that speaking in tongues serves as the unique evidence of Spirit baptism. Many of these individuals did not have a problem with the idea that speaking in tongues is one possible evidence of Spirit baptism but did not support the idea that it is the only such evidence. Others, especially those who viewed conversion and Spirit baptism as synonymous spiritual experiences, did not believe that speaking in tongues was an evidence of Spirit baptism at all. Some, like Trevor from Freedom in Christ, viewed tongues as something that might happen, but largely saw it as a spiritual excess and disruption in public church services. Others, like Derek from Elevation and Thomas from Freedom in Christ, viewed tongues as a beneficial gift that might contribute to one's spiritual development but also believed that glossolalia's evidentiary connection with Spirit baptism was a mistake.

It is important to note that, while Purdie clearly claimed that glossolalia was the chief evidence of the baptism of the Holy Spirit and that empowerment for service was this experience's primary aim, he also explicitly mentioned additional evidences of Spirit baptism. According to Purdie, the evidences of Spirit baptism are (1) glossolalia, (2) power for witnessing, (3) a greater passion for souls, (4) a greater reverence for the Word of God and zeal to study it, (5) a greater love toward all Christian people and to help others, and (6) a deeper prayer life (1951, 44; 1954, 22–23). That being said, Purdie took special care in both his catechism and in *What We Believe* to distinguish glossolalia as the first and primary evidence of Spirit baptism by listing it as the first evidence, devoting more space to its discussion, and grouping all of the additional evidences together into a single paragraph, denoting their secondary importance after tongues speech. Additionally, Purdie was more specific regarding the purpose of Spirit baptism, which he singularly identified as power to witness. It is possible, however, that he may not have made a definite distinction between the evidences and purposes of Spirit baptism, as many of the evidences that he mentions are clearly practical in orientation.

Conversely, the *Statement of Fundamental and Essential Truths* is emphatic about there only being a single evidence of Spirit baptism—speaking in tongues—while it lists three possible purposes of this experience: (1) to know Christ in a more intimate way, (2) to receive power to witness, and (3) to grow spiritually (PAOC 1994, 4–5). If one accepts both Purdie's writings and the *Statement of Fundamental and Essential Truths* as authoritative sources within traditional Canadian Pentecostalism, then one is left with a matrix of both traditional Pentecostal evidences and purposes of the baptism of the Spirit that exceed, although remain secondary to, speaking in tongues and empowerment for witness. The recognition of the multiplicity of both evidences and purposes of Spirit baptism in the traditional sources, however, does not minimize either the primacy of speaking in tongues in these sources or the apparent shift in opinion concerning these experiences that exists between these historical sources and the individuals that I interviewed.

The Purpose of Spirit Baptism

WHAT IS PERHAPS EVEN MORE INTERESTING than participants' opinions regarding the relationship between speaking in tongues and Spirit baptism are their thoughts regarding the purpose of the baptism of the Holy Spirit. As previously mentioned, research by Allan Anderson (2007) and Gary McGee (2010) convincingly demonstrates that the single most important priority for early Pentecostals around the world was the role that Spirit baptism played in providing power for the evangelization of the world. As Anderson explains, "The theological link between Spirit baptism and missions has always been made in the Pentecostal movement. It is very important to understand the significance of this, because just as Spirit baptism is Pentecostalism's central, most distinctive doctrine, so mission is Pentecostalism's central, most important activity" (2007, 65). Put more simply, "The power of the Spirit in Pentecostal thinking is always linked to the command to preach the gospel to all nations" (Anderson 2007, 212).

This is again confirmed in the Canadian Pentecostal tradition by Purdie, who asked in question 255 of his catechism, "What is the purpose of the Infilling of the Holy Spirit?" to which he replied, "It means that God gives us additional power and liberty for service enabling us to freely and efficiently witness for Christ–Acts 1:8" (1951, 44). Similarly, the *Statement of Fundamental and Essential Truths* states, "The baptism of the Holy Spirit is an experience in which the believer yields control of himself to the Holy Spirit. Through this he comes to know Christ in a more intimate way, and receives power to witness and grow spiritually" (PAOC 1994, 4).

Only fourteen interview participants (a third) indicated that they believed the purpose of Spirit baptism was to receive power to witness. Many of these same individuals also understood empowerment to be only one of several other possible purposes of Spirit baptism. James from Elevation, for instance, affirmed the traditional Pentecostal understanding of the purpose of Spirit baptism as empowerment. He also listed several other purposes of Spirit baptism.

> **Author:** What do you think the purpose of the baptism of the Holy Spirit is?
>
> **James:** The difficulty in answering that question is that I don't think of the baptism of the Holy Spirit as a one-time thing. I believe that we are meant to live the Christian life continually being filled, to keep on being filled with the Holy Spirit. So the presence of God's Holy Spirit in our lives, to me, is supposed to be, you know, as I understand it, an absolutely vital and central aspect of Christian living. So, the question is, "What is the purpose?" To me that question means, "What is the purpose of the Holy Spirit in our lives?" The purposes of the Holy Spirit in our lives are many. The Holy Spirit is the seal that we belong to God. The Holy Spirit is our guide. The Holy Spirit empowers us. The Holy Spirit convicts us. The Holy Spirit works in me spiritually and is vitally at work in my spiritual formation. To me it's one of the most important aspects of being a Christian and to live without that you are living a decidedly less exciting, less interesting, less vital Christian experience than you were meant to be.

Tracy from Freedom in Christ affirmed the traditional purpose of Spirit baptism as receiving power to witness, but, like James, she thought that there were additional purposes, namely the provision of a unique prayer language with God.

> **Author:** What do you think the purpose of the baptism of the Holy Spirit is?

Tracy: Well, I mean, Scripture tells us, of course, this was given to us so that we would have power to witness, and I would agree with that in real life. I think that there is a deeper place of courage to be able to share what I need to share when I feel I need to share it. Also, another purpose that has been very real in my life has been having a prayer language. Being able to pray things that I don't understand, but knowing that I'm doing a better job communicating with God through speaking in tongues than on my own with my own words. That kind of intimate prayer language thing has been a huge benefit, but also having an extra boost, I guess, that's such a stupid way to say that, but a power to be able to know what to say and to know that I can call on that. That's a part of my life now that I can call on to witness and to speak about Christ in the world and wherever I need to and wherever I'm being called to do that.

While there were a number of interview participants who held this type of hybrid understanding of the purposes of Spirit baptism that wedded the traditional power to witness with a wide range of other purposes, the majority of participants, like Derek from Elevation, primarily emphasized the individual benefits of Spirit baptism.

Author: What do you think the purpose of the baptism of the Holy Spirit is?

Derek: The purpose of the baptism is a seal to receive the Spirit when you become a Christian, to both seal yourself for eternity and to have the counsellor or convictor, or someone to come along with you in life to have the Spirit in you as first fruits of the promise and as the beginning of your sanctification, or purification, or just becoming a better person, if you want to just look at it that way. So, I would rephrase that question as saying, "What is the purpose of the Holy Spirit being in our lives, or Christ living in our heart?" The purpose is to counsel, convict, and to be a comfort.

Colin from Elmira Pentecostal Assembly explained the purpose of Spirit baptism in extremely individualistic terms. While Derek understood the role of Spirit baptism to be the reception of a moral and spiritual guide, Colin perceived Spirit baptism (which he clearly did not understand as a singular event) as a way for God to directly communicate with him or to manifest his reality in a powerful way.

> **Author:** What do you think the purpose of the baptism of the Holy Spirit is?
>
> **Colin:** I would say, for myself anyway—I can't speak for everybody, and I know everybody's experience with the baptism is different—for myself, whenever I am usually baptized by the Holy Spirit it's during a time of devotion and I think it's just more or less God coming to, you know, speak a word or give revelation or more or less just say, "Hey, I'm showing up in a big real way." So I think it's those three main purposes basically. Whether it's God giving revelation, just showing up in a big way, or just saying, "Hey, I'm an awesome God and this is who I am." So, yeah, it can be a variety of purposes.

A number of other participants also interpreted the baptism of the Holy Spirit in primarily individualistic terms but, like Arthur from Freedom in Christ, were more ambiguous about exactly what the purpose of the experience was or even when it occurred.

> **Author:** When would you say this experience happened?
>
> **Arthur:** As for a date, I couldn't give you an exact date. As for a time period, I would say I became more attuned to the Spirit's moving in the latter years of high school.
>
> **Author:** How would you define the nature of that experience?
>
> **Arthur:** I couldn't even define it for you, exactly what it was. I just know that my Christian walk significantly changed towards the mid to end of high school. You know, that's when I got into it a little more than just, "This is what I believe."

Alice from Freedom in Christ similarly described her Spirit baptism as occurring at an imprecise time in her life when she decided to focus more sincerely on her faith, and she could not fully articulate what this experience entailed.

> **Author:** What do you think the purpose of the baptism of the Holy Spirit is?
>
> **Alice:** I guess for me, it was kind of the turning point in my life where I kind of laid it all out and said, "Okay, I'm going to do this." For the first time I gave up a job to pursue school and study and stuff like that. So it was kind of in that whole period where I was, I don't want to say "super-religious," but we have ups and downs. We have peaks. So it was one of those periods where I was very gung-ho and very, okay, this is what I'm going to do. God is moving in my life. All these things are happening. So, it's kind of, I don't know, a whole lot of stuff was going on and it just sort of happened. I didn't really understand it at the time. I had to ask a lot of questions afterwards. I don't necessarily know if all those questions were answered.

Other participants echoed James, Tracy, Derek, Colin, Arthur, and Alice's convictions that the baptism of the Holy Spirit was, in the words of Edward from Elevation, "a very personal thing." Gwen from Freedom in Christ, for instance, explained that the purpose of Spirit baptism was, "Just to have a more personal relationship with God. I think it makes your relationship and dependence on him much deeper than, perhaps, someone who isn't seeking those things." Similarly, Lucy from Elmira Pentecostal Assembly told me that the purpose of Spirit baptism was so that "you know that God is there and that he is always with you. If you have the baptism of the Holy Spirit, you would have that." Finally, Mike, also from Elmira Pentecostal Assembly, described Spirit baptism as "a direct connection with the Spirit in a different mindset. It's a direct connection; hardwired versus wireless, maybe."

While the specific purposes of the baptism of the Holy Spirit varied from individual to individual, the vast majority of these participants emphasized the individual emotional, relational, and spiritual benefits that this experience had for them personally, rather than the corporate role that the experience played in providing power and boldness for evangelism and foreign missions that might strengthen the Church overall. Generic evangelicalism's emphasis on therapeutic individualism was apparent in the responses of the members from the three congregations regarding the purpose of Spirit baptism.

Evidence of the changing conception of the purpose of Spirit baptism was not confined to the individual responses of interview participants. During the course of my fieldwork, I observed, most commonly, the complete absence of discussion related to Spirit baptism, and, less frequently, the leadership of the three congregations directly reinterpret the experience of Spirit baptism through their public teaching and preaching ministries. A series of mid-week Bible studies led by Del Wells and Tracy Dunham in the fall of 2009 at Freedom in Christ illustrated some of the ways that the religious leadership at the three churches attempted to reframe the experience of Spirit baptism for their members and potential members.

Over his thirty years of pastoral ministry, Del Wells has developed four of what he calls "Life Transformation Courses." The four courses are titled "First Steps," "Life in the Spirit," "Learning to Serve," and "Learning to Lead." Wells has also developed a private company called Life Transformations Unlimited, which he uses as a means of advertising and distributing his courses in addition to marketing himself as a workshop, seminar, and retreat leader. In the fall of 2009, Wells offered his course "Life in the Spirit" to the members of Freedom in Christ. These mid-week courses were also sometimes attended by one or two individuals who were interested in the church but who had not yet become committed members of the congregation. The objective of the course, according to the introduction found in the course booklet, was to assist Christians to discover how the Holy Spirit, "enables you to live a life that is pleasing to God" and to "teach us and assist us in living our new life to the full" (Wells 2009, 1).

Each Wednesday evening from six thirty to eight o'clock, thirty to forty people would gather in the sanctuary at Freedom in Christ, where they would first listen to a short fifteen-to-twenty-minute teaching delivered by Wells or his daughter, Tracy. This short teaching—intended to orient participants to the general theme of the weekly lesson—was followed by groups of six to eight people gathered around circular tables discussing a series of questions that

Wells had arranged in order to encourage discussion relating to the lesson. The small-group discussion component of the lesson lasted about fifty minutes, and the evening was concluded with a few short remarks and a prayer given by either Wells or Dunham. As I attended these weekly lessons, and later skimmed through the course booklet written by Wells, I assumed that this course was simply intended to reinforce the traditional denominational views on Spirit baptism and speaking in tongues. As my participation in the course continued, however, it became clear that both Wells and Dunham had a very different agenda in mind.

In the first lesson, titled "Controlled by the Spirit," Wells introduced the idea that a life that is controlled by the Spirit is characterized by life, peace, freedom, and hope. It is, however, in the second lesson, "Led by the Spirit," that Wells more explicitly unpacked a number of the "benefits of following the Holy Spirit's leading" (Wells 2009, 5). In addition to freeing the believer from fear, Wells explains that a life controlled by the Spirit "enables you to cry 'Abba, Father,'" and means that the Holy Spirit, "testifies with your spirit that you are God's child" (Wells 2009, 5–6). He elaborates: "*Abba* is a very personal word that a Hebrew child would use to speak to his own father.[18] Jesus, God's Son, used this same word in addressing the Heavenly Father in the garden of Gethsemane just before His crucifixion (Mark 14:36). *Abba* is a word that reveals trust in someone else's care" (Wells 2009, 6; emphasis original). Wells included the following questions in order to help stimulate discussion during the group component of the lesson: "Why is it important that the Holy Spirit helps you to grow in your relationship with Father God? . . . At what times might you want to cry out 'Abba, Father'? . . . What benefit is it to you that the Holy Spirit confirms in your spirit that God has fully adopted you as His own child?" (Wells 2009, 6).

In the next lesson, "Helped by the Spirit," Wells continued to develop the benevolent fatherly image of the person of the Holy Spirit. The introduction to this lesson in the course booklet explains:

> Perhaps you have been so overwhelmed with an issue or situation in your life that you were almost spinning in circles. You wondered what you should do next. Maybe you thought about praying for what you were facing but you were so confused that you were unsure of how

to pray. Be encouraged. There is support available in these difficult circumstances of life for those who put their trust in Jesus Christ. The Holy Spirit living in you is ready and willing to help you in your most trying and difficult days. You prepare yourself to receive this assistance by making the conscious decision to live under the Holy Spirit's control . . . and by seeking the Holy Spirit for His direction for that which is ahead of you. (Wells 2009, 8)

Here Wells emphasizes being "overwhelmed" and "confused" and the role that the Holy Spirit plays in providing "support" and "assistance" in order to help one cope with life's difficulties. Some of the discussion questions for this lesson included "Why do you need the Holy Spirit to help you in your weakness? . . . How Will the Holy Spirit's help encourage you in your prayer life? . . . How intensely does the Holy Spirit pray through you? . . . What does this tell you about His interest in you?" (Wells 2009, 9).

Each of these lessons promotes an understanding of the person of the Holy Spirit as someone who is ultimately concerned with the immanent, relational task of helping individuals navigate the difficult aspects of their lives. God is not described as someone who often kills people for disobeying his commandments, such as Uzzah, who was struck dead because he mistakenly touched the ark of the covenant;[19] the forty-two small children who were mauled by bears for making fun of the prophet Elisha's baldness;[20] or Ananias and Sapphira, who were killed by God for lying to the apostles.[21] Rather, God— through the person of the Holy Spirit—is presented as a benevolent fatherly figure who exists largely to love, help, and encourage individuals. This image of God is a common feature in generically evangelical, and particularly seeker, churches like Freedom in Christ. Kimon Howland Sargeant explains: "The most common way that seeker churches portray God is as father. God is our 'heavenly father who sees what is done in secret' and will 'reward you.' God is not an angry father, eager to judge and condemn. Instead, God is an understanding and compassionate father" (2000, 83).

The Bible does, of course, often present God as a peaceful, loving, benevolent father. My point is not to claim that Wells's portrayal of the Holy Spirit is his own creation with no basis in the Christian tradition. Rather, my aim is to point out that his presentation of the person and character of the Holy Spirit is a selective one, and it casts the Holy Spirit as a largely innocuous figure that lacks the sense of awe, power, energy, otherness, and exhilaration—Rudolf Otto's *mysterium tremendum*—that was characteristic of the experience of early Pentecostals (Otto 1958, 12–40). Wells's description of God remarkably mirrors a large swath of Americans that Paul Froese and Christopher Bader encountered in their research, who, as described by one participant, "felt no sense of sublime awe in the presence of God but rather described a sensation similar to hugging a devoted parent" (2010, 16). Sargeant similarly explains: "The vast majority of seeker messages stress God's immanence, those aspects of God's character that are culturally appealing, over and above those aspects of God's character that inspire fear and are more culturally problematic" (2000, 86; see also Desjardins 1997; Ellingson 2007, 120).

The transformation of the God-image from awesome to largely pedestrian is confirmed by a long-time member from Freedom in Christ.

> It used to be that the gifts of the Spirit were what would attract people and draw them to the church, draw them to Christ. Today it seems that it is very much the opposite. Now we downplay the gifts of the Spirit. So what do I think? I think sometimes we underestimate the Spirit, but it's a whole lot more comfortable to do what we are doing right now . . . I think that—within most people—there is a longing for a sense of assurance that there is something beyond ourselves. Sometimes a supernatural manifestation is what a person needs in order to believe. My husband walked into a Pentecostal church as a university student and heard somebody speak in tongues and was totally wowed and sat there crying not knowing why he was crying. I don't always walk into our church and have a sense of the Holy Spirit—it just doesn't feel holy. And I think that is what I miss more than anything. Because it's just church—people are talking, people are socializing. Sometimes it would be nice to walk in and just, I don't know, get a sense that God is there.

The implications of the concept of the person and role of the Holy Spirit developed by Wells in the first half of the eight-week Bible study had interesting consequences when our class reached lesson five, titled "The Baptism in the Holy Spirit." Over the course of this Bible study, a number of the participants had openly expressed their concerns that they did not support the traditional Pentecostal teaching that an individual had to be baptized in the Holy Spirit or speak in tongues in order to be a fully functioning Christian. As already pointed out, this was the majority opinion among the people that I interviewed within all three of the congregations. In an attempt to address this concern of a significant number of the participants, Wells allowed his daughter to facilitate the class that focused on the baptism of the Holy Spirit.

Dunham opened this lesson by stating, "Our traditional teaching on the baptism of the Holy Spirit is not helpful for the average Canadian." She also suggested that this might be remedied if we "changed our thinking of divine encounters." Dunham then argued that there exist two major categories of divine encounters: (1) "regular spiritual disciplines," such as Bible reading and prayer, and (2) "extraordinary spiritual encounters," such as conversion, water baptism, baptism in the Holy Spirit, and "refillings" of the Holy Spirit. She continued by explaining that "the baptism of the Holy Spirit is a wonderful encounter with God, but it is not the only divine encounter" and that "God gives this gift according to his sovereign will." At one point in the teaching, Wells chimed in to stress that "the baptism of the Holy Spirit is an important experience, but it is not the only experience." Dunham concluded the lesson by telling those gathered that "as a young minister in the Pentecostal Assemblies of Canada, I have felt for a long time that our distinctive doctrine is dying and I am so happy that we can view this experience in this new way."

Dunham and Wells effectively reframed the experience of Spirit baptism from its traditional place as the most distinctive and sought-after spiritual experience in the life of a Pentecostal to "simply something worth pursuing"— a statement which both Wells and Dunham repeated several times over the course of the evening. Throughout this lesson, Dunham and Wells referred to Spirit baptism as one of the gifts of the Holy Spirit that God may or may not decide to give someone. As I have already demonstrated, however, traditional Canadian Pentecostals viewed Spirit baptism and its associated evidence of tongues speech as a distinct and normative event in the life of the believer, one which every Pentecostal—in fact, every Christian—is expected to receive. In response to a number of members who openly did not support the traditional view of Spirit baptism, and perhaps reflecting their already changed positions on the experience, Wells and Dunham reinterpreted the doctrine according to the concept of God already displayed in the earlier weeks of the course: God as a peaceful, loving, benevolent father who desires only to help and encourage, rather than demand and convict, his children.

Conclusion

MY GOAL IN THIS CHAPTER is not to argue that the members of Freedom in Christ, Elmira Pentecostal Assembly, and Elevation have totally abandoned traditional Pentecostal positions surrounding the experiences of Spirit baptism and glossolalia (although many certainly have done this). The churches that I studied have clearly chosen to emphasize certain elements of their traditional teachings while minimizing others, insofar as they support the largely therapeutic understanding of both the person of God and their individual relationships with God, which is a common feature of the generic evangelical subculture. The responses of interview participants clearly show that most of the individuals with whom I spoke believed that the primary role of the baptism of the Holy Spirit and speaking in tongues was no longer to provide power for evangelism and the evidence of the authenticity of this experience. Rather, most participants opined that the purpose of Spirit baptism was to provide a deepening relationship with God and that the chief benefit of speaking in tongues was its provision of a private channel of communication between the believer and God. Comfort appears to have replaced power as the most urgent need among the members of the three congregations.

Unlike a Canadian Pentecostal from one or two generations earlier, whom Philip Rieff might have called the "religious man" who was "born to be saved," the contemporary Canadian Pentecostal, whom Rieff might have called the "psychological man," is "born to be pleased" (Rieff 1966, 24–25). The majority of the individuals I interviewed indicated that it was not the dissemination of the salvation message—the driving force of the early Pentecostal movement—but the fulfillment of felt needs that was the rubric used for evaluating and understanding the value of Spirit baptism and speaking in tongues. Sensing this fundamental religious transition from the desire for salvation to the desire for self-fulfillment, many pastors, Rieff explains, "become, avowedly, therapists, administrating a therapeutic institution—under the justificatory mandate that Jesus himself was the first therapeutic" (1966, 251). Rieff believed that this attitude results in a Church that is "committed, both culturally as well as economically, to the gospel of self-fulfillment" (1966, 252).

To simply describe Del Wells, Hansley Armoogan, or Brandon Malo as "therapists, administrating a therapeutic institution" who are committed "to the gospel of self-fulfillment" would be completely unfair. The transformation of beliefs and practices surrounding Spirit baptism and glossolalia within Canadian Pentecostalism that is reflected in the above narratives has taken place over several decades and has occurred through dialogue with other ministers across the denomination and members within their own congregations who share similar beliefs about Spirit baptism and glossolalia. That being said, both the opinions of individual members and the paucity of traditional teaching on the part of their leaders relating to these traditional Pentecostal beliefs reveal that these historic commitments and understandings did not place highly in either the individual or congregational lives of those that I spoke with and observed. Both the pastors and the members of Freedom in Christ, Elmira Pentecostal Assembly, and Elevation were much more interested in what these experiences had to offer them personally than what role they might play in worldwide evangelism. ➤

6

Healing, Miracles, and Other Supernatural Phenomena

In this chapter, I detail participants' encounters with divine healing, miracles, and other supernatural phenomena such as angels, demons, and the practice of exorcism. Given the trajectory of the previous two chapters, it would be reasonable to assume that the pattern of homogenization that I have documented would continue in relation to traditional Pentecostal beliefs and practices regarding supernatural phenomena. This, however, was not the case. To my surprise, the interviews, surveys, and my observations all revealed that commitment to beliefs and practices surrounding supernatural phenomena were very high among members of Freedom in Christ, Elmira Pentecostal Assembly, and Elevation.

For instance, in addition to the 97 percent of survey respondents who indicated that they believed in the reality of divine physical healing, 65 percent indicated that they pray for someone else's divine healing in a public church service at least once a year or more, 41 percent claimed that they have actually witnessed someone's divine healing, 34 percent claimed they have experienced divine healing in their own bodies, 33 percent indicated that they receive prayer for healing in a public church service at least once a year or more, 17 percent believed they have been used as an instrument of divine healing in

TABLE 5. Highlights from the congregational surveys on healing, miracles, and other supernatural phenomena

	Freedom in Christ (%)	Elmira Pentecostal Assembly (%)	Elevation (%)
Completely or generally agreed that Jesus made provision for divine physical healing	97.8	100.0	95.1
Completely or generally agreed that angels, demons, and Satan are real beings	100.0	100.0	93.6
Pray for spiritual deliverance in a church service at least once a year	65.1	51.9	41.9
Receive prayer for divine healing in a church service at least once a year	43.2	48.0	19.4
Pray for someone else to receive divine healing in a church service at least once a year	74.3	73.1	55.7
Reported having experienced divine healing in their own body	50.0	63.0	9.5
Reported having been used as an instrument for divine healing in someone else's body	25.6	14.8	12.7
Reported having witnessed someone else's divine healing	50.0	48.1	30.6
Reported having heard what they consider to be authentic accounts of divine healing	88.6	100.0	77.8
Reported having witnessed the casting out of a demon	27.9	25.9	14.3

someone else's body, 97 percent believed that angels, demons, and Satan are real beings, and 21 percent said that they have witnessed the casting out of a demon (see table 5).

It would, again, be entirely reasonable to view the fact that commitment to these beliefs and practices were as high as they were among the members of the three congregations as a possible source of counterevidence against my claim that Canadian Pentecostals were experiencing a transformation of religious identity and experience from traditionally Pentecostal to generically evangelical categories. In this chapter, however, I will provide evidence that demonstrates that the members of Freedom in Christ, Elmira Pentecostal Assembly, and Elevation that I interviewed, surveyed, and observed did not express commitment to these beliefs and practices due to any real devotion to, or even understanding of, traditional Pentecostalism.

Rather, I argue that, unlike Spirit baptism and speaking in tongues, traditional Pentecostal belief and practice regarding divine healing, miracles, and other supernatural phenomena may have been as prominent as they were because the idea that God wishes to heal, protect, and deliver already fits nicely into the therapeutic understanding of religion common within the generic evangelical subculture of the three congregations. The Pentecostals that I interviewed did not present lower levels of commitment to beliefs and practices regarding Spirit baptism and glossolalia because they became "less religious," but rather because these more traditional forms of belief and practice did not coalesce with their commitment to the values of therapeutic individualism. Beliefs and practices relating to healing, miracles, and other supernatural phenomena, I argue, were more readily expressed because they could easily be incorporated into this generically evangelical framework.[22]

Divine Healing

DURING MY FIELDWORK I encountered no shortage of opinions from the members of Freedom in Christ, Elmira Pentecostal Assembly, and Elevation regarding divine healing. While the majority of the individuals that I spoke with demonstrated strong commitments to divine healing, a few, such as Amy from Freedom in Christ, struggled with the concept.

Author: Have you ever personally experienced divine healing?
[*long pause*]
Amy: No.
Author: That was a long pause.
Amy: Well, divine healing, you know—have I ever been healed from something or recovered from something? Have I ever been ill and recovered after praying about it? Yes. Have I been cured of cancer? No. So, it's kind of a funny question, because I believe that God heals people in a lot of ways. I believe he heals through doctors; I believe he heals through medicine; I believe that he can heal divinely.
Author: Do you ever pray for divine healing for you or anyone else?
Amy: You know, again, you've got to take the word "divine" out of there for me. I do believe that God heals people through medicine and I believe that he can also completely reverse physics.
Author: Let me put this another way, then. Do you ever pray for anyone's healing?
Amy: Yeah, I do. But I don't beat them up about it. And I don't think that just because I ask God for divine healing for myself or someone else that he's obligated to do it. I don't know—I have real issues with that from personal experience. So I struggle with putting the "divine" in front of healing. I really do, because this is one thing that I think Pentecostals abuse and hurt people with because I've personally been hurt with the whole divine healing thing. We attended Kennedy Road Tabernacle in Brampton before we went to Immanuel Pentecostal Church. We were a young, married couple and already had one daughter at the time, but we had another baby who was born with spina bifida and died a few days after birth. It was devastating, but the way the church prayed and talked about it—"If we just have enough faith then she will be healed"—made it much worse. So, it's the guilt and the expectation that if you don't have enough faith you've somehow caused this illness by your lack of faith.

Author: Your problem was with the church putting the pressure on the individual, placing healing within the realm of human potentiality, rather than with God?

Amy: Exactly. They put this pressure on us when healing is not in the realm of human potential to begin with. And thinking that we can somehow cause God to move by our faith or cause him not to move by our lack of faith, and therefore being guilty of not receiving a healing. Living with a family with several severe illnesses, I have a hard time with that. I struggle with that.

Amy is a clear example of someone who was a member of a congregation that held to some version of the "health and wealth gospel" or the "prosperity gospel." Proponents of this theology are sometimes referred to as being a part of the "word of faith movement" because they believe that if Christians only exhibit enough faith, God will supernaturally bless them with perfect health and abundant financial rewards (Harrison 2005). At the same time, word of faith advocates often chastise the ill or poor for not demonstrating the prerequisite faith that is believed to be necessary in order to move God to heal their illnesses or restore their finances. While I did not detect any support for word of faith theology among the leadership at Freedom in Christ, Elmira Pentecostal Assembly, or Elevation, these beliefs are not uncommon within many Canadian Pentecostal churches. As the example given by Amy aptly demonstrates, these theologies can have a negative impact on the personal and emotional lives of individuals whose life trajectories do not conform to the expectations of the advocates of these theologies.

While two or three individuals that I spoke with had some reservations about divine healing, the vast majority of participants recounted numerous instances where they claimed that either they or people they knew had been the recipients of divine healing. There was a vast range among the types of illnesses that participants believed they or others they knew were healed from. These included minor concerns, such as common colds and sprained ankles, to more serious conditions, such as neuromuscular diseases and other chronic illnesses, all the way to life-threatening illnesses, the most common being cancer.

Shane from Elmira Pentecostal Assembly recounted witnessing some teenagers being healed from some rather minor injuries at a youth convention.

"I guess the biggest thing that I've witnessed first-hand were people being healed in a service of different things. Even just at junior-high-school convention this year there were four or five junior highs that were healed. They had everything from sprained ankles to one kid's knee. He wasn't able to walk because he had fallen and hit his kneecap and they were picking him up and putting him in the car and putting him to bed. After being healed, he was running around on the platform."

Similarly, Tracy from Freedom in Christ recounted some rather vague experiences of divine healing, in which she believed that God helped her to gradually recover from minor illnesses much more quickly than she would have otherwise under normal circumstances.

> **Author:** Have you ever personally experienced divine healing?
> **Tracy:** Yes, I believe that I have been healed over time. I've never had an experience where I was healed instantly of something. But I absolutely believe that God works in process as well. So, there have been times when things should have taken much longer to heal from that have been much shorter and those kinds of things, because I know that I was being prayed for. So, I believe in divine healing that way. Never like an instant Benny Hinn[23] sort of a moment, getting up out of a wheelchair. But I do believe I've been divinely healed, yeah.

Others, such as Ruth from Elmira Pentecostal Assembly, described instances of divine healing from more serious illnesses, such as her husband's chronic back pain:

> Barry, my husband, was healed. When he was sixteen, he had a back injury. He worked on a farm and fell off of a beam. I didn't know him then. He was flat on his back and I guess people must have prayed for him because he came out of that. He could have been paralyzed. I just know that when we got married he'd be on the farm working and he would come home and his back would hurt after haying. He would lie on the floor and I used to rub his back and say, "It sure would be

nice if you could get healed." That was whenever haying season was, probably in June.

So in July, I believe, we were having tent meetings in our church. For three weeks they had different speakers and we went every single night. I don't know which week it was, whether it was the first or the second, but Bill Prankard,[24] who had a healing ministry, was there. I had never heard of him. Barry's aunt and uncle were there and so we sat with them. It started to just sprinkle rain a wee bit after we sat down and then Barry felt his back starting to hurt. He didn't say anything to me, but he used to say that anytime it would rain his back would hurt. I think that was a sign to remind him that his back hurt.

So Bill Prankard was preaching, really going into it, and God was really moving and healing people while he was preaching. While this was going on, Barry was healed sitting beside me and I didn't even know it. When the service was getting near the end, God was telling Bill Prankard that he had healed people, and he was saying, "In this section over here I've healed people of a back problem, I've healed them of a knee problem." You name it, whatever it was, I don't remember. Then he went into this section and he said that God told him that he wanted those people to stand up to confirm their healing. Then he got to our section and he said, "God is telling me that he has healed somebody of a back problem." Nobody stood up, and I'm thinking, "Oh, it would be nice." But Barry didn't get up and I didn't say anything. He said it three times, then said, "Well, I'm really being prompted that someone has been healed of a back problem and I want you to stand to your feet." Then Barry stood up. I asked him why he didn't do it before and he said, "I wanted to make sure that it was me." Nobody else stood up but he said, "When that rain started my back hurt and then all of a sudden I felt a warmth go from my head to my feet and the pain went away." So he knew something was going on and that he was healed. He has never complained about his back since that day.

The story of Ruth's husband is rather typical of those participants who told me about experiences where they or someone they knew was healed through the work of a travelling or itinerant faith healer in a public setting.

These events typically begin with a long period of time devoted to praise and worship music, which sets the mood for the occasion. This is followed by a rather rousing sermon preached by the faith healer, often with the aim of presenting the theological basis for divine healing. These services usually conclude with the faith healer calling out various illnesses that he or she believes that God is in the process of healing people from. It is also common for faith healers to ask individuals seeking healing to approach the altar of the church or the front of the venue in order to be anointed with oil and prayed over by the healer and other individuals.

Trevor from Freedom in Christ described a much less quintessentially Pentecostal experience of divine healing. He placed less emphasis on healing as a distinct event, and, echoing Tracy's explanation, put much more emphasis on the idea of healing as a process, reminiscent of earlier, radical evangelical conceptions of divine healing predating Pentecostalism.

>**Author:** Do you believe in divine healing?
>
>**Trevor:** Yeah, I think so. I actually have Crohn's disease and I've had people pray for me a number of times. I really believe that things have happened. I've had people lay hands on me and pray for me and that was one thing that I found really exciting in the Pentecostal Church was we, you know, get around and pray. I still struggle with that because it's a real level of intimacy with people you don't know very well. But I believe it's been really good.
>
>>It's hard to do. I still have to kind of convince myself to do it because it feels so intimate to me. It's not something that I take really casually, but that's the one thing I really like about the Pentecostal Church. I think it's really important. They don't do that in the Lutheran Church. My brother studied at a Lutheran seminary for years. He and the other guys at the seminary never got together to pray very often. My brother said he was kind of disappointed with that. He kind of thought that they would.
>
>**Author:** Do you think that receiving prayer for your disease has had an effect?
>
>**Trevor:** Yeah, I do.
>
>**Author:** Can you explain?

Trevor: Not really. I had people pray for me and I'd say, "Hey, you know, I went for some tests and they couldn't find anything. I'm feeling really good. I mean, it probably won't last forever and everything." Sometimes God giving me Crohn's disease is kind of a gift in a lot of ways. It kind of focused me on other important things besides what I was doing at the time in my career and all that other kind of stuff. When your health is affected you are forced to focus on what is really important in your life. God really refocused me through that. I also believe God doesn't necessarily heal you. Sometimes the way he heals you is to lead you to doctors and medications and stuff. Well I got on a great medication about four years ago and I feel like a million bucks now. I had a test two weeks ago and there are no signs of Crohn's. It's Remicade. It's pretty amazing stuff. It's been around for ten years, but it's only the last few years that they started to give it out. I take it every eight weeks as an infusion. I take it for two or three hours and it works great. God leads you to people who can help you out, I think.

While Trevor clearly believed in the reality of divine healing and that he has even personally experienced divine healing himself, he was also careful to explain that he does not believe that God will always heal someone. Trevor, like the majority of the participants I interviewed, believed that God sometimes works through modern medicine and medical professionals and that these medical interventions are a part of, rather than contrary to, God's plan for divine healing.

On the more extreme end of the spectrum were those participants who described the healing of life-threatening illnesses. Harold from Freedom in Christ recounts a particularly memorable experience while working on a Christian humanitarian aid project in Central Asia.

Author: Have you ever known anyone else who has experienced divine healing?

Harold: Okay. I'm in Kyrgyzstan a couple of years ago and we went into this home and there was this young girl lying there who looked like death warmed over. I said to Sergei, our translator, "What's her problem?" He said, "Oh, she's really sick. She's been sick for a couple of days." We were there to see her grandmother, who was in the next room. I think her grandmother was on her deathbed. So we sang a song, and I'm not kidding you, I think I could count on my hand the times in my life where I had felt the presence of God like that. I looked over at another member of the team. He was already on his knees, kneeling at the bed of this lady that was laying there and I said, "Do you feel that?" He said that he felt the same way.

I didn't think anything of it. We sang another song, we brought them some groceries, prayed with the lady, and left. I didn't even notice the young girl wasn't in her bed when I went by. We went outside and were standing by the van and I said to Sergei, "Who is that girl trying to climb the fence over there?" And he said, "That's the girl who was laying in bed." I said, "Come on, you're jerking my chain. There is no possible way that is the same girl that is climbing that fence over there." So I asked, "What happened?" He said, "We were singing and praying for her and she got right up out of bed." And I said, "You're kidding. She was death warmed over. There was no way she should have got up, and then to be climbing a fence!" Literally, Sergei had said she got out of bed, went to the little sink there and combed her hair—it didn't look like the same girl. I was shook.

Similarly, Jane remembered when she was used as an agent of divine healing in a Sunday morning service at Freedom in Christ.

Author: Have you ever witnessed anyone experience divine healing?
Jane: Yeah. I'm going to go way back to when I started to attend Freedom. This was actually not even something that I knew about until much later. There was a young girl at the altar and I was sitting in my pew. I didn't know very many people; in fact I don't even think I knew the young girl's name. They called people up for prayer and they were at the altar praying and everything,

and I was sitting in my chair just watching and singing with my hands raised. And the Lord specifically spoke to me to go over and pray for that girl. You know, I did this reluctantly. I was not reluctant because I was being disobedient, but I actually don't like the spectacle and don't like eyes on me unless I'm doing a presentation. I went over to pray for her and I touched her and she fell on the floor. I bent down to pray with her and I immediately started to feel horrible pains in my stomach. I was like, "Oh, goodness." I couldn't understand it, but I held her down on the ground with my hands just over her stomach. I was holding my hand over her stomach and praying in the Spirit, praying and crying, and I didn't know what I was praying and I didn't understand any of it. Well, I learned months later from her mom that she had stomach cancer and that she was healed that day. That does something for you as a person that God uses. But also for me to be able to share that with others so that their faith can be built up. God does answer prayer, and he does stuff when you don't even know what he's doing.

Not all of the experiences of divine healing that participants told me about referred to the healing of a physical condition or illness. Several individuals told me of experiences where they believed that God healed them of emotional or psychological illnesses. This further reflected the idea of God as someone who is concerned with not only the physical but also the psychological or therapeutic wellness of human beings, which was expressed by an experience recounted to me by Colin from Elmira Pentecostal Assembly:

I used to have anxiety and panic attacks. It probably started when I was about fourteen or fifteen, I would say. For the longest time I prayed for healing from it and nothing would happen. By the time I was about twenty-five or maybe twenty-six, I was still praying for healing, but more out of habit and desperation than anything else. And then, finally, I came across the passage in the book of James where it says to go to your elders and they will anoint you with oil and their prayers and faith will heal you.[25] I read that and all of a sudden

I felt God saying, "Now is your time to go get anointed with oil and to be prayed over." And, to be honest, I got a little ticked off at God and thought, "Why now and not twelve or thirteen years earlier when I could have used the healing back then?" God showed me the story where the woman who was subject to bleeding for twelve years, how she prayed to God for healing, but it wasn't until twelve years later that she was actually healed.[26] And God was just saying, "It's just my timing." He never said why I had to wait, but it was just his timing and maybe there was a learning process there, who knows, right? So I went and I got anointed with oil and was healed from my panic and anxiety attacks.

The participants that I spoke with accepted the reality of divine healing more than any other traditional Pentecostal experience. Even individuals like Amy who had negative encounters with the word of faith movement's interpretation of divine healing continued to believe that it was completely possible for God to heal people. Amy's somewhat restrained commitment to divine healing, however, proved to be an exception to the rule of overwhelming support for divine healing. Also, divine healing was the only traditional element of Pentecostal belief and practice that was ever given any special degree of emphasis during the public services that I attended at the three congregations. Even though divine healing was clearly given the most priority by clergy and laity alike, it was certainly not the only element of traditional Pentecostal belief and practice expressed by the members of Freedom in Christ, Elmira Pentecostal Assembly, and Elevation.

Miracles

IN THE SPRING OF 2009, I designed both the interview questionnaire and the congregational survey that I later used to conduct the personal interviews and to survey the members of the three congregations. In the midst of this preparation, and without much thought, I included a question at the end of the section relating to religious practice in my interview questionnaire that read, "Have you ever experienced any other kind of miracle?"

I was well aware that miracles played an incredibly important role within the religious culture of early Pentecostalism. As Gary B. McGee appropriately writes, "If liberals celebrated the spirit of the age—happily shorn of all superstition, Pentecostals believed the age of the Spirit (the advancing kingdom of God) had come, complete with miracles" (2010, 203). Understanding the historical importance of miracles within early Pentecostalism, I still did not expect this question to yield very much usable information, particularly given the barrage of questions about supernatural practices such as healing, Spirit baptism, and glossolalia that preceded it. Nonetheless, as fall approached and I carefully re-examined my interview questionnaire, I thought it might be a good idea to retain this question in order to give participants the opportunity to mention any other spiritual experiences or supernatural phenomena they had experienced that my other questions might not capture. As it turns out, this was a very good decision. Participants responded to this question by telling me about all kinds of supernatural experiences that I would never have otherwise anticipated. I was clearly wrong to have assumed that such a question might prove to be superfluous.

Harold from Freedom in Christ, for instance, told me about a miracle that he was a part of while visiting Uzbekistan that is reminiscent of the biblical miracles of the meal and the oil[27] and the feeding of the multitude.[28] Participants often viewed experiences of divine healing and other supernatural events through the lens of biblical literature. These biblical narratives appeared to give participants a framework through which to understand and retell a great deal of their religious experiences.

Author: Have you ever witnessed something that you believe was a miracle?

Harold: Yeah. I was part of it, although I didn't actually witness it happen. It was during a missions trip to Uzbekistan. We had taken a bunch of medication over to an orphanage in Uzbekistan and we had two or three nurses who were doing examinations on all of the kids. I remember one night one of the nurses saying to me, "I don't know what we are going to do, but a lot of the kids that we are seeing require this one medication and I don't think that we have enough. It's going to run out. We've only got enough to treat another three or four kids and we've got to see another sixty kids yet." I remember saying to her, "Don't worry about it, just do whatever you can and that's all we can do." It was about ten thirty or eleven a.m. the next day and I was working on a project outside when she came running across the yard and grabbed me by both shoulders and said, "You'll never believe what has happened. That medication that I was telling you about, it's multiplying in the cupboard." I said, "Oh, okay." She shook me and said, "No. You're not listening to me. That medication should have been gone an hour ago, and every time I go back to the cupboard and take one, I'm looking around and I know we have no more left. I'm asking people if they've found more medication and they say that they haven't. It's multiplying in the cupboard."

I'll never forget that day as long as I live. It was crazy. We had enough medication to treat every one of those kids. To this very day she has no idea where that medication came from. She said, "I was the one responsible for packing the medication, and I asked if someone else had brought more with them. No one knew what I was talking about." She said that they started the day with four or five packages, and she would go and get them and it took her three or four trips to realize, "Hold on a second, I keep taking one and when I go back there are still four or five there." She told me later that she just got to the point where she admitted that this was going to sound crazy, but she began to expect that it would be there, and didn't even think about it anymore. Just, here's another kid and she grabbed more of it.

Edward from Elevation recounted an equally dramatic experience that took place while he was on a family vacation as a child.

Author: Have you ever witnessed something that you believe was a miracle?

Edward: When I was younger, my family and I camped at Algonquin Park a lot. So, long story short, one day we were hiking and we were on a cliff that was probably fifty, sixty feet of straight, sheer rock. I walked over to the edge, turned around, and accidentally fell off the cliff. I fell off up to about my chest. It was a sheer drop and I didn't fall to the bottom. I stood on something and there was nothing there. I'm freaking out and my parents are losing it because I had just fallen off a cliff. I was probably about nine or ten when this happened and I honestly believe—to me there is no other explanation—that this was a supernatural intervention. Somehow, whatever it was, whether it was an angel holding my feet up or whatever—I don't know how to explain it—something happened. I should have died; I should have fallen off the cliff and hit the rocks at the bottom and died. I stood on something on the side of this cliff and my parents pulled me up and they were like, "That was just crazy. What just happened? How did you not fall? You should have been gone." The falling off the cliff thing, that was really pretty intense. My mom used to remind me of that event all the time, mostly after I had done something bad: "You have no idea the power of your mother's and your grandmother's prayers. It's protecting you when you don't even know it." So, maybe it is. In that particular instance with me, who knows? I believe stuff like that can happen.

The most common types of miracles that participants told me about were specifically related to divine protection, particularly while driving or travelling in foreign countries. Gordon from Elmira Pentecostal Assembly, for instance, remembered a harrowing near-accident on a rural road while travelling with his family:

One time I was travelling with my family and my older brother was at home. He later told us that he felt very impressed upon his heart to pray for our safety while we were driving. While we were driving we approached an intersection with stoplights, and we were going through the intersection on a green light, and, all of a sudden, there was a vehicle that went right through the red light coming from the opposite direction. It was incredible that we didn't get hit because, I mean, if we had of been there just a split second sooner we would have been totally T-boned, and it would not have been good. We believe it was a miracle. When we got home to tell my brother he said, "Oh man, I was just praying like crazy for you guys at that time." And that was the exact time when it happened.

Gordon's story shows a striking resemblance to an experience that James from Elevation had while travelling on the highway with a group of friends.

Author: Have you ever witnessed something that you believe was a miracle?

James: There have been times when I have had close calls that I believe were a miraculous save. I was in an accident on Highway 401 where another friend was driving and it looked like we should have been wiped out, but instead we were saved. We were driving at night on a very busy highway and there were two cars in front of us. This guy fell asleep and drifted and hit the concrete median. Sparks flying, just flying off of his car, and then he overcompensated and turned right into another guy, hit him, and that guy started spinning 360 degrees. We were coming straight at them doing something like 130 or 140 kilometres per hour. I just saw the two cars coming, one spinning and the other one coming at us. My one friend was driving, I was in the passenger seat, and I had a friend in the back who just leapt forward and grabbed the dashboard and said, "Jesus!" and we just barely made it through these two cars. I don't know how we did it. So to me, that was a hand of God kind of thing. And, amazingly, the guy who started the whole thing took off and the other guy ended up stopped, facing traffic on the 401. So he's in this lane and did several turns and ended up in a 180 looking backwards. And, again, amazingly, no one hit him. The oncoming traffic all managed to sort of part the waters and slow down and stop, allowing him to turn around, get off the road, and get going. So, it could have been bad.

Not unlike the experiences described by Gordon and James, Tracy from Freedom in Christ told me about a time when she was on a missions trip in Central Asia and, she believed, God intervened in order to protect the members of her group. Tracy's story is representative of a number of participants who recounted similar experiences in which they felt that they were miraculously protected while travelling.

> **Author:** Have you ever witnessed something that you believe was a miracle?
>
> **Tracy:** Yes. There is a time that comes to mind right away when we were on a missions trip and we were stopped by the police for no reason, as happens often in a lot of countries. We were about to be in a lot of trouble. All of the North Americans were being kicked out of the country, and there was a lot of stuff going on. All of a sudden, someone appeared out of nowhere and started talking with the cop and gave him something, we don't know what happened, and then, all of a sudden, he was gone. So, I believe that I saw an angel that day. He came and dealt with whatever the situation was. Our bus driver, our interpreters, nobody knew what was going on except that there was someone talking to the man and then he was gone and everything was fine.

These stories represent just a sampling of the different types of miraculous events that participants from Freedom in Christ, Elmira Pentecostal Assembly, and Elevation claimed to have experienced. The most common type of miracle was divine protection from some kind of accident, most often related to driving and other forms of travel. Others, however, included supernatural provision, most often in the area of finances, and dreams that were thought to contain direct revelations from God. Though not as common as experiences of divine healing, the miraculous events reported by the participants were still numerous, and they formed an important aspect of both the individual and corporate spirituality of each of the three congregations.

Angels, Demons, and Exorcism

THE EXISTENCE AND ACTIVITY OF SUPERNATURAL BEINGS such as angels and demons, and particularly experiences such as demonic possession and exorcism, was one of the most fascinating topics that I discussed with interview participants during the course of my research. From a personal perspective, these conversations were stimulating because of the conviction with which the participants recounted their experiences, replete with tears, trembling, and obvious physical distress, more than once requiring that interviews be discontinued. After one particularly vivid description of a participant's encounter with a demonic being, this self-described sober-minded researcher lost more than a few nights of sleep.

More than simply titillating, these discussions were also fascinating from a sociological point of view, because there is arguably no other belief or practice that I observed that better refutes the prediction put forth by Peter Berger and other scholars that religion in modern societies such as Canada would become predominantly demythologized and mystically sterile (1967, 146). What I find even more interesting about this topic is that the people I spoke with who earnestly told me about their beliefs and experiences relating to supernatural phenomena were not the indigent dregs that earlier historians and sociologists had commonly associated with such beliefs (Anderson 1979; Glock 1964). Rather, they were public school teachers and college professors, firefighters and police officers, nurses and scientists, social workers and engineers, accountants and civil servants. The majority of the participants I interviewed were middle- and upper-middle-class Canadians who wanted for little in the way of material possessions or social status, which severely challenges theories of deprivation previously used to explain Pentecostals' commitments to such beliefs and practices.

As might be expected, the accounts given by many of the participants who indicated that they believed in some kind of supernatural beings were either vague, uncertain, or second-hand (Bramadat 2000, 106). Mavis from Freedom in Christ, for instance, did not want to dismiss the possibility that she had witnessed such an occurrence, but her recollection of the experience remained extremely vague.

Author: Have you ever witnessed the casting out of a demon?

Mavis: Not that you could put your finger on it and say that was a demon for sure. I've witnessed occasions where that's what was said to have been going on, I suppose. With the yelling and all that stuff.

Tracy, also from Freedom in Christ, likewise provided a rather vague account of her experiences with the supernatural.

Author: Have you ever witnessed the casting out of a demon?

Tracy: I don't know. There was a time that I was with a leader when supposedly that was happening and I wouldn't deny it, but nor would I confirm it, because I probably wasn't mature enough in my own faith to be able to know the difference. I was much younger. I wasn't discerning one way or the other, but that was supposed to be what was happening and I was there and there was something crazy going on. I just don't know exactly what was happening, so I would say I don't know. I believe in it. I just don't know if I've ever witnessed it.

There were also other participants like James from Elevation who described with a great amount of detail experiences that they believed may have involved supernatural beings but who were ultimately uncertain of the veracity of these events.

Author: Have you ever witnessed the casting out of a demon?

James: Yes, I have.

Author: How many times?

James: Directly, only once. I know someone who worked for Teen Challenge[29] and they had lots of really screwed up people there and he had lots of stories about that, but those are not first-hand experiences. So the one time I did see it happen was actually very early in my Christian experience when I was still a Catholic Charismatic.

Author: In a church setting?

James: It was in a church setting, but it wasn't a pastor who performed the exorcism. It was just some guy. And to this day, looking back, I think, "Was that what was going on there?" I don't know. Is that what really happened there? I don't know. But it seemed to me that that was what happened. Somebody was upset and agitated and couldn't compose themselves, couldn't stand up, couldn't stop crying, couldn't stop shrieking. We were all only Christians for six months and thought, "What do we do now?" There was nobody of authority or leadership there, and then some guy came over and said, "In the name of Jesus, I command you to leave." And then [*snap of the fingers*] she sobered up right away and sat up. So, who knows? That would be the one time that I saw something that looked like it was the casting out of a demon.

Author: Would you say that it is possible for a demon to possess someone?

James: I think, yeah, that demons can possess people and that they can be cast out. I think it's probably fairly rare, and I also think that casting out is more rare than it should be [*laughter*], but I do think those are real. Those are very rare things and most of my knowledge of them is third-hand, but I do believe that those things are real, yeah.

Edward from Elevation echoed both James's degree of detail and his degree of doubt.

Author: Have you ever witnessed the casting out of a demon?

Edward: I believe I did one time. But I'm very skeptical about stuff like that. Like, I believe it; I believe it can happen; I believe it does happen; I believe there is lots of supernatural stuff going on that I have no understanding of; I believe it is reality. It was an experience in youth group, I believe. Some guy was just going like Hollywood possessed on the floor. It was scary. Really, there was a very uneasy feeling and there were a couple of pastors and just some other people that you would consider strong in their faith and that type of thing. Again, it wasn't a big, flashy, like, Benny Hinn, "Demon out!" type of thing. They prayed for him. They spoke directly to the "entity" that was supposedly possessing this guy. It was both scary and pretty powerful at the same time. Like, I said, I'm a skeptic about a lot of that stuff and I could probably be skeptical about even that particular situation, but I believe it was real. It was freaky. It was like a Hollywood movie. The guy was having a seizure and he was freaking out and he was talking in these funky voices. It was really weird—really weird. I was kind of looking around for the cameras or something. I didn't know the guy who was possessed very well, but I knew him, and it wasn't like this guy is putting on a show. It was pretty powerful.

In addition to those participants whose recollections of supernatural activity were either vague or uncertain, there were a number of people who attested to the veracity of demon possession and the practice of exorcism as a result of second-hand accounts told to them by people whom they trusted. Interestingly, many of these second-hand accounts originate from foreign mission trips, where I was commonly told that demonic and other supernatural encounters were common. Gwen from Freedom in Christ, for instance, remembered a story told to her by a companion while on a missions trip to Haiti.

Author: Have you ever witnessed the casting out of a demon?
Gwen: No. But when I was in Haiti, someone that I was travelling with did. I don't know if I would want to see that, but I found the story quite interesting. But no, I've never witnessed it personally.

Mike from Elmira Pentecostal Assembly shared a similar experience.

Author: Have you ever witnessed the casting out of a demon?
Mike: No, but I just missed it, apparently. I was in Africa three weeks ago and we walked into a classroom there and apparently an exorcism had happened just minutes before.

Not all of the individuals that I spoke with were as uncertain or hesitant as these participants regarding the question of supernatural experiences. The reports of others, such as Hansley from Elmira Pentecostal Assembly, contained no ambiguity whatsoever regarding the veracity of what was seen.

> **Author:** Have you ever witnessed the casting out of a demon?
> **Hansley:** Yes.
> **Author:** How many times?
> **Hansley:** Six to eight. The first time was in Bible College with a student, actually. We gathered together and around. One or two of these times were while on the mission field working with other Christian leaders who were there. Actually, the rest would have been in northern Ontario. There were a group of young ladies who were connected—their parents were connected with the church that I pastored—and they had become involved in some dark things. There was a particularly poignant experience that involved different manifestations and different personalities coming from the individuals who were possessed. This was one of those definite growth areas in my life where I was the only evangelical Christian leader in a probably 30-kilometre range. Aside from the Roman Catholics, who may have practised exorcism—I've never seen the movie—but whatever they do there, I was the go-to person for this group of people.

Similarly, Kelly from Elevation expressed no sign of doubt regarding her experiences with the supernatural.

> **Author:** Have you ever witnessed the casting out of a demon?
> **Kelly:** Yes, I have, a couple of times. Maybe five times. One was at a youth retreat, someone who had been involved heavily with drugs and alcohol. That was probably the most real experience because he was very strong. One time—actually it's interesting—at the Embassy we prayed for somebody after our service once in a similar situation. And then a few times probably at altar calls at Waterloo Pentecostal Assembly.

The vast majority of those participants who claimed that they had witnessed the manifestation of supernatural beings indicated that these events occurred within a public church setting. A much smaller number of participants claimed that they had more personal encounters with supernatural beings, either in their own homes or even through what they described as personal demonic possession. Some participants asked me not to share their stories about demon possession. The following two accounts that I was given permission to include, however, are representative of these more intense encounters with supernatural beings that participants shared with me. Toby from Elevation, for instance, believed that he has had a continual struggle with personal demonic possession.

Author: Have you ever witnessed the casting out of a demon?

Toby: I would say that deliverance has been a huge theme in my life. I would say that my entire spiritual life has been a series of deliverances. When I was sixteen I remember I always suffered from a strange anxiety; I would call it a binding anxiety. In my childhood I knew that I was never capable of doing my best because I would suffer from premature anxiety. Like—I will give you an example. I would go to a wrestling match and I wouldn't have eaten for three days prior to that wrestling match. And I knew that if I had of been able to eat and think properly before that match I would have done very well. But by the time it got around for me to go into that particular match, after not eating for three days due to this extreme anxiety, I would not be able to perform my best. The same with public speaking, ironically, as now people laugh to hear that I would be scared to speak in public, but I would get up in front of people and my knees would shake violently. The first time I ever sang publicly my lower body shook more than Elvis on cocaine. I held it together. I remember I was at Cold Water Music Festival, and I won that year, but I remember choking out the words because my lower body was convulsing like a Quaker. I was in complete horror because I was a teenager. It was very embarrassing and I was having a mini seizure of some sort while singing up on stage and I couldn't control it. The more I tried to grip down on it, the more I wiggled and moved. I remember when I was sixteen, one of my sort of defining moments in taking personal initiative with my faith, I'll call it a confirming moment. When I was in worship one time, all of a sudden, I remember this anxiety that I had in my gut that I had just considered was part of life, it just fell off or flew away like you'd scare a bunch of bats out of a cave—it left. And all I know is that I remember saying, "Whatever got rid of that, I'm sticking close to." If I had to say that there is a single characteristic that has defined my entire spiritual walk, it is deliverance.

Author: So do you think that was a demonic presence?

Toby: I think that, yeah, there was definitely something spiritual there and it wasn't good. It was nasty and ugly. Yeah, I think that probably was demonic. I think there was something nesting in me, some kind of parasitic spiritual thing just trying to make itself comfortable.

After that event, avenues of my life opened up that were closed to me before, where I was prohibited. Suddenly I was able to speak publicly and I started leading worship in a band up in front of people. Now I am a musician and I have played in front of lots of people and have no fear of public spaces. But back then it was impossible for me to do that. I oftentimes find that the people who like my music are the oddballs. Very rarely does the Church latch on to a particular piece of music that I've played, but I get people coming up to me saying, "I listened to your song and something left me." So I have had a couple of cases when I have been playing music and actually had deliverances specifically occur as a result of the music. That is something that I tend to be very aware of, almost to the point of wondering sometimes about exorcisms. I wonder about deliverance ministries and I wonder what my relationship is with that, but it's not something that you talk about a lot because it is kind of creepy, let's face it. I do know that it's a huge factor in my spiritual walk and I usually think of things in my life in terms of a scrap. Where a lot of people think of Jesus as their lover or these kinds of weird things, I think that if we are going to move anywhere it is going to be the result of a scrap and it is going to be some kind of violent encounter.

Ruth from Elmira Pentecostal Assembly also told me about an experience when she believes her home was visited by both demons and an angel.

I believe that a couple of times God sent me an angel in disguise. The first time that I will tell you about happened when my son was about nine years old. I was putting him to bed on a Sunday evening and he was asking me all about heaven, God, and angels. I'm not sure why he was asking, all that I could think of was that maybe the subject came up in Sunday school. As I was talking about this, all of a sudden, he looked frightened. He leaned back away from me and his eyes got very large. I immediately knew something was wrong. I then asked him, "What is the matter?" At that moment he started to cry and said to me, "Mom, you looked different." He gave me a hug and I said, "What do you mean, I looked different?" He said, "You were scary." I then asked more questions about how I looked. He said, "You had horns on your head, fiery eyes, huge pointed ears, and warts on your face." He also told me that the whole time he was looking at this scary face, my voice still sounded like my own—I sounded like Mom, but I sure did not look like Mom. My normal face appeared back to him right when I asked him what was wrong.

I knew that I needed to cast the demons and Satan out of the room right then, because I was fully aware now who was attacking. At this point, I could sense that these demons were holding hands and circling around us, and I felt trapped. I immediately started to rebuke Satan to leave at once, in the name of Jesus. It took a little while, but not too long before this heavy feeling left the room. I knew that they were gone; however, I was bothered as to why this image was on me. I thought I was doomed to hell. My son did not want to stay in his bed, so I let him stay up with us for a while. He would not sleep in his bed. He wanted to be in our bed, in the middle. Meanwhile, he thought that I had not got rid of what he had just seen, so I had to rebuke them again. I never felt them at this point, but to reassure him that they were gone, I tried to rebuke them again.

Everything was fine after that, but the next morning, just after my children left for school, I heard the aluminum door open and close. I went to check and I saw a person standing at my door—a side profile with something in this person's arm. I looked at this person, but this person did not look at me. I will call this person a "her" because she had short, curly, golden hair, and a white round hat and a red coat. I was impressed to watch her leave. As soon as I saw her, she proceeded to leave to the left down my sidewalk. I watched to see if she was leaving down the laneway, but she did not. I waited; no one went down the driveway. I was curious, so I went to look out the window at the carport. No one was there. I had to know where she went, so I went outside. Now, this was February. There was a light snow covering everything. I followed the tracks of the lady, down the sidewalk, across the driveway and over about two feet onto the snow covered grass. I noticed another set of footprints on top of the first set of footprints. They were directly on top. I could see the heel marks and toe marks pointing out toward the garden and the set of footprints pointing back toward my house. There were no more prints coming back to the house and there were no more footprints anywhere else. My children's footprints left the house near the door and went down across the grass. I could see those, but I could not figure out why this lady's prints did not go anywhere. They were too far from any other prints, which were way over on the right side of the driveway and these prints were over on the left of the driveway at the house.

I pondered over this for some time. I tried shovelling the light fallen snow off the driveway, but to my amazement, only the snow left, not the footprints. While I was still trying to figure this out and thinking about the evening before, I thought, well this must be an angelic visit, because I felt terrible about it and I knew that God had sent me a messenger. I knew God was with me and that I had done nothing wrong. This was for me, but it was connected with events from the night before. Meanwhile, a lady from across the street came over while she was on her way to a Bible study. I said, "Come here, look at these footprints. Can you tell me where they go?" She looked down at me with a big smile and said to me, "It must be an Angel." I said, "Really? That is what I am thinking." Of course, I had to fill in all the details. This person was not a normal human being because no one could just puff away into the air and disappear. I believe that the point of these events was to send a message to my son, to let him see the other side—evil—in order to keep him out of trouble. And I can assure you that he has not had any of the troubles that people get into. I'm thankful to God for that.

Whether or not these participants actually experienced or witnessed the supernatural encounters that they so earnestly recounted to me is irrelevant for the purposes of this chapter. What is relevant, as sociologist Christian Smith explains, is that, "*they* believe these things to be true and real" (1998, 176; emphasis original).

Conclusion

THE ARGUMENT that I have attempted to make in this chapter is simple. The Pentecostals that I interviewed, surveyed, and observed did not display religious beliefs and practices completely bereft of any influence from the Canadian Pentecostal tradition. Rather, participants exhibited a few important traditional Pentecostal emphases, as long as these appeared to conform to the values of therapeutic individualism. When we examine the material presented in chapters 5 and 6 as a whole, we can see how traditional Pentecostal beliefs and practices were either absent or present among the members of Freedom in Christ, Elmira Pentecostal Assembly, and Elevation due to, in large part, the degree to which these traditional elements either conflicted with or supported generic evangelicalism's implicit commitments towards the values of therapeutic individualism.

This fact was perhaps most obviously displayed in relation to participants' beliefs and practices surrounding Spirit baptism and tongues speech. As I demonstrated in chapter 5, most of the participants who expressed a commitment to these experiences preferred to emphasize their therapeutic and individual—emotional, relational, and spiritual—benefits, rather than the corporate role that these experiences traditionally played in providing power for evangelism and foreign missions. Similarly, I believe that support for divine healing, miracles, and other supernatural phenomena were as high as they were at Freedom in Christ, Elmira Pentecostal Assembly, and Elevation because these beliefs and practices are particularly easy to align with the values of therapeutic individualism. In other words, these traditional Pentecostal commitments survived the sterilization of traditionally Pentecostal religious culture during the process of homogenization involved in the migration towards generically evangelical norms because they were not antithetical to generic evangelicalism's underlying emphases.

7

Conclusion

THE OVERARCHING OBJECTIVE OF THIS STUDY has been to answer just one central question that has perplexed me from the time that I took my first undergraduate course on the study of religion in Canada: "What accounts for the dramatic decline in Canadian Pentecostal religious affiliation recorded by Statistics Canada between 1991 and 2001?" The realization that there existed no empirical evidence to support the idea that this decrease in affiliation was the result of a real decline in Canadian Pentecostal church attendance led me to develop the central hypothesis of this study: Canadian Pentecostals are undergoing a transformation of religious identity and experience from traditionally Pentecostal to generically evangelical categories.

I thought that, perhaps, just as many people were attending Canadian Pentecostal churches in 2001 as they were in 1991, but that a number of them no longer thought of themselves as Pentecostals, and, as a result, this term was reported less to census takers. I wondered if it was possible that the same movement towards religious homogenization observed within other denominations in both Canada and the United States had also found its way into Canadian Pentecostal churches, resulting in a significant number of adherents who prefer to describe their religious commitments using less denominationally specific terms. If this was indeed the case, I also wondered how this development might have affected not only Canadian Pentecostal identity but also belief and practice. I had significant anecdotal evidence that such a shift was taking place within Canadian Pentecostalism, but I needed empirical evidence to support this intuition.

Although the primary research presented in chapters 4, 5, and 6 in no way proves the transformation of Canadian Pentecostal identity and experience from traditionally Pentecostal to generically evangelical forms on a national scale, it does offer one very rich set of data that illustrates what this change might look like on the ground, data that can be used as a baseline for the broader, national investigation of this question. In October 2014, Andrew Gabriel and I launched a national survey of clergy within the PAOC that received 1,730 responses—nearly half of all clergy within the denomination. Among other things, the survey was designed to measure to what extent the beliefs and practices of this cohort adhered to traditional Canadian Pentecostal types. Preliminary analysis of the data shows that, much like the participants in the present study, commitment to some key traditional beliefs and practices are declining among clergy within the denomination, providing another important piece of evidence to support my hypothesis.

I strongly suspect that the levels of commitment to traditional Pentecostal identity and experience that I observed at Freedom in Christ, Elmira Pentecostal Assembly, and Elevation, and that were reported by clergy within the denomination more broadly, would be similar to those found within Pentecostal congregations across Canada. Moreover, I suspect that this transformation of identity and experience is facilitated by the pervasive adoption of the generic evangelical subculture, which acts as a carrier for therapeutic individualism. Without further confirmatory research, however, my theorizing remains only suggestive and tentative.

The ubiquity of generically evangelical forms of identity, belief, and practice in other Canadian Pentecostal congregations is perhaps intimated by the leadership of the current General Superintendent of the PAOC, David Wells. In addition to being the national leader of the PAOC, Wells is also a former chair of the board of directors for the Evangelical Fellowship of Canada (EFC). His past leadership within the EFC appears to be more than coincidental, given that his writings and public communication reveal a clear commitment to bringing the PAOC more in line with mainstream Canadian evangelicalism.

Shortly after his election as the new General Superintendent of the PAOC on 6 May 2008, Wells distributed a pamphlet to the clergy of the denomination in December 2008, titled *What I See*. This pamphlet outlines, in Wells's words, the "vision, mission and values that the Lord is putting in my heart for our Fellowship" (2008, Preface). In the opening pages of the pamphlet, Wells explains that a major component of his vision, mission, and values is to see the PAOC transition from a "denomination," which he understands to be dominated by "bureaucracy" and "maintaining constitutions and programs," to an "undenomination" or rather a "postdenominational" organization that is "relational and missional" (2008, 1-2). Wells refers to this new organization as a *"relationally based mission family"* (2008, Preface; emphasis original), by which he means a group of churches that are not bound together so much by their shared Pentecostal history or theology as by a spirit of mutual co-operation and commitment to church growth. Throughout this pamphlet, Wells unfolds a vision for the PAOC as an organization that is not very distinctly "Pentecostal" at all, but rather as a "family" that is part of a larger Canadian "evangelical movement" with which it is united by a shared set of beliefs and values (2008, 67-68).

In June 2009, Wells organized a Theological Study Commission in order to address the issue of the changing nature of religious identity within the PAOC. The commission was composed of four pastors, two New Testament scholars, and David Wells. I was first made aware of the commission through a conversation I had with Brandon Malo, the senior pastor of Elevation, who just happened to be one of the four pastors that Wells asked to be a part of the national commission. The Theological Study Commission produced a number of discussion papers as well as another pamphlet distributed to the clergy of the denomination in December 2010, titled *Authentically Pentecostal: Here's What We See—A Conversation* (Wells and Johnson 2010).[30] Given the composition of the commission, and perhaps because it did not include or consult individuals trained in social research methodology, the members of the commission mainly chose to focus their attention on biblical and historical questions. Additionally, the lack of proper research protocols meant that the few pieces of data that the commission collected that might have been potentially useful for trying to ascertain the source of the recent identity crisis within the denomination were, in the end, unreliable and impossible to validate.

What the Theological Study Commission did accomplish, however, was to provide some insight into the way that Wells and some of the other members of the commission understood Pentecostal identity. On the surface, these documents appear to reassert the denomination's commitment to the fourfold gospel. Wells, for instance, concludes *Authentically Pentecostal* by stating, "I am happy to be a Pentecostal serving the Lord Jesus—my Saviour, my Baptizer, my Healer, and my Coming King" (Wells 2010b, 94). What is interesting about the documents produced by the Theological Study Commission is that they contain a considerable degree of ambiguity surrounding what commitment to these historical Pentecostal emphases might actually look like. A traditional Pentecostal who read these documents could easily see a reaffirmation of the traditional understanding of these values, while a Pentecostal practitioner influenced by generic evangelicalism would be free to see in these documents a licence to broaden their interpretation of these historical commitments.

The work of the Theological Study Commission appears to allow Canadian Pentecostals the freedom to develop the kind of congregations and religious content that would be the most effective for meeting the denomination's overarching goals of mutual co-operation and commitment to church growth, rather than perpetuating historical Pentecostal forms of commitment. For instance, Wells writes in the introduction to *Authentically Pentecostal*, "I am at peace that we are not a franchise anymore. As I travel nationally and internationally, it is clear to me that we do not have a fixed, 'bounded set' identity" (Wells 2010c, 7). In an interview in July 2010 on the Canadian evangelical television show *100 Huntley Street*, Wells similarly explained, "We can't do the franchise thing. . . . The majority of Canadians probably aren't going to connect with that" (Wells 2010a). Also, in an email sent to me in July 2010, Wells explained that he believed "identity shifts need to be made to be effective in mission."

According to Wells, then, Pentecostal identity takes second place to whatever is needed in order to bring the tradition more in step with the broader Canadian evangelical movement as well as contribute to the goal of facilitating church growth. If the Pentecostal tradition contains elements that will help congregations to achieve these objectives, then these may certainly be retained. If the tradition, however, contains elements that hinder congregations in these efforts, then these must be either removed, or, more likely, sufficiently sanitized. While David Wells certainly does not speak for all Canadian Pentecostal pastors, and certainly not all Canadian Pentecostal practitioners, if his opinions about the future of the denomination are any indication of the direction in which it is headed, then the movement from traditional Pentecostalism towards generic evangelicalism evidenced in just three of the denomination's churches might become an increasingly more common phenomenon.

It is my hope that other scholars pick up these important questions where I have left off. I am very aware that the present study—limited to just three racially homogeneous congregations located only thirty minutes apart and belonging to the same denomination—has barely scratched the surface of the work that needs to be done in order to come to more concrete conclusions regarding the changing nature of Canadian Pentecostal identity and experience. I can think of at least three important areas where further empirical research is needed.

First, additional qualitative studies within specific congregations belonging to the PAOC in other regions of Canada need to be conducted in order to determine if the trends that I uncovered exist on a broader national scale. We are well aware that there exists a significant regional variation in religious attendance in Canada (Clark 1998, 2000, 2003; Clark and Schellenberg 2006), and it is quite possible that there exist other regional differences that might geographically limit my conclusions.

Second, further studies need to be conducted within congregations that belong to other Canadian Pentecostal denominations, such as the United Pentecostal Church, the Pentecostal Assemblies of Newfoundland and Labrador, the Apostolic Church of Pentecost, the Church of God (Cleveland, Tennessee), the Independent Assemblies of God–Canada, the Italian Pentecostal Church of Canada, the Church of God of Prophecy in Canada, the Foursquare Gospel Church of Canada, the Apostolic Church in Canada, the Open Bible Standard Church of Canada, the Elim Fellowship of Evangelical Churches and Ministers, and the Pentecostal Holiness Church in Canada. While the PAOC represents the majority of all Pentecostals in Canada, and, as a result, is a significant bellwether of religious change within the spectrum of Canadian

Pentecostalism, this does not mean that very different trends could not exist in other Canadian Pentecostal denominations.

Third, much could be learned about the nature of Canadian Pentecostal religious identity and experience by conducting a large-scale national survey of Canadian Pentecostals who belong to a variety of denominations. Such a project would require a tremendous amount of preparation, scholarly collaboration, and funding. However, combined with targeted qualitative congregational studies, it would provide the best possible source of data in order to confirm, modify, or reject the hypothesis developed in this study.

Bearing these important qualifications and the need for further confirmatory research in mind, it is my firm suspicion that a significant transformation is currently taking place within Canadian Pentecostalism. This transformation is reconfiguring at least some Canadian Pentecostals into practitioners who are less concerned with denominational affiliation, tradition, and established definitions of what it means to be a Pentecostal. These new Canadian Pentecostals are more concerned about autonomy, individualism, and actively engaging with culture in order to develop new understandings of what it means to be a part of this ever-growing and continuously evolving global religious movement.

NOTES

1. See chapter 2 for a definition of Pentecostalism.
2. It was always my intention to make use of the data from the 2011 Census of Canada in this study. In 2010, however, the Government of Canada replaced the mandatory long-form census questionnaire (containing the religion question) with the voluntary National Household Survey. The voluntary nature of the National Household Survey makes the data collected from this instrument scientifically incomparable with previous mandatory long-form census questionnaires. As a result, I was, unfortunately, unable to compare the data on religion collected by Statistics Canada in 1991 and 2001 with the most recent data collected in 2011.
3. Chandler reserves the term "spiritual definitely not religious" for the relatively smaller portion of individuals who "are more inclined to view religion and spirituality as distinct, separate spheres" (2011, 42).
4. I understand religious identity as religious affiliation or religious self-identification, and I define religious experience as belief and practice.
5. Despite close attention on my part during both participant observation and the personal interviews, I was unable to find evidence of any way that gender played a role in the change toward generic evangelicalism within the three congregations.

6. Interestingly, when I discussed the self-reported attendance and giving figures provided by survey respondents with the senior pastors of the churches, they indicated that these numbers, particularly those regarding giving, were greatly exaggerated.
7. Some of the first and most enduring definitions of Pentecostalism were social scientific and attempted to define the tradition according to some of its most common social and cultural characteristics. Perhaps the most unusual Pentecostal practice is glossolalia, or speaking in tongues, causing many early observers to define Pentecostals as those who spoke in tongues, which they believed to be the result of either demon possession or mental instability (McCloud 2007, 90–91). While a glossolalic definition of Pentecostalism is certainly too simplistic to explain all of the global varieties of the movement, it is not entirely inaccurate, particularly within the North American context. As we will see later in this chapter, many early Pentecostals explicitly chose the practice of glossolalia in order to differentiate themselves from other Christians.

Other early assessors argued that Pentecostals were not simply the demonic or mentally depraved, but rather the either culturally, economically, or psychologically deprived, who found in Pentecostalism the social compensation for what they lacked in the other aspects of their lives (Anderson 1979; Calley 1965; Lalive d'Épinay 1969; Rolim 1985). "For Pentecostals," Robert Mapes Anderson wrote, "ecstasy was a mode of adjustment to highly unstable circumstances over which they had little or no control" (1979, 231). Pentecostalism was believed to provide an oasis in what was for many living during the early twentieth century an otherwise brutal existence consisting of long hours of work, low pay, and squalid working and living conditions.

Defining Pentecostals simply as those who were deprived, however, failed as an adequate explanation of Pentecostal affiliation on several empirical and theoretical levels (Stewart 2010b, 144–54), not the least of which was the fact that, as historian Grant Wacker rightly observes, "Contrary to stereotype, the typical convert paralleled the demographic and biological profile of the typical American" (2001b, 205). In other words, the average American Pentecostal was nearly identical to the average American. While more recent social scientific understandings of Pentecostalism have improved on the poor track record of their disciplinary ancestors (see, for instance, Coleman 2000; Droogers 2001; Freston 2001; Martin 2002; Poloma 2003), the faults of these earlier social scientific attempts cause many of the leading scholars of Pentecostalism to seriously question whether or not social scientists are capable of providing a robust, non-reductionistic explanation of the movement.

Other scholars have attempted to define Pentecostalism theologically. One of the most prominent examples of a theological definition of Pentecostalism was developed by Donald W. Dayton. He took issue with social scientific definitions of Pentecostalism that attempted to explain Pentecostal affiliation as a result of some amalgam of economic, psychological, or social antecedents. He especially rejected a strictly glossolalic definition of Pentecostalism, which he argued had three major limitations. First, it fails to differentiate Pentecostals from other Christians, not to mention members of other religions, who also practise tongues speech. Second, it promotes ahistorical and hagiographical accounts of Pentecostal origins and ignores a close examination of the historical record that may lead to other non-traditional points of origination. Third, it ignores theological understandings of the movement and instead prioritizes social scientific perspectives, which view glossolalia as an "abnormal response" to either real or relative deprivation (Dayton 1987, 15-16).

Conversely, Dayton explained that a careful examination of the historical and theological roots of Pentecostalism, particularly within North American Methodism, but also within Anglicanism, Puritanism, and Pietism, reveals a basic gestalt or pattern of theological commitment that provides a much more robust theological definition of Pentecostalism (1987, 17-18). Early Pentecostals eventually developed a Christological construct called the full gospel or the fourfold gospel, which, Dayton argued, served as a theological definition of the movement and included the beliefs in Jesus as (1) saviour, (2) baptizer in the Holy Spirit, (3) healer, and (4) soon-coming king (1987, 17-28).

One obvious problem with Dayton's definition of Pentecostalism, or any other definition that attempts to define Pentecostalism according to a particular set of theological commitments, is that it will ultimately fail to include the diversity of individuals and traditions around the world that are often subsumed under the rubric "Pentecostal." Such a definition, Allan Anderson explains, "can only neatly be applied to 'classical Pentecostalism' in North America" (2004, 10). Dayton's definition works best to understand and define North American classical Pentecostalism, but fails to accurately describe Pentecostalism's many global permutations.

Another important approach to defining Pentecostalism is the historical, which defines Pentecostals as those who share a historic connection with particular events in Pentecostal religious history. The first generation of Pentecostal historians, such as Zelma Argue, Frank Ewart, Stanley Frodsham, Donald Gee, Gloria Kulbeck, and B. F. Lawrence, developed largely hagiographical accounts of Pentecostal origination in which it was believed that God's supernatural outpouring of the Holy Spirit, usually upon the members of the Azusa Street Revival in Los Angeles, was thought to mark the beginning of the movement (Stewart 2010a, 17–18). This position was eventually challenged by another generation of historians, such as Vinson Synan (1997), William W. Menzies (1971, 1975), David Bundy (1975), and Donald W. Dayton (1987). These scholars traced the origins of the movement more broadly to also include the Methodist Holiness and Keswick movements of the nineteenth and early twentieth centuries. Definitions of Pentecostalism that require direct, historical links to Western evangelicalism, however, are problematic, because they exclude a whole range of so-called Pentecostal movements and institutions around the world that developed independently of these religious traditions (Anderson 2007; 2010, 23–25).

More recently, the German historian of Pentecostalism Michael Bergunder has argued that Pentecostalism must be defined according to the dual criteria of diachronicity (historical connections with Pentecostal beginnings) and synchronicity (contemporary interrelations with other Pentecostals) (2008, 2010). He explains: "The first criterion demands that everything we count as Pentecostal must be connected within a vast diachronous network that goes back to the beginning of Pentecostalism.... The second criterion demands that only that which is linked together in a synchronous network can be called Pentecostalism" (2008, 12). Put more simply, Bergunder defines Pentecostalism as a network of individuals, churches, and institutions that share a common historical root and are also recognized by other Pentecostals as being part of the same loose network that they themselves inhabit.

The obvious problem with Bergunder's definition is that whomever the scholar studying Pentecostalism, or the adherent practising it, perceives as comprising or controlling these two networks is granted the representational power of defining the tradition and determining who is and who is not a Pentecostal. In other words, if at any point the individuals, churches, and institutions that most scholars or adherents consider most accurately define the diachronic or synchronic Pentecostal networks do not for some reason include other individuals, churches, and institutions who also consider themselves to be Pentecostal, then, according to Bergunder's definition, we must exclude this latter group from being considered Pentecostal. For instance, in a particular geographical region or historical era in which those holding the representative power within the dominant Pentecostal networks consider Trinitarian theology a criterion for network status, then non-Trinitarian, Oneness Pentecostals would necessarily be excluded from being considered Pentecostal. For this reason, Bergunder's his-

torical definition of Pentecostalism is also inadequate to describe the global, and often mutually contested, composition of the contemporary Pentecostal movement.
8. Matthew 28:19 (NRSV).
9. Acts 2:38 (NRSV).
10. Before it is possible to determine whether or not a religious tradition has changed, one must first establish an ideal-typical construction of that tradition that can then be used to compare the current characteristics of the tradition in order to determine if any change has indeed occurred. There exist a limited number of ways in which this can be done, such as gathering the oral history of individuals who possess a living memory of an earlier version of the tradition, or, more commonly, examining textual sources that describe the tradition during the era of interest. Because I was unable to find an adequate number of individuals in each of the churches that possessed a living memory of the Pentecostal tradition that reached more than just a decade or two into the past, I was forced to rely largely on textual sources for this task. No matter which method one chooses, they all fall prey to the same basic critique: the reliance on either the memory of individuals who attempt to remember details from their lives many decades in the past, or the written accounts of, most often, religious elites, who have a vested interest in portraying the tradition as being much more coherent than it likely was.

Here is where Max Weber's concept of the ideal type is particularly helpful. During his various socio-historical studies of religion, Weber found it useful to construct hyperrational and idealized conceptualizations of institutions and other phenomena that could then be used as comparative tools in order to analyze such phenomena as they exist in other social and historical contexts. Using this method he was able to demonstrate that Protestantism contained certain characteristics that differentiated it from, for instance, Buddhism. By using this same method on a much smaller scale, it is possible to create an ideal-typical construction of Pentecostalism that can subsequently function as a sort of baseline and be used to determine if a specific expression of Christianity contains the same or similar characteristics as the ideal type, and, thus, if it can appropriately be described as Pentecostal.

It is crucially important to understand that Weber was not naive enough to suppose that these ideal-typical constructions represented the empirical reality of religious traditions as they actually existed in the real world. Regarding the ideal type, Weber wrote:

> It is not a *description* of reality but it aims to give unambiguous means of expression to such a description. . . . An ideal type is formed by the one-sided

accentuation of one or more points of view and by the synthesis of a great many diffuse, discrete, more or less present and occasionally absent *concrete individual* phenomena, which are arranged according to those one-sidedly emphasized viewpoints into a unified *analytical* construct (*Gedankenbild*). In its conceptual purity, this mental construct (*Gedankenbild*) cannot be found empirically anywhere in reality. It is a *utopia*. Historical research faces the task of determining in each individual case, the extent to which this ideal-construct approximates to or diverges from reality. . . . When carefully applied, those concepts are particularly useful in research and exposition. (1949, 90; emphasis original)

Following Weber, I do not wish to suggest that the normative construction that I present below is a description of the actual, lived reality of Canadian Pentecostal identity, belief, and practice of a previous era, but rather it is an earnest attempt to provide an impression of the tradition as it previously existed as accurately and fairly as possible given the many existing constraints. Some readers may have serious reservations regarding the ability of textual sources to provide an appropriate source of data with which to compare the type of contemporary ethnographic data contained in this study for the purpose of making conclusions regarding the ways in which the tradition may have changed. Although this is a valid concern, the fact remains that if meaningful discussions regarding how religious traditions change over time are ever to occur, this requires first coming to at least a rudimentary, if imprecise, definition of the primary characteristics of that tradition using whatever sources are available.

11. Ephesians 4:5 (NRSV).
12. 1 Corinthians 12:8–10, 28, 29 (NRSV).
13. James 5:13–16 (NRSV).
14. In the fall of 2012, two years after the conclusion of my fieldwork, Elevation entered into a facility-sharing agreement with St. John's Lutheran Church (interestingly, this was the childhood church of senior pastor, Brandon Malo) located at 22 Willow Street, Waterloo, Ontario. It will be interesting to see if the decision to adopt a more permanent and definitively "sacred" space will affect the nature of Elevation's ministry, as sociologists of religion normally predict of religious groups that take these steps towards institutionalization.
15. The Canadian theologian John G. Stackhouse Jr. was probably the first scholar to make use of the term "generic evangelicalism" in any kind of systematic way. Stackhouse differentiated between two basic types of twentieth-century Canadian evangelicals. The

first type is a group of more ecumenically minded evangelicals who are willing to compromise specific denominational elements within their traditions in order to, Stackhouse argues, promote the idea of a united evangelicalism for the purpose of exerting a greater, more concerted influence upon the moral future of Canadian society. Stackhouse identifies these evangelicals as "evangelica*lists*" and as being a part of a "transdenominational evangelicalism" (1998, 9–10; emphasis original). The second type is a group of evangelicals who, although they share with transdenominational evangelicals a commitment to the same basic set of evangelical beliefs, practices, and values, nonetheless prioritize particular denominational emphases over the ideology of a united evangelicalism, and, as Stackhouse writes, "would be seen as generic 'evangelicals' per se, members of the set one might call (with apologies to C. S. Lewis) 'mere evangelicality'" (1998, 10).

In short, Stackhouse uses the term "generic evangelicalism" to identify what I and other sociologists of religion most commonly refer to as either traditional or denominational evangelicalism. What Stackhouse refers to as "transdenominational evangelicalism" is actually what most contemporary sociologists of religion have in mind when they use the term "generic evangelicalism"—evangelicals who modify their traditions often at the expense of diluting traditional denominational characteristics. Stackhouse's usage of the term "generic evangelicalism," then, is out of step with the way that it is now most commonly used. His impact on the present discussion lies in the role that he played as an early progenitor of the idea of a "transdenominational evangelicalism" in both Canada and the United States, which was picked up and furthered by later scholars (Reimer 2000, 231; 2003, 21, 119; Stackhouse 2000, 113–28).

16. Not to be confused with the term "emergent church," which refers to a group of churches formally organized under the banner Emergent Village. Founded in 2001, this organization seeks to intentionally promote many of the values represented in the much broader "emerging church" movement.
17. Wuthnow defines young adults as those between twenty-one and forty-five years of age (2007, 6–7).
18. It is interesting to note the way that many boomer evangelical pastors frequently and inaccurately use the Aramaic term *Abba* in order to provide biblical support for their therapeutic understanding of the human-divine relationship. The late Canadian evangelical theologian Stanley Grenz, for instance, explained, "Preachers are fond of asserting that *Abba* is equivalent to the English designation 'Daddy.' In fact, however, *Abba* does not carry overtones of a small child addressing a parent that are evoked by the

English 'Daddy'" (2005, 16). Rather, James Barr explains that the word *Abba* "was more a solemn, responsible, adult address to a Father" (1988, 46).
19. 2 Samuel 6:3-7 (NRSV).
20. 2 Kings 2:23-24 (NRSV).
21. Acts 5:1-11 (NRSV).
22. The members of Freedom in Christ, Elmira Pentecostal Assembly, and Elevation engaged in what Stephen Ellingson calls, "selective isomorphism" (2007, 107-43). This process entailed incorporating only those traditional Pentecostal beliefs and practices that, in Ellingson's words, "dovetailed with their own understanding of what is essential and what is nonessential" (109), which, in the particular case of these three congregations, appeared to be centred around how well these beliefs and practices corresponded with generic evangelicalism's emphasis on therapeutic individualism.
23. A popular Charismatic faith healer and televangelist.
24. A popular Canadian Pentecostal faith healer.
25. James 5:13-16 (NRSV).
26. Mark 5:25-34 (NRSV).
27. 1 Kings 17:8-16 (NRSV).
28. 2 Kings 4:42-44; Matthew 14:13-21; Mark 6:31-44; Luke 9:10-17; John 6:5-15 (NRSV).
29. Teen Challenge is a Christian organization first developed by David Wilkerson, author of the popular book, *The Cross and the Switchblade*. It aims to rehabilitate young adults suffering from drug and alcohol addiction.
30. For the resulting discussion papers, see http://mpseminary.com/papers/.

REFERENCES

Althouse, Peter. 1996. "The Influence of Dr. J. E. Purdie's Reformed Anglican Theology on the Formation and Development of the Pentecostal Assemblies of Canada." *PNEUMA: The Journal of the Society for Pentecostal Studies* 19(1): 3-28.

———. 2003. *Spirit of the Last Days: Pentecostal Eschatology in Conversation with Jürgen Moltmann*. London: T&T Clark.

———. 2010. "The Ecumenical Significance of Canadian Pentecostalism." In Wilkinson and Althouse 2010, 55-78.

Ammerman, Nancy T. 1997. "Golden Rule Christianity: Lived Religion in the American Mainstream." In *Lived Religion in America: Toward a History of Practice*, edited by Donald G. Hall, 196-216. Princeton, NJ: Princeton University Press.

Anderson, Allan. 2004. *An Introduction to Pentecostalism: Global Charismatic Christianity*. Cambridge: Cambridge University Press.

———. 2007. *Spreading Fires: The Missionary Nature of Early Pentecostalism*. Maryknoll, NY: Orbis.

———. 2010. "Varieties, Taxonomies, and Definitions." In *Studying Global Pentecostalism: Theories and Methods*, edited by Allan Anderson, Michael Bergunder, André Droogers, and Cornelis van der Laan, 13-29. Berkeley: University of California Press.

Anderson, Ray. 2006. *An Emergent Theology for Emerging Churches*. Downers Grove, IL: InterVarsity Press.

Anderson, Robert Mapes. 1979. *Vision of the Disinherited: The Making of American Pentecostalism.* New York: Oxford University Press.

Atter, Gordon F. 1965. *The Third Force*, 2nd ed. Peterborough, ON: College Press.

Bainbridge, William Sims. 1997. *The Sociology of Religious Movements.* New York: Routledge.

Baldwin, James. 1952. *Go Tell It on the Mountain.* New York: Bantam Dell.

Barr, James. 1988. "'Abba Isn't 'Daddy.'" *Journal of Theological Studies* 39(1): 28–47.

Barrett, David B. 1988. "The Twentieth-Century Pentecostal/Charismatic Renewal in the Holy Spirit, with Its Goal of World Evangelization." *International Bulletin of Missionary Research* 12: 119–29.

Bebbington, David W. 1989. *Evangelicalism in Modern Britain: A History from the 1730s to the 1980s.* London: Unwin Hyman.

Belcher, Jim. 2009. *Deep Church: A Third Way beyond Emerging and Traditional.* Downers Grove, IL: InterVarsity Press.

Bell, Rob. 2005. *Velvet Elvis: Repainting the Christian Faith.* Grand Rapids, MI: Zondervan.

———. 2007. *Sex God: Exploring the Endless Connections between Sexuality and Spirituality.* Grand Rapids, MI: Zondervan.

———. 2011. *Love Wins: A Book about Heaven, Hell, and the Fate of Every Person Who Ever Lived.* New York: HarperCollins.

Bellah, Robert N., Richard Madsen, William M. Sullivan, Ann Swidler, and Steven M. Tipton. 2008. *Habits of the Heart: Individualism and Commitment in American Life*, 3rd ed. Berkeley: University of California Press.

Berger, Peter L. 1965. "Toward a Sociological Understanding of Psychoanalysis." *Social Research* 32(1): 26–41.

———. 1967. *The Sacred Canopy: Elements of a Sociological Theory of Religion.* New York: Anchor Books.

Bergunder, Michael. 2008. *The South Indian Pentecostal Movement in the Twentieth Century.* Grand Rapids, MI: Eerdmans.

———. 2010. "The Cultural Turn." In *Studying Global Pentecostalism: Theories and Methods*, edited by Allan Anderson, Michael Bergunder, André Droogers, and Cornelis van der Laan, 51–73. Berkeley: University of California Press.

Bernard, H. Russell. 2006. *Research Methods in Anthropology: Qualitative and Quantitative Approaches*, 4th ed. Lanham, MD: AltaMira Press.

Beyer, Peter. 2000. "Secularization from the Perspective of Globalization." In *The Secularization Debate*, edited by William H. Swatos and Daniel V. A. Olson, 81–94. Oxford: Rowman and Littlefield.

Blumhofer, Edith. L. 1993. *Restoring the Faith: The Assemblies of God, Pentecostalism, and American Culture.* Urbana: University of Illinois Press.

Blumhofer, Edith L., Russell P. Spittler, and Grant A. Wacker, eds. 1999. *Pentecostal Currents in American Protestantism.* Urbana: University of Illinois Press.

Bramadat, Paul A. 2000. *The Church on the World's Turf: An Evangelical Christian Group at a Secular University.* New York: Oxford University Press.

Bruce, Steve. 2002. *God Is Dead: Secularization in the West.* Malden, MA: Blackwell.

Bundy, David. 1975. *Keswick: A Bibliographic Introduction to the Higher Life Movements.* Wilmore, KY: B. L. Fisher Library of Asbury Theological Seminary.

———. 1993. "Keswick and the Experience of Evangelical Piety." In *Modern Christian Revivals,* edited by Edith L. Blumhofer and Randall Balmer, 118–44. Urbana: University of Illinois Press.

Burgess, Stanley M., and Eduard M. van der Maas, eds. 2002. *The New International Dictionary of Pentecostal and Charismatic Movements,* rev. ed. Grand Rapids, MI: Zondervan.

Calley, Malcolm J. 1965. *God's People: West Indian Pentecostal Sects in England.* London: Oxford University Press.

Campbell, Colin. 1987. *The Romantic Ethic and the Spirit of Modern Consumerism.* Oxford: Blackwell.

Carroll, Jackson, and Wade Clark Roof, eds. 1993. *Beyond Establishment: Protestant Identity in a Post-Protestant Age.* Louisville, KY: Westminster John Knox Press.

Cavey, Bruxy. 2007. *The End of Religion: Encountering the Subversive Spirituality of Jesus.* Colorado Springs, CO: NavPress.

Chandler, Siobhan. 2011. "The Social Ethic of Religiously Unaffiliated Spirituality." PhD diss., Wilfrid Laurier University.

Chaves, Mark. 2011. *American Religion: Contemporary Trends.* Princeton, NJ: Princeton University Press.

Clark, Warren. 1998. "Religious Observance, Marriage and Family." *Canadian Social Trends* 50: 2–7.

———. 2000. "Patterns of Religious Attendance." *Canadian Social Trends* 59: 23–27.

———. 2003. "Pockets of Belief: Religious Attendance Patterns in Canada." *Canadian Social Trends* 68: 2–5.

Clark, Warren, and Grant Schellenberg. 2006. "Who's Religious?" *Canadian Social Trends* 81: 2–9.

Coleman, Simon. 2000. *The Globalization of Charismatic Christianity: Spreading the Gospel of Prosperity.* Cambridge: Cambridge University Press.

Curtis, Heather D. 2007. *Faith in the Great Physician: Suffering and Divine Healing in American Culture, 1860–1900.* Baltimore: Johns Hopkins University Press.

Davie, Grace. 1994. *Religion in Britain since 1945: Believing without Belonging.* Oxford: Blackwell.
——. 2000. *Religion in Modern Europe: A Memory Mutates.* Oxford: Oxford University Press.
Dayton, Donald W. 1987. *Theological Roots of Pentecostalism.* Peabody, MA: Hendrickson Publishers.
——. 2009. "Methodism and Pentecostalism." In *The Oxford Handbook of Methodist Studies,* edited by William J. Abraham and James L. Kirby, 171-87. New York: Oxford University Press.
Desjardins, Michel. 1997. *Peace, Violence and the New Testament.* Sheffield, UK: Sheffield Academic Press.
DeYoung, Kevin, and Ted Kluck. 2008. *Why We're Not Emergent: By Two Guys Who Should Be.* Chicago: Moody Publishers.
Di Giacomo, Michael. 2009. "Pentecostal and Charismatic Christianity in Canada: Its Origins, Development, and Distinct Culture." In *Canadian Pentecostalism: Transition and Transformation,* edited by Michael Wilkinson, 15-38. Montreal and Kingston: McGill-Queen's University Press.
Droogers, André. 2001. "Globalisation and Pentecostal Success." In *Between Babel and Pentecost: Transnational Pentecostalism in Africa and Latin America,* edited by André Corten and Ruth Marshall-Fratini, 41-61. Bloomington: Indiana University Press.
Eagle, David E. 2011. "Changing Patterns of Attendance at Religious Services in Canada, 1986-2008." *Journal for the Scientific Study of Religion* 50(1): 187-200.
Ellingson, Stephen. 2007. *The Megachurch and the Mainline: Remaking Religious Tradition in the Twenty-First Century.* Chicago: University of Chicago Press.
Fetterman, David M. 2010. *Ethnography: Step-by-Step,* 3rd ed. Thousand Oaks, CA: Sage.
Freston, Paul. 2001. *Evangelicals and Politics in Asia, Africa and Latin America.* Cambridge: Cambridge University Press.
Froese, Paul. 2008. *The Plot to Kill God: Findings from the Soviet Experiment in Secularization.* Berkeley: University of California Press.
Froese, Paul, and Christopher Bader. 2010. *America's Four Gods: What We Say about God—and What That Says about Us.* New York: Oxford University Press.
Fuller, Robert C. 2001. *Spiritual, but Not Religious: Understanding Unchurched America.* New York: Oxford University Press.
Gibbs, Eddie, and Ryan K. Bolger. 2005. *Emerging Churches: Creating Christian Communities in Postmodern Cultures.* Grand Rapids, MI: Baker Academic.
Glock, Charles Y. 1964. "The Role of Deprivation in the Origin and Evolution of Religious Groups." In *Religion and Social Conflict,* edited by Robert Lee and Martin W. Marty, 24-36. New York: Oxford University Press.

Grenz, Stanley J. 2005. *Prayer: The Cry for the Kingdom*, rev. ed. Grand Rapids, MI: Eerdmans.

Griffith, R. Marie. 1998. "'Joy Unspeakable and Full of Glory': The Vocabulary of Pious Emotion in the Narratives of American Pentecostal Women, 1910-1945." In *An Emotional History of the United States*, edited by Peter N. Stearns and Jan Lewis, 218-40. New York: New York University Press.

Harrison, Milmon F. 2005. *Righteous Riches: The Word of Faith Movement in Contemporary African American Religion*. New York: Oxford University Press.

Hervieu-Léger, Danièle. 2006. "The Role of Religion in Establishing Social Cohesion." In *Religion in the New Europe*, edited by Krzysztof Michalski, 45-63, vol. 2 of *Conditions of European Solidarity*. Budapest: Central European University Press.

Hewett, James Allen. 2002. "Pentecostal Assemblies of Newfoundland." In Burgess and van der Maas 2002, 964-65.

Hillman, James. 1989. *A Blue Fire: Selected Writings*. New York: Harper & Row.

Hollenweger, Walter J. 1997. *Pentecostalism: Origins and Developments Worldwide*. Peabody, MA: Hendrickson Publishers.

———. 1998. "The Rise of Pentecostalism: *Christian History* Interview—Pentecostalism's Global Language." *Christian History*, April 1. http://www.christianitytoday.com/ch/1998/issue58/58h042.html.

Jacobsen, Douglas. 1999. "Knowing the Doctrines of Pentecostals: The Scholastic Theology of the Assemblies of God, 1930-1955." In Blumhofer, Spittler, and Wacker 1999, 90-107.

———. 2003. *Thinking in the Spirit: Theologies of the Early Pentecostal Movement*. Bloomington: Indiana University Press.

———. 2011. *The World's Christians: Who They Are, Where They Are, and How They Got There*. Malden, MA: Wiley-Blackwell.

Janes, Burton K. 1996. *History of the Pentecostal Assemblies of Newfoundland*. St. John's: Pentecostal Assemblies of Newfoundland.

Jenkins, Philip. 2002. *The Next Christendom: The Coming of Global Christianity*. New York: Oxford University Press.

Johnson, Todd M., and Kenneth R. Ross, eds. 2010. *Atlas of Global Christianity*. Edinburgh: Edinburgh University Press.

Kärkkäinen, Veli-Matti. 2008. "The Pentecostal View." In *The Lord's Supper: Five Views*, edited by Gordon T. Smith, 117-35. Downers Grove, IL: InterVarsity Press.

Kulbeck, Gloria G. 1958. *What God Hath Wrought: A History of the Pentecostal Assemblies of Canada*. Toronto: Pentecostal Assemblies of Canada.

Kydd, Ronald A. N. 1997. "Canadian Pentecostalism and the Evangelical Impulse." In *Aspects of the Canadian Evangelical Experience*, edited by G. A. Rawlyk, 289–300. Montreal and Kingston: McGill-Queen's University Press.

———. 2002a. "Canada." In Burgess and van der Maas 2002, 48–51.

———. 2002b. "Pentecostal Assemblies of Canada." In Burgess and van der Maas 2002, 961–64.

Kyle, Richard. 2006. *Evangelicalism: An Americanized Christianity*. New Brunswick, NJ: Transaction Publishers.

Lalive d'Épinay, Christian. 1969. *Haven of the Masses: A Study of the Pentecostal Movement in Chile*. London: Lutterworth.

LeCompte, Margaret D., and Jean J. Schensul. 2010. *Designing and Conducting Ethnographic Research: An Introduction*, 2nd ed. Lanham, MD: AltaMira Press.

Lindbeck, George. 1986. "Barth and Textuality." *Theology Today* 43(3): 361–76.

Lugo, Luis, Sandra Stencel, John Green, Timothy S. Shah, Brian J. Grim, Gregory Smith, Robert Ruby, Allison Pond, Andrew Kohut, Paul Taylor, and Scott Keeter. 2006. *Spirit and Power: A 10-Country Survey of Pentecostals*. Washington, DC: Pew Forum on Religion and Public Life.

Marsden, George M. 2006. *Fundamentalism and American Culture*, 2nd ed. New York: Oxford University Press.

Marti, Gerardo. 2005. *A Mosaic of Believers: Diversity and Innovation in a Multicultural Church*. Bloomington: Indiana University Press.

Martin, David. 2002. *Pentecostalism: The World Their Parish*. Oxford: Blackwell.

McCloud, Sean. 2007. *Divine Hierarchies: Class in American Religion and Religious Studies*. Chapel Hill: University of North Carolina Press.

McGee, Gary B. 1991. "Early Pentecostal Hermeneutics: Tongues as Evidence in the Book of Acts." In *Initial Evidence: Historical and Biblical Perspectives on the Pentecostal Doctrine of Spirit Baptism*, edited by Gary B. McGee, 96–118. Peabody, MA: Hendrickson Publishers.

———. 2010. *Miracles, Missions, and American Pentecostalism*. Maryknoll, NY: Orbis.

McKnight, Scot. 2007. "Five Streams of the Emerging Church: Key Elements of the Most Controversial and Misunderstood Movement in the Church Today." *Christianity Today*, January 19. http://www.christianitytoday.com/ct/2007/february/11.35.html?start=1.

McLaren, Brian. 2001. *A New Kind of Christian: A Tale of Two Friends on a Spiritual Journey*. San Francisco: Jossey-Bass.

———. 2004. *A Generous Orthodoxy*. Grand Rapids, MI: Zondervan.

———. 2006. *The Secret Message of Jesus: Uncovering the Truth That Could Change Everything*. Nashville, TN: Thomas Nelson.

———. 2010. *A New Kind of Christianity: Ten Questions That Are Transforming the Faith*. New York: HarperCollins.

Menzies, William W. 1971. *Anointed to Serve: The Story of the Assemblies of God*. Springfield, MO: Gospel Publishing House.

———. 1975. "The Non-Wesleyan Origins of the Pentecostal Movement." In *Aspects of Pentecostal-Charismatic Origins*, edited by Vinson Synan, 83–97. Plainfield, NJ: Logos International.

Menzies, William W., and Robert P. Menzies. 2000. *Spirit and Power: Foundations of Pentecostal Experience*. Grand Rapids, MI: Zondervan.

Miller, Donald. 2003. *Blue Like Jazz: Nonreligious Thoughts on Christian Spirituality*. Nashville, TN: Thomas Nelson.

Miller, Donald E. 1997. *Reinventing American Protestantism: Christianity in the New Millennium*. Berkeley: University of California Press.

Miller, Donald E., and Tetsunao Yamamori. 2007. *Global Pentecostalism: The New Face of Christian Social Engagement*. Berkeley: University of California Press.

Miller, Thomas William. 1994. *Canadian Pentecostals: A History of the Pentecostal Assemblies of Canada*. Mississauga, ON: Full Gospel Publishing House.

Moore, Thomas. 1992. *Care of the Soul: A Guide for Cultivating Depth and Sacredness in Everyday Life*. New York: HarperCollins.

Murchison, Julian M. 2010. *Ethnography Essentials: Designing, Conducting, and Presenting Your Research*. San Francisco: Jossey-Bass.

Niebuhr, H. Richard. 1929. *The Social Sources of Denominationalism*. New York: Henry Holt.

Opp, James. 2005. *The Lord for the Body: Religion, Medicine, and Protestant Faith Healing in Canada, 1880–1930*. Montreal and Kingston: McGill-Queen's University Press.

Otto, Rudolf. 1958. *The Idea of the Holy*. Translated by John W. Harvey. New York: Oxford University Press.

Pagitt, Doug. 2003. *Reimagining Spiritual Formation: A Week in the Life of an Experimental Church*. Grand Rapids, MI: Zondervan.

PAOC (Pentecostal Assemblies of Canada). 1994. *Statement of Fundamental and Essential Truths*. Mississauga, ON: Pentecostal Assemblies of Canada.

Patterson, Eric. 2007. "Conclusion: Back to the Future: U.S. Pentecostalism in the 21st Century." In *The Future of Pentecostalism in the United States*, edited by Eric Patterson and Edmund Rybarcyk, 189–210. Lanham, MD: Lexington Books.

Poloma, Margaret M. 1989. *The Assemblies of God at the Crossroads: Charisma and Institutional Dilemmas*. Knoxville: University of Tennessee Press.

———. 2003. *Main Street Mystics: The Toronto Blessing and Reviving Pentecostalism*. Walnut Creek, CA: AltaMira Press.

———. 2006. "Charisma and Structure in the Assemblies of God: Revisiting O'Dea's Five Dilemmas." In *Church, Identity, and Change: Theology and Denominational Structures in Unsettled Times*, edited by David A. Roozen and James R. Nieman, 45-96. Grand Rapids, MI: Eerdmans.

Poloma, Margaret M., and John C. Green. 2010. *The Assemblies of God: Godly Love and the Revitalization of American Pentecostalism*. New York: New York University Press.

Poloma, Margaret M., and Ralph W. Hood, Jr. 2008. *Blood and Fire: Godly Love in a Pentecostal Emerging Church*. New York: New York University Press.

Purdie, James Eustace. 1951. *Concerning the Faith*. Toronto: Full Gospel Publishing House.

———. 1954. *What We Believe*. Toronto: Full Gospel Publishing House.

"Questions Answered." 1908. *The Apostolic Faith* 1(11): 1-4.

Reed, David A. 2008. *In Jesus' Name: The History and Beliefs of Oneness Pentecostals*. Blandford Forum, UK: Deo Publishing.

Reimer, Sam. 1995. "A Look at Cultural Effects on Religiosity: A Comparison between the United States and Canada." *Journal for the Scientific Study of Religion* 34(4): 445-57.

———. 2000. "A Generic Evangelicalism? Comparing Evangelical Subcultures in Canada and the United States." In *Rethinking Church, State, and Modernity: Canada Between Europe and America*, edited by David Lyon and Marguerite Van Die, 228-46. Toronto: University of Toronto Press.

———. 2003. *Evangelicals and the Continental Divide: The Conservative Protestant Subculture in Canada and the United States*. Montreal and Kingston: McGill-Queen's University Press.

Rieff, Philip. 1966. *The Triumph of the Therapeutic: Uses of Faith after Freud*. Chicago: University of Chicago Press.

Robeck, Cecil M., Jr. 2002. "National Association of Evangelicals." In Burgess and van der Maas 2002, 922-25.

Rolim, Francisco Cartaxo. 1985. *Pentecostais no Brasil*. Petrópolis: Vozes.

Rollins, Peter. 2006. *How (Not) to Speak of God*. Brewster, MA: Paraclete Press.

———. 2008. *The Fidelity of Betrayal: Towards a Church beyond Belief*. Brewster, MA: Paraclete Press.

———. 2009. *The Orthodox Heretic: And Other Impossible Tales*. Brewster, MA: Paraclete Press.

———. 2011. *Insurrection: To Believe Is Human; to Doubt, Divine*. New York: Howard Books.

Roof, Wade Clark. 1999. *Spiritual Marketplace: Baby Boomers and the Remaking of American Religion*. Princeton, NJ: Princeton University Press.

Roof, Wade Clark, and William McKinney. 1987. *American Mainline Religion: Its Changing Shape and Future*. New Brunswick, NJ: Rutgers University Press.

Sargeant, Kimon Howland. 2000. *Seeker Churches: Promoting Traditional Religion in a Nontraditional Way*. New Brunswick, NJ: Rutgers University Press.

Smith, Christian. 1998. *American Evangelicalism: Embattled and Thriving*. Chicago: University of Chicago Press.

———. 2005. *Soul Searching: The Religious and Spiritual Lives of American Teenagers*. With Melinda Lundquist Denton. New York: Oxford University Press.

Spittler, Russell P. 1994. "Are Pentecostals and Charismatics Fundamentalists? A Review of American Uses of These Categories." In *Charismatic Christianity as a Global Culture*, edited by Karla Poewe, 103-16. Columbia: University of South Carolina Press.

Stackhouse, John G., Jr. 1998. *Canadian Evangelicalism in the Twentieth Century: An Introduction to Its Character*, 2nd ed. Vancouver: Regent College Publishing.

———. 2000. "Bearing Witness: Christian Groups Engage Canadian Politics since the 1960s." In *Rethinking Church, State, and Modernity: Canada Between Europe and America*, edited by David Lyon and Marguerite Van Die, 113-28. Toronto: University of Toronto Press.

Statistics Canada. 2001. *Religions in Canada*. Catalogue 97F0022XIE2001041. Ottawa: Statistics Canada.

Steinbeck, John. 1939. *The Grapes of Wrath*. New York: Viking Press.

Stewart, Adam. 2010a. "A Canadian Azusa? The Implications of the Hebden Mission for Pentecostal Historiography." In Wilkinson and Althouse 2010, 17-37.

———. 2010b. "Re-Visioning the Disinherited: Pentecostals and Social Class in North America." In *A Liberating Spirit: Pentecostals and Social Action in North America*, edited by Michael Wilkinson and Steven M. Studebaker, 136-57. Eugene, OR: Pickwick.

———. 2012a. "A Brief Introduction." In *Handbook of Pentecostal Christianity*, edited by Adam Stewart, 3-8. DeKalb: Northern Illinois University Press.

———. 2012b. "Azusa Street Mission and Revival." In *Handbook of Pentecostal Christianity*, edited by Adam Stewart, 43-48. DeKalb: Northern Illinois University Press.

———. 2014. "From Monogenesis to Polygenesis in Pentecostal Origins: A Survey of the Evidence from the Azusa Street, Hebden, and Mukti Missions." *PentecoStudies: An Interdisciplinary Journal for Research on the Pentecostal and Charismatic Movements* 13(2): 151-72.

Synan, Vinson. 1997. *The Holiness-Pentecostal Tradition: Charismatic Movements in the Twentieth Century*, 2nd ed. Grand Rapids, MI: Eerdmans.

"To the Baptized Saints." 1907. *The Apostolic Faith* 1(9): 1-4.

Tomlinson, Dave. 2003. *The Post-Evangelical*, rev. ed. Grand Rapids, MI: Zondervan.

Turner, Bryan S. 2011. *Religion and Modern Society: Citizenship, Secularisation and the State*. Cambridge: Cambridge University Press.

Wacker, Grant. 2001a. "Are Pentecostals Sex-Crazed?" *Christianity Today*, September 1. http://www.christianitytoday.com/ct/2001/septemberweb-only/9-10-25.0.html?start=1.

———. 2001b. *Heaven Below: Early Pentecostals and American Culture*. Cambridge, MA: Harvard University Press.

Wagner, Melinda Bollar. 1997. "Generic Conservative Christianity: The Demise of Denominationalism in Christian Schools." *Journal for the Scientific Study of Religion* 36(1): 13–24.

Warrington, Keith. 2008. *Pentecostal Theology: A Theology of Encounter*. London: T&T Clark.

Weber, Max. 1949. *The Methodology of Social Sciences*. Translated by Edward A. Shils and Henry A. Finch. Glencoe, IL: Free Press.

Wells, David. 2008. *What I See: Relationally Based Mission Family*. Mississauga, ON: Pentecostal Assemblies of Canada International Office.

———. 2010a. "Olympics Chaplain: David Wells." Interview by James Cantelon. *100 Huntley Street*. CTS. July 13. http://www.100huntley.com/video.php?id=9blI012_tTg.

———. 2010b. Conclusion to Wells and Johnson 2010, 89–94.

———. 2010c. Introduction to Wells and Johnson 2010, 1–8.

Wells, David, and Van Johnson, eds. 2010. *Authentically Pentecostal: Here's What We See—A Conversation*. Mississauga, ON: Pentecostal Assemblies of Canada International Office.

Wells, Delbert. 2009. *Life in the Spirit*. Kitchener, ON: Freedom in Christ.

Westerlund, David, ed. 2009. *Global Pentecostalism: Encounters with Other Religious Traditions*. London: I. B. Tauris.

Wilkinson, Michael. 2006. *The Spirit Said Go: Pentecostal Immigrants in Canada*. New York: Peter Lang.

———. 2009. "Pentecostalism in Canada: An Introduction." In *Canadian Pentecostalism: Transition and Transformation*, edited by Michael Wilkinson, 3–12. Montreal and Kingston: McGill-Queen's University Press.

Wilkinson, Michael, and Peter Althouse, eds. 2010. *Winds from the North: Canadian Contributions to the Pentecostal Movement*. Leiden: Brill.

Wuthnow, Robert. 1988. *The Restructuring of American Religion*. Princeton, NJ: Princeton University Press.

———. 1998. *After Heaven: Spirituality in America since the 1950s*. Berkeley: University of California Press.

———. 2007. *After the Baby Boomers: How Twenty- and Thirty-Somethings Are Shaping the Future of American Religion*. Princeton, NJ: Princeton University Press.

INDEX

100 Huntley Street, 168

altar calls, 40-41, 58, 144, 146-47, 158
Althouse, Peter, 33, 35, 37, 42
Ammerman, Nancy T., 9
Anderson, Allan, 22, 25, 125, 173n7, 174n7
Anderson, Robert Mapes, 3, 154, 172n7
angels, 20, 138-39, 151, 153, 161-64
Anglicans, 2, 4, 22, 36, 173n7
Apostolic Faith Mission, 26, 37
Apostolic Faith, The, 37
Armoogan, Hansley, 11-13, 53-55, 136, 158
Assemblies of God, 27, 29, 32, 33, 82
attendance, 3, 74, 83, 92, 165, 169, 172n6; Elevation, 62, 66-68, 73; Elmira Pentecostal Assembly, 52; Freedom in Christ, 44-47; New Hope Community Church, 70. *See also* church growth

Authentically Pentecostal (Wells and Johnson), 167-68
authenticity, 48, 73, 75; divine healing, 138; Spirit baptism and speaking in tongues, 24, 26, 119, 135
Azusa Street Revival, 26, 28-29, 174n7

baby boomers, 73, 75, 82, 83, 86, 178n19
Bader, Christopher, 133
Bainbridge, William Sims, 32
baptism. *See* water baptism
baptism in/of the Holy Spirit. *See* Spirit baptism and speaking in tongues
Baptists, 4, 7, 8, 22, 27, 72, 84, 90, 93, 103, 119
Bebbington, David W., 80
Bellah, Robert N., 85
Berger, Peter L., 85, 154
Bergunder, Michael, 174n7

Beyer, Peter, 2
Bible, 4, 9, 33, 45, 56–58, 102, 113, 132, 134, 149, 167, 178n19; Spirit baptism and speaking in tongues, 36, 118–19, 121, 122
Bible colleges, 33, 47, 53, 54, 65, 68–69, 101, 103, 158. *See also* education
Bible study, 40, 43, 46, 53, 130, 133–34, 162. *See also* small groups
Blumhofer, Edith L., 9, 31
Bolger, Ryan, 72, 84, 85
born-again, 4, 15, 78, 89, 100, 115, 117. *See also* conversion
Bramadat, Paul, 154
Brethren churches, 8, 51, 68–72
Buddhism, 175n10
buildings. *See* church facilities

Catholics, 22, 40, 80, 84, 93–95, 103–4, 155, 158
Census of Canada, 2–5, 7, 11, 16, 98, 107–8, 165, 171n2. *See also* Statistics Canada
Chandler, Siobhan, 5, 171n3
Charismatic movement, 22–23, 31, 78–79, 84, 94, 155, 178n24
charitable giving, 22, 46, 52, 58, 60, 172n6
Chaves, Mark, 10
children, children's ministry. *See* youth, youth ministry
Christian and Missionary Alliance, 8
Christian Reformed churches, 2, 84, 90, 113
church facilities: Elevation, 59–61; Elmira Pentecostal Assembly, 50–52; Freedom in Christ, 43–45; New Hope Community Church, 69–70
church growth, 44, 47, 54, 56, 81, 167–68. *See also* attendance

Coleman, Simon, 172n7
Concerning the Faith (Purdie), 33–36, 39–42, 115, 124–25
conservative Protestantism, 2, 8–9, 51, 54, 80–85
consumerism, 73–75, 83
conversion, conversionism, 56, 134; Armoogan, Hansley, 53; evangelicalism, 81; evangelical quadrilateral, 30, 80; Methodism and Holiness movement, 24–27; Spirit baptism and speaking in tongues, 35, 36–37, 49, 80, 110, 112, 113–14, 114–17, 118, 121–24, 134, 177n18; typical Pentecostal convert, 172n7; water baptism, 113–14. *See also* born-again
credentials. *See* ministerial credentials
curriculum, 8, 18, 33, 81

Dallas Theological Seminary, 69
Davie, Grace, 7
Dayton, Donald W., 23–28, 34, 173–74n7
demographics, 12–18, 73, 86, 172n7
demons, 20, 137–39, 154–61, 163–64, 172n7. *See also* exorcism
Desjardins, Michel, 133
differentiation: Brethren churches, 71–72; evangelicalism, 80, 176–77n15; Pentecostalism, 9, 20, 34, 48, 57, 58, 89, 109, 118, 120–21, 125, 134, 172–73n7; Protestantism, 175n10. *See also* marketing; religious marketplace
Di Giacomo, Michael, 29
disease. *See* divine healing
distinctiveness. *See* differentiation

divine healing, 20, 137-48, 153, 163-64, 168, 178n24; Bible 149; early Pentecostalism, 27, 30; Elmira Pentecostal Assembly, 57-58; Freedom in Christ, 48-50; traditional Pentecostal views, 33-42, 118, 173n7. *See also* healing home movement

Dunham, Tracy, 11-12, 14, 46, 107, 126-27, 129, 130-35, 142, 144, 153, 155

Eagle, David E., 5
Eastern Orthodox Church, 22, 104
Eastern Pentecostal Bible College. *See* Master's College and Seminary
education: Armoogan, Hansley, 54; attainment among Pentecostals, 3, 13-16; discrimination, 31; Malo, Brandon, 64-65; Tulloch, Steve, 68-69; Wells, Del, 47. *See also* Bible colleges
EFC (Evangelical Fellowship of Canada), 166-67
Elevation: description, 59-75
Ellingson, Stephen, 4, 9, 75, 81, 110, 133, 178n23
Elmira Pentecostal Assembly: description, 50-59
embarrassment. *See* identity; Spirit baptism and speaking in tongues
Embassy, The, 65-68, 75, 101, 105, 158
emerging church, 72-73, 82-85, 177n16
eschatology, 27, 30, 33, 34, 42, 48, 49, 57, 168, 173n7
ethnicity, 12-15, 18
Evangelical Fellowship of Canada. *See* EFC
evangelical quadrilateral, 30, 80

evangelism, 33, 48, 56, 72, 73, 75, 84; Spirit baptism and speaking in tongues, 34-36, 49-50, 103, 118, 119, 124-27, 130, 135-36, 163-64
exorcism, 20, 137-39, 154-64. *See also* demons

family night. *See* Bible study; small groups
film. *See* Pentecostalism
fourfold gospel, 27-28, 30, 34, 168, 173n7
Freedom in Christ: description, 43-50
Freston, Paul, 172n7
Froese, Paul, 3, 133
Fuller, Robert C., 4

Gabriel, Andrew, 166
gender, 12, 17-18, 171n5
generic evangelicalism: defined by Reimer, 79-81; described, 79-86; Elevation, 72, 74-75; Elmira Pentecostal Assembly, 55-59, 74-75; Freedom in Christ, 48-50, 74-75; gender, 171n5; healing, miracles, and other supernatural phenomena, 139, 163-64; PAOC, 6-10, 165-70; Spirit baptism and speaking in tongues, 20, 129-30; Wells, David, 166-69. *See also* identity; individualism; worship
Gibbs, Eddie, 72, 84, 85
gifts of the Spirit. *See* spiritual gifts
giving. *See* charitable giving
glossolalia. *See* Spirit baptism and speaking in tongues
Griffith, R. Marie, 31

Harrison, Milmon F., 141
healing home movement, 23-24. *See also* divine healing
heaven, 9, 33, 49, 57, 63, 161
Heaven's Gates and Hell's Flames, 63
Hebden Mission, 28-29
Hebden, Ellen, 28
hell, 33, 49, 57, 63, 83, 113, 161
Hervieu-Léger, Danièle, 7
Hinduism, 22
Hinn, Benny, 142, 157
Holiness movement, 24-27, 28
homogenization, 9-10, 79-86
Hybels, Bill, 82

ideal type, 19, 34, 175-76n10
identity: congregational, 90-92; embarrassment identifying as Christian, 104-6; embarrassment identifying as evangelical, 103-4; embarrassment identifying as Pentecostal, 93-98, 103-4, 106-7; generically evangelical, 4-10, 19-20, 77-108, 165-70; religious, 1-6, 13-15, 171n4; traditionally Pentecostal, 30-42, 77-79, 86-89
illness. *See* divine healing
immigration, 53
individualism: generic evangelicalism, 5, 19, 81-86, 163-64, 166, 178n23; Spirit baptism and speaking in tongues, 110, 127-36, 139, 163-64
isomorphism, 178n23

Jacobsen, Douglas, 1, 26, 32-33, 38
Jenkins, Philip, 1
Jesus Camp, 30-31, 94-95

Keswick movement, 23, 27, 32, 35, 36, 174n7
Kydd, Ronald A.N., 30

Life in the Spirit (Wells, Del), 130-35
Lutherans, 2, 4, 22, 63, 81, 91, 103-4, 122, 144, 176n14

mainline Protestantism, 31, 80, 84
Malo, Brandon, 11-13, 62-68, 69-70, 71, 106, 136, 167, 176n14
marketing, 8, 50, 81, 83, 130. *See also* differentiation; religious marketplace
market niche. *See* differentiation
Marti, Gerardo, 83
Martin, David, 172n7
Master's College and Seminary, 54, 65
McCloud, Sean, 172n7
McGee, Gary B., 35, 118, 125, 149
McKnight, Scot, 84-85
McLaren, Brian, 5, 83, 84; *A New Kind of Christian*, 83
medical science, 39-40, 140, 145, 149-50
mega-church, 75
Mennonites, 8, 53, 91
Methodists, 4, 22, 24-26, 35, 93, 173-74n7
mid-week programs. *See* Bible study; small groups
Miller, Donald E., 4, 9, 22, 61, 81-82
Miller, Thomas William, 28, 30, 33
ministerial credentials, 35, 64, 71-72

miracles, 20, 39, 137-39, 148-53, 163-64
missional, 70, 167
missions, 23, 26, 28-29, 37, 45, 61-62, 71, 125, 130, 145-46, 149-50, 153, 157, 158, 164, 168
movies. *See* Pentecostalism
music. *See* worship

New Kind of Christian, A (McLaren), 83
Niebuhr, H. Richard, 3

ordination, 54, 71
orthodoxy, orthopraxy, 32-33, 35, 58, 41-42, 70-72, 82, 85, 102, 118-19, 123
Otto, Rudolf, 133

PAOC (Pentecostal Assemblies of Canada): clergy, 166; congregations, 8, 11, 53, 54, 70, 89, 108, 169; loyalty, 98; membership, 3; origins, 29-30; *Statement of Fundamental and Essential Truths*, 33-35, 37-42, 115, 118, 124-25; Theological Study Commission, 167-68; Wells, David, 166-69. *See also* generic evangelicalism; Master's College and Seminary; ministerial credentials; ordination; orthodoxy, orthopraxy; Purdie, James Eustace
Parham, Charles F., 23, 26, 37
Pentecostal Assemblies of Canada. *See* PAOC
Pentecostal Assemblies of Newfoundland, 27, 29-30, 169
Pentecostalism: defined, 21-23, 172-75n7; growth, 1-2, 12; origins, 23-30; in television and film, 30-31, 94-95, 107, 114, 156-57, 168

persecution, 30-31, 87-88
pluralism, 86
politics, 80, 104
Poloma, Margaret M., 9, 82, 83, 109, 172n7
postmodernism, 83
praise. *See* worship
Prankard, Bill, 143
prayer: benediction, 46; divine healing, 22, 39-41, 137-38, 140, 142, 144-48; Dunham, Tracy, 131, 134, 142; evidence of Spirit baptism, 36-37, 124; exorcism, 157-58; Hindu, 22; Malo, Brandon, 65; Pentecostal, 63; praying in the Spirit, 38-39, 126-27; for protection, 151-53; for Spirit baptism, 111; for spiritual deliverance, 138; Wells, Del, 131-32
Presbyterians, 4, 22
prophecy, 8 39, 58
prosperity gospel, 139-41
Purdie, James Eustace, 33-42; *Concerning the Faith*, 33-36, 39-42, 115, 124-25; *What We Believe*, 33, 36, 41-42, 118, 124-25

Region of Waterloo, 6, 11, 16, 45, 51, 53, 73
Reimer, Sam, 4, 9, 79-82, 177n15
religious marketplace, 74-75. *See also* differentiation; marketing
Rieff, Philip, 85, 135-36
rock and roll, 82-83
Roman Catholic Church. *See* Catholics
Roof, Wade Clark, 85

Salvation Army, 2
Sargeant, Kimon Howland, 4, 9, 73, 82, 132–33
Satan, 102, 138–39, 161
second coming. *See* eschatology
secular, secularization, 10, 84
seekers, seeker churches, seeker-sensitive, 5, 8, 72–75, 82–83, 132–33
sex, 31
Seymour, William J., 23, 26, 28–29, 37
sickness. *See* divine healing
small groups, 62, 83, 131. *See also* Bible study
Smith, Christian, 9, 163
speaking in tongues. *See* Spirit baptism and speaking in tongues
Spirit baptism and speaking in tongues, 20, 109–36; compared with healing, miracles, and other supernatural phenomena, 139; decline of, 8, 109–11; early Pentecostalism, 26–28; Elmira Pentecostal Assembly, 56–58; embarrassment regarding, 93–95, 104; Freedom in Christ, 48–49, 130–36; ignorance and confusion, 110–14; Methodism and Holiness movement, 25–26; other evidences of Spirit baptism, 36–38; purpose of Spirit baptism, 125–35; role in defining Pentecostalism, 22, 24, 172–73n7; speaking in tongues as evidence of Spirit baptism, 26, 30–31, 34–39, 110–11, 113–14, 116, 118–25, 134–35; subsequence of Spirit baptism to conversion, 24, 34–35, 49, 110, 114–17, 121–24, 177n18; traditional Pentecostal views, 30–39, 41–42, 70, 88, 134. *See also* authenticity; Bible; evangelism; generic evangelicalism; individualism

spiritual gifts, 24, 35, 38–39, 48–50, 57–58, 111–12, 117, 120–21, 123, 124, 133, 134. *See also* charitable giving; divine healing; evangelism; miracles; prophecy; Spirit baptism and speaking in tongues

spiritual tinkering, 86
Stackhouse, John G., Jr., 176–77n15
Statement of Fundamental and Essential Truths (PAOC), 33–35, 37–42, 115, 118, 124–25
Statistics Canada, 2–10, 15, 165, 171n2. *See also* Census of Canada
Stewart, Adam, 22, 26, 28, 172n7, 174n7
subsequence. *See* Spirit baptism and speaking in tongues
Sunday school, 161; Elevation, 59; Elmira Pentecostal Assembly, 51, 53; Freedom in Christ, 43–44

television. *See* Pentecostalism
Theological Study Commission. *See* PAOC
therapeutic individualism. *See* individualism
tithes. *See* charitable giving
Tulloch, Steve, 11–13, 68–72
Turner, Bryan S., 85

United Church of Canada, 2, 3–4
United States, negative views of, 103–4

University of Toronto: discrimination, 31
University of Waterloo, 12, 113; discrimination, 31; Elevation, 59, 66-68

voluntarism, 61, 66-67

Wacker, Grant, 31, 34, 40, 118, 172n7
Warren, Rick, 82
Warrington, Keith, 34, 38-39, 40
water baptism: Christian Reformed churches, 113-14; confusion with Spirit baptism, 110, 113-14; Elmira Pentecostal Assembly, 52; Freedom in Christ, 49, 52, 134; Lutheran, 62-62, 103; Oneness Pentecostalism, 27-28
Weber, Max, 175-76n10
Wells, David, 166-69; *Authentically Pentecostal*, 167-68; *What I See*, 167
Wells, Del, 11-13, 47-48, 130-36; *Life in the Spirit*, 130-35
What I See (David Wells), 167
What We Believe (Purdie), 33, 36, 41-42, 118, 124-25
Wilfrid Laurier University: Elevation, 59; Malo, Brandon, 64-66, New Hope Community Church, 69-70
Wilkinson, Michael, 2-4, 11

witnessing. *See* evangelism
worship: Catholic, 94; demonic possession, 159-61; Elevation, 60-62, 67; Elmira Pentecostal Assembly, 52-53; emerging church, 84-85; Freedom in Christ, 45-46, 49-50; generic evangelicalism, 81-82; healing services, 41, 144; Lutheran, 63; Pentecostal, 63, 94, 122; preferences of young adults, 73; Satanic, 102; seeker churches, 83; singing in the Spirit, 38
Wuthnow, Robert, 73, 85, 86, 177n17
Wycliffe College, 36

young adults: Armoogan, Hansley, 54-55; defined, 177n17; Elevation, 67-68, 75; Freedom in Christ, 91; Malo, Brandon, 65; perceptions of Pentecostalism, 119; recruitment, 73; Teen Challenge, 178n30. *See also* spiritual tinkering; worship
youth, youth ministry: Armoogan, Hansley, 54-55; Elevation, 67; Elmira Pentecostal Assembly, 52-53, 73; exorcism, 156-58; Freedom in Christ, 46, 73, 90, 92; healing, 141-42; *Jesus Camp*, 30-31; Lutheran, 63, 103; Malo, Brandon, 65; Tulloch, Steve, 69

Series Published by Wilfrid Laurier University Press
for the Canadian Corporation for Studies in Religion/
Corporation Canadienne des Sciences Religieuses

Editions SR

Comparative Ethics Series / Collection d'Éthique Comparée
Studies in Christianity and Judaism / Études sur le christianisme et le judaïsme
The Study of Religion in Canada / Sciences Religieuses au Canada
Studies in Women and Religion / Études sur les femmes et la religion

SR Supplements

For information and availability please visit the WLU Press website:
http://www.wlupress.wlu.ca